PLUTARCH

THE LIVES OF POMPEY,
CAESAR AND CICERO

PLUTARCH
THE LIVES OF POMPEY, CAESAR AND CICERO

A Companion to the Penguin Translation

M.J. Edwards

Bristol Classical Press

This impression 2003
First published in 1991 by
Bristol Classical Press
an imprint of
Gerald Duckworth & Co. Ltd.
61 Frith Street, London W1D 3JL
Tel: 020 7434 4242
Fax: 020 7434 4420
inquiries@duckworth-publishers.co.uk
www.ducknet.co.uk

Translations in bold type from *Plutarch: Fall of the Roman Republic*
translated by Rex Warner (© Rex Warner, 1958) are reprinted
by kind permission of Penguin Books Ltd

A catalogue record for this book is available
from the British Library

ISBN 1 85399 128 7

Printed and bound in Great Britain by
Antony Rowe Ltd, Eastbourne

Cover illustration: (top left) gold coin depicting Pompey, in use 42-38 BC;
(right) silver denarius of Caesar styled as general, struck in 44 BC;
(bottom left) Cicero, from a bust in the Uffizi Gallery, Florence.

Contents

Acknowledgments

John Betts has cheerfully offered advice, and the stemmata and maps have been prepared by the staff of Bristol University Department of Classics. To these I am sincerely grateful, also to John Wilkins and my colleagues at the Accordia Research Centre for their encouragement. The MS was read by John Moles, and his extensive list of suggestions has considerably improved the final version: the imperfections which remain are entirely due to the author. Most of all I am indebted to Helen for many hours of help with the typing and for bearing with me, especially at the weekends.

NOTE

Words marked with * are to be found in the Glossary. References to modern commentaries (e.g. Moles' commentary on the *Cicero*) are made simply to the author — the reader should consult the note(s) on the relevant passage. Ancient texts and modern journals are referred to by standard abbreviations; simple references such as *Crassus* 6.4 are to works of Plutarch, those to *Cato* signify the biography of Cato the Younger. Other abbreviations include:

c.	about
cos.	consul
frg.	fragment
MSS	manuscripts
pr.	praetor
procos.	proconsul
q.	quaestor
tr.	tribune

THE FAMILY OF POMPEY

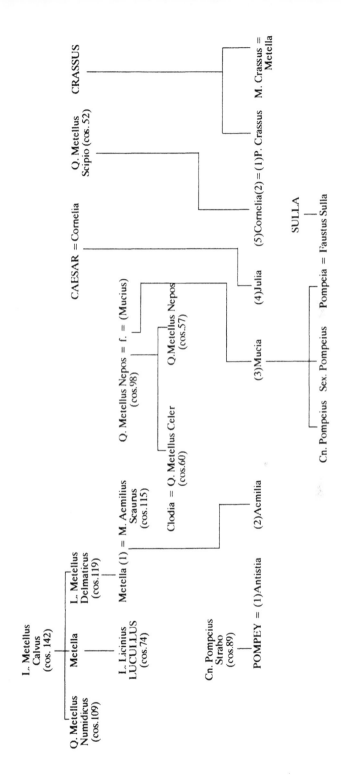

THE FAMILY OF CAESAR

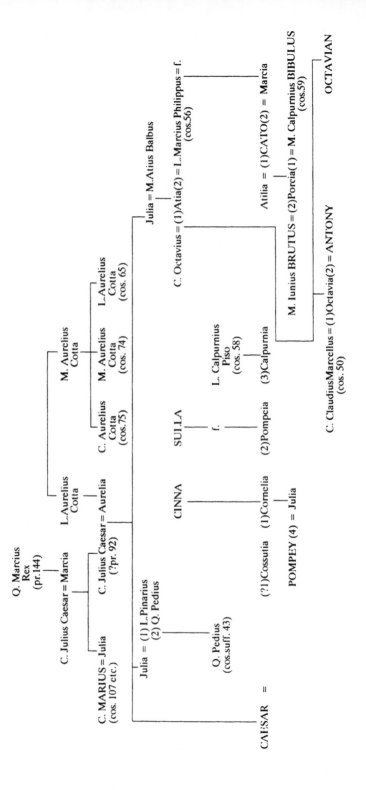

ITALY

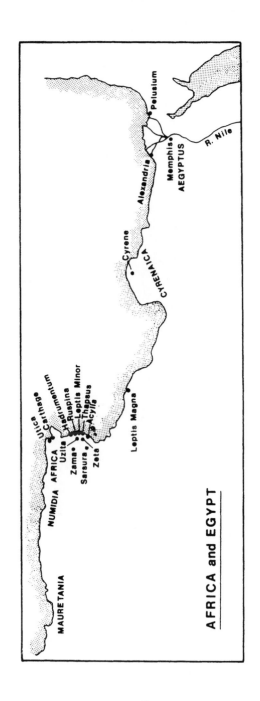

AFRICA and EGYPT

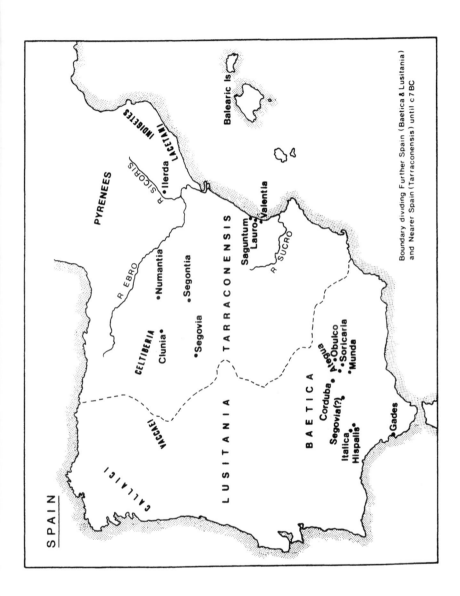

SPAIN

Boundary dividing Further Spain (Baetica & Lusitania) and Nearer Spain (Tarraconensis) until c 7 BC

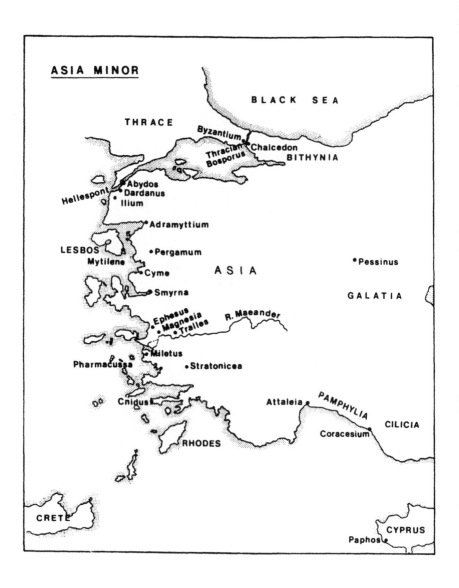

ASIA MINOR

BLACK SEA

THRACE

Byzantium
Thracian Bosporus
Chalcedon
BITHYNIA

Abydos
Hellespont
Dardanus
Ilium

Adramyttium

LESBOS
Pergamum
Mytilene
Cyme

ASIA

Pessinus

GALATIA

Smyrna

Ephesus
Magnesia
Tralles
R. Maeander

Miletus

Pharmacussa

Stratonicea

Cnidus

Attaleia
PAMPHYLIA
CILICIA

RHODES

Coracesium

CRETE

CYPRUS

Paphos

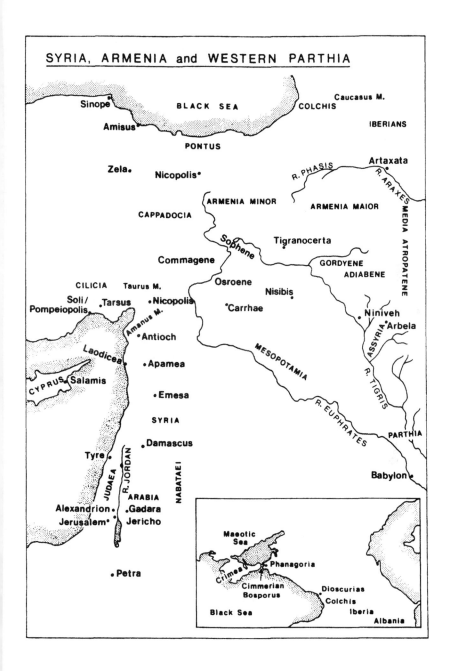

SYRIA, ARMENIA and WESTERN PARTHIA

Sinope

Amisus

BLACK SEA

COLCHIS

Caucasus M.

IBERIANS

PONTUS

Zela

Nicopolis

R. PHASIS

Artaxata

ARMENIA MINOR

ARMENIA MAIOR

R. ARAXES

MEDIA ATROPATENE

CAPPADOCIA

Sophene

Tigranocerta

Commagene

GORDYENE

ADIABENE

CILICIA

Taurus M.

Soli/
Pompeiopolis

Tarsus

Nicopolis

Osroene

Nisibis

Carrhae

Niniveh

Arbela

Amanus M.

Antioch

ASSYRIA

Laodicea

Apamea

MESOPOTAMIA

R. TIGRIS

CYPRUS

Salamis

Emesa

SYRIA

R. EUPHRATES

PARTHIA

Damascus

Tyre

R. JORDAN

NABATAEI

Babylon

JUDAEA

ARABIA

Gadara

Alexandrion

Jerusalem

Jericho

Petra

Maeotic
Sea

Phanagoria

Crimea

Cimmerian
Bosporus

Dioscurias

Colchis

Black Sea

Iberia

Albania

xi

MACEDONIA and ACHAEA

•Lissus

• Dyrrhachium

• Asparagium

R APSUS
•Apollonia

• Oricum

• Palaeste

MACEDONIA

Philippi•

Amphipolis •

Beroea•   •Thessalonica

Tempe•

CORCYRA   EPIRUS   Larissa

R PENEUS   R ENIPEUS

Gomphi•   THESSALY   Scotussa

Pharsalus•

Actium•   AETOLIA

Chaeronea   EUBOEA

Calydon   •Delphi•

BOEOTIA
Thebes•

•Patrae
Dyme•   Megara   •Athens
           Corinth•   Piraeus

Argos •

Sparta •

CATUVELLAUNI
VERULAMIUM •

TRINOBANTES

ATREBATES

USIPETES TENCTERI
SUGAMBRI
UBII

MORINI

MENAPII

EBURONES
ADUATUCI

TREVERI

ATREBATES
Nemetocenna •
VIROMANDUI

NERVII

R SABIS

AMBIANI
• Samarobriva
E
• Bibrax
BELLOVACI SUESSIONES

B

L
REMI

G
A
E

• Durocortorum

PARISII

R MEUSE

Lutetia •

SENONES

Vellaunodunum •
• Agedincum

R RHINE

SUEBI

CARNUTES

• Cenabum

LINGONES
Alesia

ANDES

Noviodunum •
R LOIRE

AEDUI

MANDUBII

Dijon

• Vesontio

VENETI

TURONES

BITURIGES

Avaricum •

A

Bibracte •

SEQUANI

JURAS

HELVETII
(Tigurini)

C E L
T
• Decetia
Gorgobina(?) •

L

BOII

E

R SAÔNE

AMBARRI
• Genava

ALLOBROGES

Gergovia •

Vienna •

E

ARVERNI

R RHONE

• Uxellodunum

NITIOBRIGES
CADURCI

AQUITANIA

• Tolosa

CEVENNES

• Arelate

Massilia
SALUVII

Narbo Martius •

GAUL and BRITAIN

Chronological Table

106 BC Birth of Cicero and Pompey
100 Birth of Caesar
91 Outbreak of Social War
89 Victories of Pompeius Strabo and Sulla
88 Sulla seizes Rome; Mithridates overruns Asia Minor
87 Cinna and Marius seize Rome; Cinna consul 87-4; Sulla in East
86 Death of Marius; Sulla captures Athens, defeats Mithridates
85 Treaty of Dardanus with Mithridates; Sulla settles Asia
84 Death of Cinna; Carbo sole consul
83 Return of Sulla, supported by Pompey; Second Mithridatic War
82 Sulla wins civil war; proscriptions; Pompey in Sicily
81 Sulla dictator, reforms constitution; Pompey in Africa
80 Cicero's *Pro Roscio Amerino*; Caesar wins civic crown
79 Sulla resigns dictatorship; Sertorius defeats Metellus Pius in Spain
78 Death of Sulla; revolt of Lepidus; Servilius Vatia sent against pirates
77 Death of Lepidus; Pompey sent against Sertorius; Caesar prosecutes Dolabella
76 Agitation over powers of tribunes; more Sertorian victories
75 Cicero quaestor in Sicily; Aurelian law opens higher offices to ex-tribunes; Caesar captured by pirates; death of Nicomedes
74 Reinforcements sent to Spain; Antonius sent against pirates; Lucullus sent against Mithridates
73 Caesar pontiff; Spartacus' slave revolt; assassination of Sertorius
72 Caesar military tribune; Pompey settles Spain
71 Crassus defeats Spartacus; Pompey returns from Spain
70 Pompey and Crassus consuls I; tribunes' powers restored and courts reorganised; trial of Verres
69 Caesar quaestor in Further Spain; successes of Lucullus in Armenia
68 Mounting discontent in Lucullus' army
67 Gabinian law
66 Cicero praetor; Manilian law; 'First Catilinarian Conspiracy'
65 Crassus censor; Caesar curule aedile; Pompey campaigns in Caucasus
64 Pompey in Syria
63 Cicero consul; Rullus' agrarian bill; Caesar Chief Pontiff; Catilinarian conspiracy; birth of Octavian; Pompey in Jerusalem; death of

xiv

Mithridates

62 Caesar praetor; death of Catiline; Bona Dea scandal; Pompey settles East and returns to Rome

61 Pompey's Eastern settlement opposed; his triumph; trial of Clodius; Caesar governor of Further Spain; revolt of Allobroges in Gaul

60 Return of Caesar, elected consul; 'First Triumvirate'

59 Caesar consul I; Pompey marries Julia; Vatinian law; Ptolemy Auletes recognised by senate as King of Egypt

58 Clodius tribune; exile of Cicero; Cato sent to Cyprus; Caesar campaigns against Helvetii and Ariovistus; Ptolemy expelled

57 Riots of Clodius and Milo; return of Cicero; Pompey commissioner of corn supply; Caesar campaigns against Belgae and Nervii

56 Renewal of 'Triumvirate' at Luca; return of Cato; Caesar campaigns in Brittany, Normandy and against the Aquitani

55 Pompey and Crassus consuls II; Caesar campaigns against Usipetes and Tencteri, crosses Rhine, first expedition to Britain

54 Rioting in Rome; death of Julia; Caesar's second British expedition, revolt in north-eastern Gaul; Gabinius restores Ptolemy

53 Rioting in Rome; Crassus killed at Carrhae; Caesar punishes Gallic rebels, crosses Rhine, exterminates Eburones

52 Milo kills Clodius; Pompey sole consul (III) until August, Pompeian legislation; trial of Milo; revolt of Vercingetorix, siege of Alesia

51 Optimates* attack Caesar; revolt of Bellovaci, siege of Uxellodunum; Cicero governor of Cilicia; death of Ptolemy

50 Curio works for Caesar; Pompey's serious illness; Marcellus calls on Pompey to save the state; Caesarian tribunes leave Rome

49 Caesar crosses Rubicon; Pompey leaves for Greece; Caesar dictator I, campaigns in Spain

48 Caesar consul II, crosses to Greece; Dyrrhachium; Pharsalus; death of Pompey; Alexandrian War

47 Caesar dictator II, installs Cleopatra in Egypt; Antony Master of the Horse; Caesar defeats Pharnaces at Zela and settles East, returns to Italy, passes legislation and sails for Africa

46 Caesar consul III, victory at Thapsus; suicide of Cato; Caesar dictator for ten years, triumphs, passes legislation and leaves for Spain

45 Caesar dictator III, consul IV, victory at Munda, receives unprecedented honours

44 Caesar dictator IV for life, assassinated; return of Octavian; Antony receives Cisalpine and Transalpine Gaul; Cicero's first *Philippics*

43 Height of Cicero's power at Rome; siege of Mutina; deaths of Hirtius and Pansa, D. Brutus; Octavian suffect consul; 'Second Triumvirate'; proscriptions and murder of Cicero

42 Brutus and Cassius defeated at Philippi

Introduction

1. PLUTARCH'S LIFE AND WORKS

Plutarch (c. AD 45-120) came from a wealthy family of Chaeronea in Boeotia, Greece (see Jones 1-64 for much greater detail on his life). Having studied philosophy at Athens under the Egyptian Ammonius, he travelled widely and went as an ambassador to the Roman governor of Achaea. His official duties also took him more than once to Rome, where influential connections secured him Roman citizenship. In addition, he became an honorary citizen of Athens and one of the two priests at Delphi, but most of his time was spent in Chaeronea. Here, as he grew older, he founded a school and became a scholar of international repute. He was devoted to his wife Timoxena, and they had at least five children. He died soon after the accession of the Emperor Hadrian.

Plutarch was the greatest post-Classical Greek writer, and his youth coincided with the beginning of the Greek cultural renaissance called the Second Sophistic. His voluminous works, of which only about half survive, are regularly grouped as the *Moralia* and *Lives*. The 'Moral Pieces', most of which were written after the death of Domitian in AD 96, cover a wide range of topics, including antiquarianism, ethics, literary criticism, philosophy, politics, religion, rhetoric and science. The *Lives* were of three kinds, firstly the earlier *Lives of the Caesars* from Augustus to Vitellius (only *Galba* and *Otho* survive); secondly the separate *Lives* of *Aratus* and *Artaxerxes;* and finally the *Parallel Lives*, biographies in pairs of famous Greek and Roman generals, politicians and statesmen also written after AD 96. Of these, twenty-two pairs survive, the first pair (*Epaminondas/Scipio*) being lost.

In writing the *Lives* Plutarch was primarily concerned with the portrayal of character. It was not always the most famous events which he chose to record, but those which best illustrated the character of his subject (*Alexander* 1, *Pompey* 8.6). Plutarch had a clear moral purpose here: to provide exemplars for himself and his readers, both to imitate if good and to avoid if bad (see further Pelling [2] 135-9, [3] 10-18; Moles 32-46). He worked on the assumption that a man's character is formed at birth and is revealed by his actions, but this raised a problem if his subject seemingly acted in a manner which was out of character, as

1

when Metellus became 'very luxury-loving' (*Pompey* 18.2). Plutarch's preferred explanation was that one set of actions reflected a man's true nature, and deviations from it were 'against nature' (see Wardman 132-40).

Plutarch composed the *Lives* in pairs, and eighteen of the twenty-two surviving pairs end with a *Comparison (synkrisis)* which summarises the similarities and differences between the two subjects. This is an essential part of Plutarch's moral purpose (*Mor.* 243B-C), though some parallels are more successful than others and the *Comparisons* themselves are often crude, in contrast with the complexity of the actual *Lives*. Thus Caesar and Cicero had obvious Greek parallels in Alexander and Demosthenes, though not as much emphasis is placed on the Alexander/Caesar pairing as might have been expected (and no *Comparison* survives), while Agesilaus is perhaps a less obvious parallel to Pompey. It is, however, beyond the scope of this *Companion* to treat this aspect of the *Lives* in detail. An excellent discussion of the Demosthenes/Cicero parallel is given by Moles, both in his Introduction (pp. 19-26) and throughout the notes. See further Russell 110-14; Wardman 234-44; Pelling [4] 18-26 (the major modern discussion is that of Erbse, H., 'Die Bedeutung der Synkrisis in den Parallelbiographien Plutarchs' *Hermes* 84 [1956] pp. 398-424).

Within the *Lives* there are also many 'internal comparisons' of the subject with other major figures, which often lead to distortions (e.g. *Pompey* 1, *Caesar* 15nn.; Moles 19).

2. PLUTARCH AS A BIOGRAPHER AND HISTORIAN

Another important aspect of Plutarch's biographical writing, which again can only be touched on here, concerns his debt to previous biographers and eulogists. Encomium (eulogy) was the forerunner of biography, and it happens that Xenophon's *Agesilaus* survives for comparison with the *Agesilaus/Pompey* pairing of Plutarch. Further on this subject see Wardman 10-18; and on the biographical tradition see Podlecki's Introduction to the *Pericles* in this series (pp. 6-9). Plutarch's works themselves were regarded as providing useful material for epideictic (display) oratory (Menander Rhetor 2.392.28-33)

Modern scholars will assess the *Lives* for their value as literature and historical sources; Plutarch himself was writing biography, with the moral purpose outlined above, and also to entertain his readers. Consequently he often selects events for their moral and entertainment value. Much of this material will be of little historical importance, and some may not even be historical at all. That said, ancient historiographical writing also contains a good deal of biographical detail and moralising, and clearly the two genres of biography and history overlap. It is not unreasonable, therefore, to attempt to evaluate biography for its historical content, especially since it forms an important part of our source material.

This immediately raises the question of Plutarch's own sources and methods: what sources did he use and how reliable were they, how many of these sources do we possess and how reliably did Plutarch use them? For the period covered by the *Lives* of this volume we have a number of primary (i.e. contemporary) sources, especially Cicero, Sallust and Caesar. It is therefore possible, for example, to check Plutarch's account of the Catilinarian Conspiracy, Caesar's Gallic campaigns and the civil war between Caesar and Pompey. Similarities and differences can be traced in the *Commentary*, but a few examples of the problems raised may be considered here. They take two main forms:

(i) Distortion of facts. There are several kinds of this, including:
    a) exaggeration of the facts (e.g. *Pompey* 3n.);
    b) conflation of similar events (*Cicero* 23n.);
    c) telescoping of chronology (*Pompey* 16n.);
    d) chronological displacement of events (*Caesar* 4n.);
    e) wrongful attribution of material (*Pompey* 28n.);
    f) omission of material (*Caesar* 22n.);
    g) use of material Plutarch knows or suspects is false (Cicero 49n.);
    h) invention of material (*Caesar* 27n.).

Further on these and similar distortions see Pelling [2]; and for a full analysis of examples in the *Cicero* see Moles 36-8. The explanation of these distortions is by no means straightforward, and they clearly serve more than merely literary or moral purposes. In an excellent discussion (pp. 38-45) Moles argues cogently that a clue to the solution lies in Aristotelian aesthetic theory. Aristotle (*Poetics 1451a36 ff.*) distinguishes between two different kinds of truth: the 'specific truths' of historiography ('what Alcibiades did or what was done to him') and the 'universal truths' of poetry ('the sort of thing that a certain type of man will do or say either probably or necessarily'). Plutarch's works are a synthesis of these specific and universal truths, with the important addition (since he is writing with the purpose of moral instruction) of the element of what should have happened. Plutarch does not go so far as to invent whole episodes, but it is clear that his 'facts' cannot simply be taken at face value.

(ii) Historical weaknesses. These again take several forms, including:
    a) factual errors and inaccuracies of various kinds (e.g. *Pompey* 52, *Caesar* 55, *Cicero* 3nn.);
    b) serious omissions of important material (*Cicero* 35n.);
    c) simplistic schematising of Roman politics (*Cicero* 11n.);
    d) Plutarch's conservative bias (*Cicero* 10n.).

For a detailed analysis see Moles (pp. 46-9), who indicates mitigating factors. Not least amongst these are the practical difficulties Plutarch faced in researching his material, e.g. using papyrus rolls was an awkward business (see further Pelling [1] 91-6). As for simplistic schematisations (which were employed by most ancient political theorists), the emphasis Plutarch places on the role of 'the people' in Roman politics is not entirely misplaced. Some of Plutarch's failings may be attributed to his Greek background and preference for Athenian and local affairs: Rome's internal politics clearly had little appeal for him, and he hardly began to understand their complexities. Indeed, he had problems even with Roman names (*Caesar* 4, *Cicero* 32n.), let alone with Latin (*Cicero* 7n.; see further Pelling [4] 6-9). Again, however, the situation is not clear-cut, and Moles points out that many Greek values, such as the striving for power and glory, are appropriately imputed by Plutarch to Roman politicians. In sum, it cannot be denied that Plutarch has weaknesses as an historian, but these may easily be exaggerated.

3. OBSERVATIONS ON THE *POMPEY, CAESAR* AND *CICERO*

From the foregoing remarks it is evident that rigorous historical standards cannot be applied to Plutarch's *Lives,* and indeed that attempts to do so are methodologically unsound. Nor, consequently, is it at all a simple matter to compare the three *Lives* of this volume for their relative historical value. However, some general observations about each life may be attempted.

The *Pompey* is an excellent example of Plutarch's biographical aims. Events are explained according to Pompey's personality and reflect the tensions between his private and public life (ch.2), and between his strength as a soldier (chs 12, 26, 34; but N.B. chs 18-19, 61, 63) and weakness as a politician (ch.13n.). The *Life* is also moralistic, praising Pompey's personal habits (chs 18, 40, 53) but censuring him when necessary (chs 10, 29, 30, 31) and making general moral observations (chs 28, 53; see further Pelling [2] 135 with nn. 40-1). Themes include Pompey's caution and vulnerability to Fortune (ch. 51n.), and his passivity (ch. 47n.). Plutarch's portrayal of Pompey, however, is one of the most favourable of all the *Lives,* and in his desire to show why Pompey was so popular amongst the people Plutarch attributes to him qualities of tact and lack of arrogance which contrast sharply with the picture we receive from Cicero's letters (ch. 1n.).

On the other hand, Plutarch makes little attempt to explain Pompey's actions in relation to the general historical background, especially the complex politics of the 50s BC, though he emphasises the effect of the deaths of Julia and Crassus (ch. 53n.) and realises that the Optimates* were using Pompey to get rid of Caesar and afterwards would have tried to eliminate him too (ch. 67). Nor does Plutarch seem fully to appreciate how Pompey, like other Roman generals and politicians, often acted in a way which was not altruistic but designed to build up his *clientela**, both in Rome (chs 21, the people; 22, the equites*) and abroad (chs 10, in Sicily; 12, in Africa; 39, in the East; see further Pelling [3] 178-9).

In the *Caesar* Plutarch makes much more of an attempt to relate his subject's career to the historical background, especially with regard to the approach of tyranny. Passages to be noted are chs 29 (seizing 'supreme power' is not mentioned in the parallel *Pompey* 57); 30 ('tyranny' is not mentioned in *Pompey* 58); and 35 (N.B. 'you are my prisoner...in my hands'). It then comes as no surprise when Plutarch says that Caesar's rule was 'an undisguised tyranny' (ch. 57, cf. 69). For Plutarch the reason that Caesar successfully achieved his aim was his championing of the people, and this is a recurrent theme of the *Life* beginning in chs 4-5. Consequently, Caesar's personal life is far less prominent than Pompey's, though his sexual habits were ideal material for biography, and there are fewer moral judgments (see Pelling [1] 78, [2] 136-7, [3] 159-60). Also, Plutarch is too ready to assume that 'Caesar was born to do great things' (ch. 58) and had planned from the beginning to seize absolute power. Plutarch's contention is that the Optimates*, with the exception of Cato (ch. 13) and perhaps Cicero (ch. 4), failed to realise Caesar's threat until it was too late. This ignores the fact that his career only became extraordinary when the short-sightedness of the Optimates* alienated Pompey and drove him into a political alliance with Caesar and Crassus. Caesar's importance before this is exaggerated (e.g. ch. 8), and Plutarch fails to give adequate weight to Crassus' backing of the young Caesar (he is only mentioned in ch. 11 before the formation of the 'Triumvirate' in ch. 13). It should be noted, however, that Plutarch knew Caesar's career took off after his alliance with Pompey (see Pelling [3] 162 with n. 10).

The emphasis on Caesar's popularity in turn distorts Plutarch's version in this *Life* of Caesar's assassination. In chs 60-1 Plutarch concentrates on the people's declining attitude towards him: it was only when he became dictator and began to act in an increasingly tactless and tyrannical fashion that he lost his popularity (contrast *Antony* 12). Even then Caesar's changed circumstances might in part be attributed to the actions of his friends (chs 51, 57, 60). Finally, however, the 'people began to turn their thoughts towards Marcus Brutus' (ch. 62). This is not Plutarch's version elsewhere (*Brutus* 10.3-4), and he clearly suppresses much material dealing with the conspirators' motives for the assassination in order to maintain the popular theme. See further Pelling [1] 77-9.

The *Cicero* has usually been seen as the least satisfactory of these *Lives* as history, and its weaknesses are examined by Moles (pp. 46-9). However, Moles attempts to rehabilitate the *Life* (pp. 49-53) and defends Plutarch's insight into several aspects of Cicero's career, contending that Plutarch was aware of the problems which faced Cicero as a 'new man'* (pp. 147-8) and understood his policy towards Octavian (pp. 52, 194, 197). Certainly Plutarch's portrait of Cicero's character, with all its virtues and defects, tensions and inconsistencies, is brilliant and compelling; and Moles also shows how several of Cicero's actions might be seen, with Plutarch, in the light of this character. Furthermore, while some episodes are clearly fictitious (e.g. the nurse's dream, ch. 2; Cicero at Delphi, ch. 5; Caesar's reaction to the Ligarius speech, ch. 39), there is a wealth of material concerning Cicero's public and private life which is reliable and often extremely important. Such material will derive from primary sources (see next section).

The value, then, of the *Cicero* as an historical source with historical insight has been underestimated, and with its moral analysis it is also a powerful work of literature. Nevertheless, there *are* definite signs within the *Life* of its inferiority as a source to the *Pompey* and *Caesar*, which have been demonstrated by Pelling [1]. The crux of the matter is the order and method of composition of the three works.

4. PLUTARCH'S METHOD OF COMPOSITION AND THE ORDER
   OF THE *LIVES*

The *Demosthenes* and *Cicero*, Plutarch tells us, formed the fifth book of his *Parallel Lives* (*Demosthenes* 3.1) and so were one of the earliest in the series of twenty-three pairs written over a long period of time (perhaps c. AD 96-120, as Jones 136). It is apparent that by the time he came to write the *Caesar* and *Pompey*, Plutarch had a far wider knowledge of Roman history and could include far more detail on the 50s BC. In fact it seems highly likely that Plutarch wrote the *Cicero* some years before a group of six which he prepared together (*Crassus, Pompey, Caesar, Cato, Brutus* and *Antony*; the final draft of the *Pompey* was written after that of *Caesar*: cf. *Caesar* 35). This hypothesis can be supported by a comparison of *Cicero* 46 and 48 with *Antony* 19-20 (see nn.). Plutarch evidently had access to new material when writing the *Antony*, and this provides the clue to his much fuller and more accurate accounts in the group of six : he had by now read the famous history of C. Asinius Pollio, which covered the civil wars from 60 BC probably down to the end of the 30s BC. Pollio seems to have been one of Appian's (and perhaps also Dio's) principal sources, and Plutarch almost certainly used him directly or indirectly as his major source for this period (cf. *Caesar* 32).

It seems, in fact, that Plutarch's method in these six *Lives* was to use the one (Pollio-)source as his basic narrative, a common practice among ancient writers. Pelling [1] 76-8 has analysed two episodes, the formation of the 'First Triumvirate' and Caesar's first consulship, and

Caesar's assassination, from which he concludes that the later accounts not only are superior to those in the *Lucullus* and *Cicero*, but also derive from the same source. Differences between the individual accounts may be explained by literary technique, with emphasis shifted according to the subject of the *Life*. Thus Lucullus, Pompey's enemy, is prominent in *Pompey* 48 but omitted in *Caesar* 13-14. Plutarch did, however, use other material, and he quotes over thirty sources in these eight *Lives*, though he clearly did not consult all of them at first hand, e.g. he probably knew Caesar and Tanusius through Pollio (*Caesar* 15, 22nn.). Nevertheless, rich biographical details in the early chapters of the *Caesar* should derive from C. Oppius (ch. 17, cf. *Pompey* 10), and those in the *Pompey* may come from Theophanes (ch. 32n.); Plutarch probably knew Livy (*Caesar* 47); and Sallust was certainly used for the *Lucullus* and *Sertorius*, probably for the early chapters of *Pompey* and to supplement the Catiline narrative in *Cicero* (see Moles 29). Plutarch evidently knew Cicero's works, including some which do not survive (*Caesar* 8, *Cicero* 24), and he seems to have used other primary sources, such as the letters of Brutus (*Cicero* 45); Tiro's collection of Cicero's jokes (id. 1n.) and biography of Cicero (id. 41, 49); Antony's reply to the *Second Philippic* (id. 41); and Augustus' *Autobiography* (id. 45). See further Moles 28-32. Finally, other biographies, memoirs, histories and to a lesser extent first-hand material such as letters and speeches might supplement his Pollio-source for the later *Lives*, as well as his own earlier *Cicero* and oral tradition (see Moles 30; *Caesar* 26n.).

In sum, we need not doubt that Plutarch carried out a considerable amount of research for his Roman *Lives*, but largely due to the difficult conditions under which he was working he will have adopted the regular ancient method and where possible will have based his account on a single source.

Commentary

Pompey

Chapter 1

Cn. Pompeius Magnus was born on 29 September 106 BC. Plutarch begins the *Life* by contrasting Pompey's popularity with the people's hatred of his father, Cn. Pompeius **Strabo** (the line of Aeschylus comes from the lost *Prometheus Unbound*, frg. 201N). Strabo was the first member of his branch of the family to be elected consul (89 BC), mainly because he showed himself to be **a most formidable soldier** as a legate of the consul P. Rutilius Lupus in 90 BC. Strabo's generalship turned the tide of the Social War against Rome's Italian allies, especially with the capture of the rebel stronghold Asculum in Picenum, the area where Strabo's estates and family influence lay. However, Strabo also displayed a readiness to use violence for his own ends; and his political double-dealing, in particular his failure to save Rome from the advance of Cinna and Marius in 87 BC (chap. 3), provided ammunition for the propaganda of enemies like Sulla. Hence the sources are hostile and attribute the riot at his funeral to his failure to help Rome and to his treachery. Plutarch mentions Strabo's unpopularity elsewhere (ch. 37, *Crassus* 6.4, *Mor.* 203B, 553C); here he puts **the hatred felt against Strabo** solely down to **his insatiable love of money,** an example of which is that he auctioned the slaves and booty from Asculum and kept the proceeds for himself, instead of donating them to the hard-pressed treasury. Strabo's death in 87 BC may have been from the plague rather than **by a thunderbolt,** but the question remains open. See now Watkins, O.D., 'The Death of Cn.Pompeius Strabo' *Rh. Mus.* 131 (1988) pp. 143-50.

The characterisation of Pompey in this chapter is clearly distorted, as Plutarch begins to paint an idealised picture of his subject. The distortion is initiated by the internal comparison of father and son, and increased by the attribution to Pompey of qualities which would surprise readers of Cicero's correspondence. Pompey could certainly be **tactful** (chs 8, 19, 39) and would court public opinion (chs 43, 45), but Cicero easily saw through him (e.g. *Att.* 1.13.4, cf. *Fam.* 8.1.3). In fact he evidently learned many lessons from his father – the use of loyal troops for protection and as a political weapon (ch. 13), techniques of betrayal and playing his opponents off against one another (e.g. his use of Clodius and Cicero, chs 46 and 49), and the value of money (ch. 52).

Chapter 2

Plutarch's description of Pompey's **appearance** fits with the portraits that have survived. **Alexander** evidently was Pompey's hero, since there are numerous examples of Pompey imitating him (e.g. his retirement to his tent, ch. 13, cf. *Alexander* 62.5; see Weinstock 37, but also ch. 46n.). For **Lucius** Marcius **Philippus** (cos. 91 BC) see chs 4, 16, 17.

Further on **Flora** see ch. 53 and on **Geminius** ch. 16; the identity of **Caecilius Metellus** is unknown. **The temple of Castor and Pollux** was a conspicuous landmark to the south of the forum, built early in the fifth century. Its steps were often used to address meetings, and it was a rallying point in the gang warfare of the 50s.

On **Demetrius** see ch. 40n. Public figures are forever the target of censure for sexual misconduct, but Plutarch later notes Pompey's **constancy as a husband** (ch. 53). Ironically, however, accusations of his **neglecting public business** then stemmed from his devotion to his fourth wife Julia.

Pompey was hardly likely to buy a **thrush** from L. Licinius **Lucullus**, one of his greatest enemies (ch. 46). Lucullus was famed for his gardens in north Rome and especially his fishponds.

Chapter 3

In 87 BC the consul L. Cornelius **Cinna** was expelled from Rome by his colleague Cn. Octavius, but he returned with C. Marius to capture the city and rule it until his death in 84 BC. Strabo was summoned to defend Rome against Cinna, and he pitched camp outside the Colline Gate; however, he failed to save Octavius and was even intriguing with Cinna just before his death. Plutarch's story here is presumably set in this camp, and its credibility is defended by Keaveney, A., 'Young Pompey: 106-79 B.C.' *L'Antiquité Classique* 51 (1982) pp. 112-13. Strabo would have remained in his tent not through fear but because he had the plague, from which he was to die; and Keaveney also accepts Pompey's role in the story. Note, however, that the story resumes the comparison of father and son in ch. 1, and whatever unrest there may have been is exaggerated in order to extol Pompey (cf. similar histrionics in ch. 13).

Pompey and **Lucius Terentius** were, in regular Roman fashion, receiving their early military training on Strabo's staff as members of his advisory council (*consilium*). Pompey, who was only eighteen in 87 BC, had already served with Terentius in the Social War at the siege of Asculum – their names appear on the Asculum inscription recording Strabo's grant of Roman citizenship to thirty Spanish cavalrymen (*ILS* 8888). See Mattingly, H.B., 'The *consilium* of Cn. Pompeius Strabo in 89 B.C.' *Athenaeum* 53 (1975) pp. 262-6.

Chapter 4

Strabo's death was certainly untimely for the young Pompey. Because his family's nobility* only began with his father, the nucleus of his potential political support lay not in the senate but in Picenum (as Plutarch notes in ch. 6). So he would have to build up for himself the nexus of friendships (*amicitiae**) that was an important element of a political career at Rome.

A more immediate problem was Strabo's unpopularity. This may have been a factor in the ransacking of Strabo's house **by Cinna's bodyguard,** though such pillaging was inevitable in these disturbed times, but Pompey's trial for misappropriation of public funds (*peculatus*) was a direct consequence of Strabo's behaviour at Asculum (it presumably took place in 86 BC, as Plutarch implies). Nevertheless, the Cinnan regime supported Pompey, adding credence to the report of Strabo's secret negotiations with Cinna just before his death: Philippus compared Pompey to Alexander (ch. 2; his son had probably served with Pompey at Asculum); the rising barrister Q. Hortensius spoke for him; and, very significantly, Cn. Papirius Carbo, Cinna's right-hand man, made one of his rare court appearances. With this support Pompey's acquittal was ensured. Plutarch typically prefers to note Pompey's **keen intelligence** and balance, which resulted in his engagement to the daughter of the judge. Antistius and his friends evidently saw Pompey's potential, and such patronage by leading families was regular in an up-and-coming politician's career (e.g. Cicero 3.2). Further on the trial see Gruen [1] 244-6; Shatzman, I., 'The Roman General's Authority over Booty' *Historia* 21 (1972) pp. 194-5 (Shatzman shows that Pompey had every right to possess the **hunting nets and books**).

Antistius is probably the P. Antistius (tr. 88 BC) who was murdered by the younger Marius in 82 BC. If so, since Velleius (2.26.2) says he had only reached the aedileship, Plutarch's description of Antistius as a **praetor** is anachronistic (praetors being the presiding officers in courts in the post-Sullan period). Plutarch's explanation of 'Talasio' derives from Livy 1.9.12 (see Ogilvie's note ad loc.).

Chapter 5

Having received Cinnan backing at his trial, Pompey **then joined Cinna's army.** Plutarch's story that his subsequent **disappearance** led to the mutiny in which Cinna was killed (84 BC) clearly overestimates Pompey's importance at this time and conflicts with the preferable version of Appian (*BC* 1.78). Appian states that the riot was caused by those of Cinna's troops who did not relish the prospect of fighting their fellow citizens. Keaveney (*L'Ant. Class.* 51 [1982] pp. 114-17) attempts to reconcile the two accounts. Cinna, who had tried to have Strabo assassinated (ch.3), would have been suspicious of Pompey's intentions, and this may help to explain the otherwise obscure **various accusations and suggestions...being made against him.** Pompey therefore went into hiding; and the Picentine troops in the camp believed the **rumour...that Cinna had killed him** and joined the rest of the troops in the riot.

Carbo now **took over and kept the supreme power** as sole consul, preventing the election of a suffect. Like Cinna, Carbo is blackened by Sullan propaganda, but he certainly made himself unpopular with the Italian cities by demanding hostages and alienated most of the moderate nobility, who deserted to Sulla after his return from Italy in 83 BC. Pompey also soon made up his mind which would be the winning side.

For civil wars taking away any **hope of freedom** see ch. 70n.

Chapter 6

Pompey waited for Sulla's return in **Picenum,** where, along with his estates, he had also inherited Strabo's friends, veterans and clients. He presumably spent his time negotiating and making preparations, so that when Carbo had recruiting agents sent into the district, Pompey **started an agitation** and was received **with enthusiasm.** He then **appointed himself** general (he was in fact still only twenty-two), and from Strabo's clients and veterans **in a short time** raised firstly one legion, then two more after his meeting with Sulla (ch. 8; the veterans would have provided the **centurions**). The proconsul Q. Caecilius Metellus Pius and the young M. Licinius Crassus had similarly raised armies and joined Sulla. On **Vedius** see Syme, R., 'Who was Vedius Pollio?' *JRS* 51 (1961) p. 30.

Chapter 7

Chs 7-8 provide a good example of Plutarch's chronological displacement of events (Intro. 2), for some at least of the events in ch. 7 must have taken place *after* the meeting of Pompey and Sulla in ch. 8. See

Tuplin, C., 'Coelius or Cloelius?' *Chiron* 9 (1979) pp. 137-45, esp. 143-4; Keaveney, L'Ant. Class. 51 (1982) pp. 117-20. Plutarch deliberately antedates these events, so that Pompey in ch. 8 can receive greater **honours from Sulla than he expected.**

The three-pronged attack on Pompey was led by C. Carrinas (pr. 82 BC), L. Iunius **Brutus** Damasippus (pr. 82 BC) and a third general whose name is unclear – either T. Cluilius (as Broughton ii. 65) or C. Coelius Antipater (as Tuplin). **Scipio** Asiaticus was also abandoned by his army at Teanum when confronted by Sulla (*Sulla* 28.1-3), casting doubt on Plutarch's account here (if genuine, this episode will have taken place after Pompey had returned to Picenum to continue recruiting); and Pompey's defeat of Carbo's **cavalry...near the River Arsis** (? the Aesis, the northern boundary of Picenum) certainly seems both misplaced and exaggerated. Plutarch is again magnifying the early career of his subject.

Chapter 8

Sulla, meanwhile, was marching towards Campania, unaware **of these successes** and probably apprehensive about the allegiance of the son of his enemy Strabo, rather than **hurrying to his help.** The offer of Pompey's legion dispelled his doubts, and he tactfully returned Pompey's greeting of him as **'Imperator'** (cf. *Crassus* 6.4). Keaveney notes (*L'Ant. Class.* 51 [1982] p. 120) that this was not the equivalent of the soldiers' acclamation of an 'Imperator'*, but a gesture of respect. Nevertheless, this flattery of Pompey, who had illegally raised a private army and was still too young to hold public office at Rome (and so **was not yet even a member of the senate**), already put him in the kind of special position which was to be his objective throughout his career. Sulla, who was already 'Imperator'* as a result of his Eastern victories not because he **was at war with such men as Scipio and Marius** (the younger), now went on to defeat the consul Norbanus and win over the army of the other consul Scipio. Pompey may have been with him, before returning to Picenum to complete his levy.

In 82 BC the proconsul Metellus engaged Carbo's forces in north Italy and Cisalpine Gaul, and Sulla sent Pompey to serve under him because of his family connections in the area. Appian's account (*BC* 1.87-92) provides a corrective to Plutarch's exaggeration of Pompey's merits, though the details are by no means clear (for Pompey's tactic of feigned reluctance **to take over the command** see ch. 13n.). Metellus defeated Carrinas at the River Aesis, was blockaded by Carbo until his withdrawal to Ariminum, then defeated C. Marcius Censorinus. Pompey, meanwhile, harassed Carbo's rearguard with his cavalry, and defeated Censorinus' remaining troops at Sena Gallica. Metellus went on to secure Cisalpine Gaul, but Pompey was transferred to Sulla's command and helped Crassus defeat Carrinas again at Spoletium. He followed this up by ambushing a large force under Censorinus on its way to relieve Marius in Praeneste. Norbanus and Carbo now fled, abandoning Clusium to Pompey, where he allegedly killed two-thirds of Carbo's troops. Appian's account, in sum, shows Pompey as Metellus' cavalry commander, then as an efficient but inexperienced legate of Sulla (both Carrinas and Censorinus escaped his blockades) – hardly yet performing deeds which **were extraordinary in themselves.**

The internal comparison of Pompey and Metellus here serves once again to highlight the character of Plutarch's subject by comparing it with a lesser one (see further ch. 17n.). Note too the athletic imagery, which recurs several times in the *Life* (chs 17, 20, 41, 51, 66; see Pelling [2] 135 n. 35; ch. 68n. on tragic imagery). The chapter is also important for Plutarch's observations on his selection of material. Selectivity is crucial to the aesthetic balance of the *Life* (**lest I should take up too much space**) and is intrinsically bound up with Plutarch's aims as a biographer (the choice of the events **best suited to illustrate his character**). See Wardman 154-61; Intro. 1.

Chapter 9

The war in Italy effectively was ended by Sulla's victory outside the Colline Gate. The infamous proscriptions followed (cf. ch.10), in which Crassus for one enriched himself, and then Sulla's dictatorship. Sulla was now faced with the problem of what to do about Pompey, who was at the head of three legions. According to Plutarch Sulla therefore attached Pompey to himself by an ill-fated political **marriage alliance** with his step-daughter Aemilia, child of his wife Metella by M. Aemilius Scaurus (cos. 115 BC), even though she was pregnant by her husband M'. Acilius Glabrio. This date, before Pompey left for Sicily, is questioned by Keaveney (*L'Ant. Class.* 51 [1982] pp. 131-2), on the grounds that Sulla was not then **Dictator** and there was not enough time for the marriage before Pompey's departure. He therefore places the marriage in 81 BC (ch. 14n.). Whatever the date Pompey was being drawn into the inner ring of Rome's nobility*, which had been so hostile to his father but which saw in him the potential to help re-establish its political dominance. Pompey would not have been blind to the opportunities which were opening up for him, however much he felt for Antistia and her plight (her father **had been murdered in the senate house** by the praetor Damasippus on the orders of Marius).

Note the apologetic tone of **rather in the interests of Sulla than in accordance with the character of Pompey**: the early chapters of the Pompey are idealised (ch. 1n.; cf. the doctrine of *Cimon* 2.4-5). Also,

Pompey's divorce and remarriage were for Plutarch a **tragedy**, and Antistia's family seems cursed, like that of Oedipus. This reflects the general influence of tragedy on biography and historiography, to which Plutarch was in fact hostile (see Wardman 168-79). Nevertheless, the second half of the *Life* from ch. 46 has an evident tragic texture, which is foreshadowed here and in ch. 38, and culminates in the tragedy of Pharsalus, and Pompey's flight and assassination. See further Pelling [2] 131-5.

Chapter 10

The continuing activities of his enemies in the provinces gave Sulla the opportunity to make further use of Pompey's military talents, while Pompey's youth and lack of official status in Rome made him, on the face of it, a less dangerous choice than the more experienced Metellus. Carbo had escaped to Africa and **was cruising off Sicily with a fleet**; M. Perperna Veiento (**Perpenna**; probably pr. 82 BC) was **occupying Sicily**; and Cn. Domitius Ahenobarbus **had invaded Libya** (i.e. Africa). So Pompey was now given his first official command, being invested by the senate with propraetorian *imperium** and six legions (ch. 11).

The first stage in Sicily was swiftly accomplished and without fighting. Perperna fled perhaps first to Liguria and Sardinia and then, after Lepidus' revolt, to Spain (ch. 16n.;Keaveney, *L'Ant. Class.* 51 [1982] pp. 125-7). Some other leaders, however, were captured and executed, including Carbo. Pompey would have been acting on Sulla's orders, but his alleged treatment of Carbo, **who had been three times consul** (85, 84 and 82 BC), and **Quintus Valerius** (? Q. Valerius Soranus, tr. 82 BC) fuelled much anti-Pompeian propaganda and gave rise to the appellation 'the teenage butcher' (*adulescentulus carnifex*, Val. Max. 6.2.8). Since Carbo had defended Pompey at his trial in 86 BC, it was **necessary for him to put Carbo to death** as proof of his loyalty to Sulla, and Carbo may have been one of the proscribed (see Seager 9-10). Pompey's ingratitude was noted, however, and Cicero would also discover to his cost how Pompey was always ready to betray old friends when circumstances dictated (*Cicero* 31.2-3). See further his treatment of Brutus (ch. 16n.). Counter-propaganda stressed Pompey's **great humanity** towards the Sicilians (**except for the Mamertines**; their alliance with Rome went back to the First Punic War); his outstanding integrity, dignity and ability (Cic. *Leg. Man.* 61); the fact that he even let many of Sulla's enemies **get away** and **actually helped them to escape**; and his firm control over his soldiers (having **their swords sealed up in their scabbards**; cf. *Mor.* 203C).

This is one of the relatively rare occasions on which Plutarch names his source, the Caesarian **Gaius Oppius** (Intro. 4), and he displays commendable awareness of the problems of source criticism. He fails, however, to state an obvious motive for Pompey's clemency: his personal *clientela** in Sicily was thereby enlarged, and his influence was extended by grants of citizenship to leading Sicilians. Prominent among these was Sthenius (**Sthenis**), the leader of **Himera**, who was one of Verres' victims in 72 BC. Sthenius and Pompey's other injured Sicilian clients would use their patron's influence to secure Verres' condemnation (ch. 22n.). Plutarch is more concerned with the opportunity afforded here to insert a typical story of *parrhesia* (i.e. **frankness of speech**) which brings its reward (cf. Lucilius at *Brutus* 50).

Chapter 11

Leaving his brother-in-law C. **Memmius** in charge of Sicily, Pompey crossed to Africa for the second stage of his mission. His receipt of **a decree of the senate and a letter from Sulla** hardly indicates a new command, since he would not have been given six legions to deal with Sicily alone, and there is no indication that he levied the majority of his force after his capture of the island. On the contrary Plutarch notes that **Pompey made his preparations quickly**, and Cicero remarks on his speed in taking Sicily (*Leg. Man.* 30). In Africa Pompey was faced with a much stiffer challenge, the influence of **Marius** being still strong. **Marius had raised** a force there in 87 BC of c. 1000 (*Marius* 41.2), but Domitius' **much larger army** numbered c. 27,000 (chs 11-12). Still, Pompey's **six legions at full strength** could imply a force of c. 36,000 (see Brunt [1] 687-93), and the odds were made better for him by the desertion of **7,000 of the enemy**. Pompey also had the support of Bogud, King of Mauretania, and the battle turned into a **great slaughter** (ch. 12).

The story of the hidden treasure reflects Plutarch's love of the striking anecdote, which he will include even if he knows or suspects it to be untrue (N.B. **they say**). See Moles 35, 38 (k). The story is included here to emphasise Pompey's superiority to greed and the devotion of his men in the first half of the *Life* (contrast chs 67-8).

Chapter 12

Pompey's refusal to accept his salutation as '**Imperator**'* until Domitius' camp was captured was perhaps a lesson learnt from the previous year – whereas Carrinas and Censorinus had escaped, **Domitius was killed**. Pompey proceeded to capture Domitius' ally, King Hiarbas (**Iarbas**) of Numidia, who was executed and replaced by the ex-king **Hiempsal**. The latter had supported the governor of Africa, P. Sextilius, when he refused to help Marius and, presumably, also aided Metellus when he raised his army in Africa. Hiarbas' support of Domitius meant the forces of a client kingdom were used in a Roman civil war, but Pompey's victory over him could be represented as one over a foreign enemy and deserving of a triumph.

This chapter is full of commonplaces (*topoi*) connected with battle: **a storm of rain;** the 'ideal general' who acts speedily and exploits his **opportunity,** fights bravely and suffers **a narrow escape**; and the general's **use of his good fortune.**

Chapter 13

With Sicily and Africa secured, Sulla seems to have thought he could simply dismiss Pompey without reward, turning him into a private citizen again. Pompey, however, may already have been hailed as '**Magnus**' in Africa (among the **others** who **say** this is Pliny, *NH* 7.96); and he will have had no intention of standing for this. Plutarch's account perhaps suggests that he skilfully tested and manipulated the feelings of his troops to ensure their backing, and such feigned unwillingness for power until being 'forced' to accept was to be one of his trademarks (as ch. 30; but his supposed use of this tactic in ch. 8 seems an anachronism on Plutarch's part). Keaveney, on the other hand (*L'Ant. Class.* 51 [1982] pp. 128-31), argues that Pompey did not engineer the mutiny, though he then used it for his own advantage: having demobilised the army in Africa, he disobeyed the instructions of the **letter from Sulla** and returned to Italy, which was illegal because he left his province without permission. He could claim in his defence that he was only able to persuade the troops to return by promising to accompany them himself; and indeed it appears that as soon as he reached Italy he discharged the army. Sulla's remark that, having defeated the younger Marius, he seemed **fated...to have boys for his antagonists,** may then imply that he initially thought of a punitive expedition; but **when he learned the truth** about how Pompey had dealt with the mutiny, he welcomed him warmly (N.B. Pompey was already, or was about to become, Sulla's son-in-law). Keaveney perhaps over-states Pompey's innocence in this affair, relying too heavily on Plutarch's account, which parallels Pompey's histrionics in ch. 3 and forms part of Plutarch's characterisation. Either way, Pompey had shown that he would not simply be discarded, and he immediately displayed his opportunism by requesting a triumph.

The story that Sulla **decided to outdo** everyone else in greeting Pompey, which parallels their meeting in ch. 8, is part of an 'escort scene': these serve as a barometer of Pompey's fortunes (chs 21, 23, 26, 27, 43, 57; contrast 73, 78). It is also an 'arrival scene': the *adventus* of a great

17

man was customarily greeted with public celebrations, and so Pompey's status is already becoming 'great'. He was still modest, however, not using the title '**Magnus**' until 77 BC.

Plutarch typically takes the opportunity here to compare his subject with famous men of the past: M'. **Valerius** Maximus as dictator in 494 BC induced the plebeians* to perform their military service after the first secession of the plebs; Q. **Fabius** Maximus Rullianus as censor in 304 BC restricted the registration of freedmen to the four urban tribes (Ap. Claudius Caecus as censor in 312 BC had admitted sons of freedmen into the senate, but these were rejected by the consuls of 311 BC). The passage also reflects Plutarch's division between **successes in war** and the higher level of **achievements in civil life**. The real test for Pompey will come in his political career, especially after his first consulship in 70 BC; and his change of lifestyle then (ch. 23) foreshadows his later failure to convert his military success in the East into political success at Rome. He will be forced to turn firstly to the demagogue Clodius (ch. 46) and ultimately to an agreement with Caesar (ch. 47). See Wardman 94-7.

Chapter 14

The request was opposed by Sulla, understandably enough though not for the technical reason given: by the late Republic triumphs were celebrated by magistrates (dictators as well as consuls and praetors) and promagistrates (proconsuls and propraetors) with *imperium**; and Pompey held propraetorian *imperium** (ch. 10n.). This was not the case at the time of Scipio Africanus, the first private citizen to be invested with proconsular *imperium** (210-206 BC) who was never praetor and did not become consul until 205 BC (some sources say he *did* receive a triumph; see Broughton i. 299). Pompey's age is also then technically irrelevant, even though he **was too young even to be a senator** (the minimum age for the quaestorship, which gave entry to the senate, was thirty after Sulla's reforms; hence **Pompey could easily have become a member of the senate** is incorrect). Pompey for his part could argue that his operations against Hiarbas were an external war (another requirement for a triumph), and according to Plutarch he persisted until Sulla gave up his resistance in exasperation. Keaveney (*L'Ant. Class.* 51 [1982] p. 133) suggests that Sulla agreed to Pompey's triumph in return for Pompey's agreement to divorce Antistia and marry Aemilia (ch. 9), and it was in this context that Pompey made his impudent 'rising sun' remark. If, on the other hand, Pompey was in fact already married to Aemilia, Sulla's change of mind would have been prompted at least in part by his private relationship with Pompey. Whatever the reason, for the first time a member of the equestrian order* celebrated a triumph.

18

During the triumph Pompey's former soldiers again **showed a tendency to mutiny**, and his reaction earned him the respect of P. **Servilius** Vatia Isauricus (cos. 79 BC; cf. *Mor.* 203F; Front. *Strat.* 4.5.1). Servilius was a leading member of the Metellan faction*, and soon after his triumph Pompey married Mucia, half-sister of the rising Q. Metellus Celer and Q. Metellus Nepos. So Pompey was now closely linked with the leading faction* behind Sulla, and he remained a Sullan for the next decade. See further Twyman 826, 835-6.

The dates of both the triumph and the marriage are disputed. The former was probably in 81 BC (as Keaveney, *L'Ant. Class.* 51 [1982] pp. 131-3); the latter probably in 80 BC (as Ward, A.M., 'The Early Relationships between Cicero and Pompey until 80 B.C. (*Phoenix* 24 [1970] p. 126 n. 37). The story that **the city gate was too narrow** to allow Pompey's **triumphal entry in a chariot drawn by four elephants** (instead of **the conventional** four **horses**) may hide Sulla's refusal to allow such a display. Pompey's circumstances already had a considerable effect in making him popular among the ordinary people, and Sulla's natural reaction, like that of the nobility* in general, would have been to try to prevent his popularity increasing any further.

On Plutarch's theme here of allaying envy by modesty see Wardman 76-8.

Chapter 15

Sulla's legislation as dictator, especially the establishment of a fixed order of magistracies (*cursus honorum*), temporarily halted Pompey's unconstitutional career at this point. Plutarch again exaggerates his importance by asserting that Sulla was ashamed to interfere and so did nothing about his growing power. If the system were rigidly enforced, Pompey would have to suffer the humiliation of waiting to stand for the quaestorship, the lowest rung on the ladder, at the age of thirty. So the newly-married Pompey may for the time being have withdrawn into private life, until the consular elections of 79 BC. At these he supported the candidature of M. Aemilius **Lepidus**, who had probably served with him at Asculum. Sulla did not attempt to influence the outcome and thereby undermine his own system (see Keaveney 210, *L'Ant. Class.* 51 [1982] pp. 135-7); and Pompey's **personal popularity** will have helped secure Lepidus' election, though once more Plutarch overestimates Pompey's role (Sulla's failure here parallels the circumstances of Pompey's triumph in ch. 14).

Sulla's rebuke perhaps stems from the fact that Lepidus won **more votes at the election than Catulus** and hence certain privileges (such as chairing senatorial debates), for Q. Lutatius Catulus was already **one of the best** men living and proved to be the backbone of the Optimates* (ch. 16). It can then hardly have come as a surprise to Pompey when Sulla proceeded to cut him out of **his will**. Pompey, however, displayed both his acumen and true loyalties by supporting Catulus against Lepidus in the matter of Sulla's **funeral**, the first to be paid for by the **state**. The precise order of events in 78 BC is unclear, but by the time of the funeral Lepidus may already have announced his anti-Sullan reform programme. Pompey had no desire yet to see the overthrow of Sulla's regulations and ended his support of Lepidus, taking up the Optimate* cause.

Chapter 16

It is difficult to reconstruct a cogent account of Lepidus' rebellion from Plutarch and the other sources. **He took up arms immediately**, for example, cannot be correct – in fact Lepidus and Catulus first continued their disagreement when sent to suppress a rising in Etruria. An alarmed senate made them swear not to fight each other. Lepidus then refused to hold the consular elections and perhaps headed northwards to recruit more troops from his allotted province of Transalpine Gaul. M. Iunius **Brutus**, Lepidus' legate in 77 BC, was probably already raising an army in **Cisalpine Gaul**, where Lepidus had important connections. Some senators (i.e. **the old factions now long enfeebled**) wanted to make an agreement with Lepidus, but Pompey's long-time supporter L. Philippus (ch. 2) induced the senate to pass its 'ultimate decree' (*senatus consultum ultimum*)* and commission Catulus as proconsul to put down the revolt (he was by this time no longer Lepidus' **colleague** in the consulship). As Catulus was not renowned for his **military leadership** and as Pompey had his large *clientela** in Picenum, the senate gave Pompey another special grant of *imperium**, probably praetorian, **to operate against Lepidus**. It is unclear whether Pompey was technically Catulus' legate or an independent general, and his refusal **to disband his troops** on Catulus' orders (ch. 17) could point in either direction (see Twyman 821).

Pompey **subdued with ease most of the rebel forces** in Cisalpine Gaul and besieged Brutus in **Mutina**, while Lepidus made a dash on Rome. On receiving news of the fall of Mutina, Catulus attacked and defeated Lepidus, who was declared an enemy (*hostis*) of Rome. After retreating to Etruria, Lepidus **crossed over to Sardinia**, where he died: Plutarch emphasises that the cause was the infidelity of **his wife** Appuleia, which reflects Plutarch's interest in such quirky detail for its own sake. Many of his supporters joined Sertorius in Spain under M. Perperna Veiento. Brutus for his part **retired** to Regium Lepidi and **was put to death by Geminius** (Pompey's friend, ch. 2), in one version while attempting to escape (Oros. 5.22.17). Brutus too may have been declared an enemy of Rome, but the episode only added to Pompey's

20

reputation as the 'teenage butcher' (ch. 10). Plutarch takes the opportunity to make another comparison of father and son which again favours the latter.

Chapter 17

A far more dangerous threat to Rome's stability lay in Spain, where the praetor of 83 BC and former governor of the Nearer province, Q. Sertorius, was prolonging **the last stages** of the Marian cause against Sulla, backed by the Lusitanians. In 79 BC his quaestor, L. Hirtuleius, had defeated and killed the **inferior** proconsul of Nearer Spain, M. Domitius Calvinus (pr. 80 BC), and Sertorius himself **was now engaged with Metellus Pius**, the **distinguished** proconsul of Further Spain, (Sulla's fellow consul in 80 BC; see Spann 40-72). Sertorius' guerrilla tactics, **unconventional** but more suited to the Spanish terrain than the **heavily armed** Roman methods, were proving highly effective. Plutarch overemphasises Metellus' inability to cope with the situation in chs 17 and 18, to heighten the need for Pompey's services and perhaps reflecting pro-Pompeian propaganda at the time. It is also noticeable that Plutarch has already in ch. 8 reported a similar story, of an ageing Metellus failing to carry out his command efficiently until the arrival of Pompey instilled fresh vigour into him (cf. *Sertorius* 13.1-2, 18.1-2; N.B. the athletic imagery here, not fully brought out in the Penguin translation **liable to be left behind**; see ch. 8n.). Nevertheless, he was unable to capture Sertorius, and Perperna's arrival with fifty-three cohorts necessitated reinforcements.

After defeating Lepidus (ch. 16) Pompey refused **to disband his troops** on Catulus' orders and **remained under arms near** Rome as his father had done. He was hardly aiming at a dictatorship, but he used this threat and his connections to obtain a command against Sertorius **with the status and power of a consul** (*imperium pro consule*).

The famous remark of **Philippus** was recorded by Cicero (*Phil.* 11.18), who also says that both consuls of 77 BC refused the command. They were perhaps reluctant to fight a guerrilla war in Spain, though both may have had Marian sympathies (see Twyman 821, 848-9). Indeed, few men of distinction appear in the war, the most famous name among Pompey's legates being that of the scholar M. Terentius Varro.

Chapter 18

Pompey marched to Spain via Transalpine Gaul, defeating the Saluvii and other tribes. Plutarch omits this campaign of autumn 77 BC and concentrates instead on the contrasting actions and characters of Pompey, Sertorius and Metellus: Pompey is energetic, popular and **temperate**; Sertorius is **contemptuous** and fearful of Pompey; while **Metellus...had given himself up entirely to his pleasures** (further on internal comparisons see Intro. 1). Fine biography, indeed, but as history the chapter is less convincing. Plutarch correctly notes the restlessness of **the Spanish tribes** (e.g. Pompey received the surrender of the Indigetes and Lacetani); however, Pompey could hardly have had much effect on **the troops on the spot**, since these were largely confined to Saguntum, Lauro (**Lauron**) and the area of Andalusia in the south. Then, although Plutarch hints at Pompey's inexperience of guerrilla warfare and over-confidence, he fails to give Sertorius due credit for his victory at Lauro, where he drew Pompey into a trap. Metellus, meanwhile, far from being idle had crushed Hirtuleius at Italica, before wintering probably at Corduba. Plutarch moves on to Pompey's **victory near Valentia**, omitting the winter of 76/5 BC; in the spring Metellus defeated and killed Hirtuleius at a Segovia in Further Spain, while Pompey captured Valentia. C. **Herennius** was killed, and Perperna fled south to join Sertorius. See Spann 84-111.

Chapter 19

Pompey now took on Sertorius himself in a **battle near the River Sucro**. Appian has Pompey and Metellus fighting together (*BC* 1.110), and his confused account can hardly be reconciled with Plutarch's. Plutarch follows an anti-Pompeian tradition that he **hastened to engage Sertorius** to deny Metellus **any share** in the victory, which in turn would reflect Pompey's continuing tactical naivety (cf. *Sertorius* 19.2). It could be, however, that Pompey realised Sertorius would not fight a pitched battle against the full Roman forces (as Plutarch also suggests) – and the next day Sertorius did indeed retire when **Metellus was approaching**. Either way Pompey took a chance, and although L. Afranius was successful on the left wing, he himself was heavily defeated by Sertorius, **wounded** in the thigh and forced into **abandoning his horse to the enemy** in order to escape. Plutarch depicts Pompey fighting bravely and says **the battle was indecisive**, but Appian makes this a Sertorian victory. See Spann 111-12.

On Metellus' arrival Sertorius reverted to his **unpredictable tactics**, which forced his opponents to retreat. This was followed by a battle probably near a city named Segontia, where Sertorius again defeated Pompey but Metellus crushed Perperna. After this setback Sertorius retreated to Clunia, where he was surrounded by Pompey and Metellus but escaped. Short of provisions the two generals then separated, and while Metellus retired to Gaul, Pompey wintered among the Vaccaei. See Spann 112-20.

Note that Metellus was not in fact **superior in rank** to Pompey, since both had proconsular status. *Lictors*, who were of low birth and often freedmen, escorted magistrates with *imperium** in varying numbers according to the officer's status (e.g. twelve with consuls). They carried **fasces**, the symbols of magisterial authority which consisted of an axe and wooden rods tied with a red thong. The axe was removed on entry within the boundary of the city of Rome proper (*pomerium*).

Chapter 20

Despite his successes Sertorius had been unable to win a decisive victory, and his hold over his troops and Spanish allies weakened as Pompey conducted a war of attrition. Pompey, however, needed supplies and reinforcements, and to back up his request for these, in a letter to the senate (cf. Sall. *Hist*. 2.98M) **threatened to come back with his army to Italy**. This probably implies not that Pompey would otherwise invade Italy but that he could not continue the war in Spain if his troops were to mutiny (see Seager 19-20). Pompey was supported by L. **Lucullus**, who had secured a joint **command against Mithridates** with his consular colleague of 74 BC, M. Aurelius Cotta - if Pompey returned unsuccessful, Lucullus might lose this potentially lucrative Eastern command. Pompey could hardly have hoped to return from Spain to claim this for **himself**; and Plutarch retrojects the hostility between the two men in anticipation of chs 30-1. **Mithridates seemed...Sertorius** is also a distortion of the facts (N.B. **proposition** in the Greek is antagonisten, which like **inveterate enemy** in ch. 41 is athletic imagery; see ch. 8n.).

The reinforcements were sent, and Pompey and Metellus gradually gained the upper hand in 74/3 BC. Plutarch omits the mounting disaffection in Sertorius' army and jumps to his assassination by Perperna and other **members of his own party** (N.B. the internal comparison of Sertorius and Perperna). Perperna took over the command, but proved no match for Pompey and was defeated in late 73 or early 72 BC. See Spann 123-36.

Plutarch is the only source for Pompey's burning of **the letters**, a very suspect item historically which illustrates the behaviour of the magnanimous victor (N.B. he reads Mithridates' **secret documents** in ch. 37 *before* the king's death). Plutarch evidently realised the threat a general returning to Rome with an army posed to the state (sim. chs 21, 43), but he is not so clear over the soldiers' desire for land and their consequent loyalties (see Pelling [3] 180-1).

Pompey's humane **settlements** involving both Sertorians and Spaniards brought him further credit and enabled him to build up loyal *clientelae** all over Spain (e.g. Caes. *BC* 1.61.3). Of those granted Roman citizenship, however, the most notable was L. Cornelius Balbus of Gades, who became one of Caesar's closest advisers (*Caesar* 17n.). These grants were ratified by a consular law, and Pompey also set up a trophy in the Pyrenees claiming the capture of 876 towns. See Spann 136-9.

In 71 BC Pompey returned to Italy, where Spartacus' **Slave War** was raging. Spartacus, a Thracian slave who had served as an auxiliary in the Roman army, escaped in 73 BC with a few companions from the training school for gladiators at Capua. Having seized Mt Vesuvius, where he was joined by runaway slaves and herdsmen, he overran Campania and Lucania before withdrawing to southern Italy for the winter. In 72 BC Spartacus defeated both consuls and the proconsul of Cisalpine Gaul, and the senate turned to M. **Crassus** (pr. 73 BC). He effectively ended the revolt by early 71 BC but allowed Spartacus to break out of southern Italy, and the senate summoned Pompey and M. Licinius Lucullus (the proconsul of Macedonia and brother of the Lucullus of chs 30-1) to help in the defence of Rome and Italy. Plutarch (*Crassus* 11.2) states that Crassus himself had originally asked the senate to send for Pompey and Lucullus, but now, galvanised by the threat to his own glory, he **precipitated the decisive battle** and crushed the revolt. However, **5,000 fugitives** fell into the hands of Pompey, and having executed them he was able to claim that **he himself had finished the war off utterly and entirely**. This gave rise to unceasing bitterness between the two men, which was not helped by the fact that Pompey was to receive a full triumph for his Spanish victory, whereas Crassus was only granted the lesser reward of an ovation. See further on their enmity Epstein 14.

Pompey now sought a consulship, and his personal popularity among the equites* and people was greatly increased by his stance on the tribunate and courts, which had become the major political bones of contention during his absence (ch. 22). Here Plutarch mentions only **the powers** of the tribunes, which **Sulla had taken away** (i.e. their legislative powers; their right to stand for higher office had been restored by the consul of 75 BC, C. Aurelius Cotta). Plutarch assigns to Pompey the altruistic motive of **expressing his thanks to the people**, but his promise to restore the tribunician powers would win him many votes: lacking family connections at Rome, Pompey needed to build up his electoral support in the face of powerful opposition from hard-line Optimates* like Catulus, the Luculli and Hortensius. For Pompey was not yet even a senator, was too young to stand for the consulship and indeed had not held any of the required preliminary offices. On the other hand his career could hardly now be expected to develop along the regular lines of the Sullan system. His popularity will have made him confident of success (N.B. the escort scene here; see ch. 13n.); but to make absolutely sure he turned to Crassus for a political alliance (ch. 22).

Plutarch notes **feelings of suspicion and of fear** as Pompey refused to disband his army until he celebrated his triumph, with the excuse that he was waiting for the return of Metellus. It is open to question, however, to what extent Pompey used the threat of his army to extort from the senate the dispensation he needed to stand against the Sullan regulations and *in absentia* (a general with *imperium** could not enter the boundary of Rome proper, the *pomerium*, before his triumph, as Plutarch notes in ch. 44). See Gruen [2] 43-5; Stockton, D.L., 'The First Consulship of Pompey' *Historia* 22 (1973) pp. 206-12.

As consul-designate Pompey prepared for his triumph and delivered a speech in which he promised to deal with the problems concerning the tribunician powers, the courts and also provincial government. In addition, he asked his friend Varro to write a handbook of senatorial procedure which would prepare the new senator for his position as chairman of the senate's debates (having headed the poll).

This is a pivotal chapter of the *Life*, in which elements already emphasised in the narrative are mixed with foreshadowings of later events. Thus the letter **to the senate** recalls Pompey's dispatch during Lepidus' rebellion (ch. 16); but while Pompey again displays his military ability, there is now the **fear** that he might march on Rome (cf. ch. 43); and despite his personal popularity there is the **fault that his enemies could find in him** (cf. ch. 53). In addition, the upstaging of Crassus both recalls Pompey's behaviour towards Metellus at the Sucro (ch. 19) and foreshadows his treatment of Metellus Creticus (ch. 29) and Lucullus (ch. 31), and his increasing desire for glory (ch. 38). On the **people...senate** antithesis in this chapter and in ch. 22 see *Cicero* 11n.

Chapter 22

Pompey celebrated his **second triumph** as an eques* jointly with Metellus on 29 December 71 BC, disbanded his army as promised and entered his first consulship with Crassus. Crassus for his part had followed the regular senatorial career and had certainly had no need to use the threat of an army to secure his office. Although Crassus' oratory and especially his wealth were of the highest order, Plutarch exaggerates his standing (**the greatest man**) to highlight Pompey's role in his election (sim. *Crassus* 12.1), but no doubt **Pompey was delighted** at this point in his political career to be allied to a man of Crassus' wealth and influence with both senators and equites*.

The alliance soon broke down, and in *Crassus* 12.2 Plutarch says that as consuls the two men were **politically ineffective and achieved noth-**

ing. His account here is preferable, recording the legislation which finally overturned the Sullan system and helped shape the future politics of the Republic.

The bill to restore the powers of the **tribunes**, a measure probably promoted by both consuls for fear of the other gaining all its attendant popular favour, met no opposition in the senate, even from Catulus, and was supported by the young C. Iulius Caesar (Suet. *Caesar* 5). See further McDermott, W.C., 'Lex de tribunicia potestate (70 B.C.)' *CP* 72 (1977) pp. 49-52 (who argues for a bill of Pompey alone). It was not so easy to deprive the senate of its control of the **juries**, which had come under fire as a result of the trial of Oppianicus in 74 BC and its record in several trials of provincial governors. The situation was brought to a head by the trial for extortion of C. Verres, propraetor of Sicily 73-1 BC. His victims included clients of Pompey, notably Sthenius of Himera (ch. 10n.), and this had prompted action by friends of Pompey, the consuls of 72 BC (L. Gellius Publicola and Cn. Cornelius Lentulus) and a tribune of 71 BC (M. Lollius Palicanus). See Badian [1] 282-3. Pompey now was content to remain in the background in the summer, when Verres was finally prosecuted by Cicero (*Cicero* 7-8 nn.), and in fact he does not seem to have been eager to carry out his promised judicial reform. It was not until after Verres' trial, in the autumn, that the bill was finally promulgated, and then it was done so **under his auspices** by the praetor L. Aurelius Cotta.The bill ended the senatorial monopoly by dividing the composition of the juries between senators, equites* (**gentlemen outside the senate**) and a third group, the obscure *tribuni aerarii* (perhaps those whose property qualification fell just below that of the equites*). See Wiseman, T.P., 'The Definition of "eques Romanus" in the Late Roman Republic and Early Empire' *Historia* 19 (1970) pp. 67-83.

This year also saw the revival of the censorship, in abeyance since 86 BC. The harsh censors were **Gellius and Lentulus**, the consuls of 72 BC who had supported Pompey by validating his grants of citizenship in Spain, as well as by attempting to check Verres (above). They expelled sixty-four members of the senate, including C. Antonius Hibrida, P. Cornelius Lentulus Sura and Q. Curius (*Cicero* 11, 14, 16nn.); and they staged for the benefit of Pompey's vanity the traditional equestrian* parade (*recognitio equitum*; on the **lictors** see ch. 19n.).

Chapter 23

The failure of Plautius' bill granting land to Pompey's and Metellus' veterans was a warning to Pompey that his influence was not boundless (see Marshall, B.A., 'The *lex Plotia agraria*' *Antichthon* 6 [1972] pp. 43-52). Hence he was ready to go through the charade of a reconciliation with Crassus, especially as Crassus **made the first move** (cf. *Crassus* 12.4, where Plutarch calls the instigator **Onatius Aurelius**; see further Ward 108-9 with n. 37).

Both men then retired into private life instead of accepting provincial commands. Pompey, whose forte was his military prowess, was awaiting a new command, to which Plutarch jumps in chs 24-5. Clearly, however, Pompey was not as inactive as Plutarch suggests and at the very least would have been building up his *clientela**. This is perhaps hinted at by **he was always accompanied by a large crowd**, though this is another escort scene (ch. 13n.). His reticence, seen here as **giving the impression of a majesty and pomp surrounding him**, is described in *Crassus* 7.3 as **a certain arrogance and haughtiness**.

In 67 BC Pompey may have been behind the scenes in the attempt of his former quaestor, the tribune C. Cornelius, to end electoral corruption. More important was Pompey's connection with another tribune of 67 BC, A. Gabinius. His involvement in the continuing campaign to undermine Lucullus' position in Asia Minor (ch. 30n.) may well have been prompted by Pompey, and he then began working for him in the matter of the pirates.

This chapter provides a good example of Pompey's passivity in politics (**it was Crassus who made the first move**): Pompey is much more decisive when in a military situation (ch. 47n.). The excursus on the great general in **civilian life** seems to foreshadow events after Pompey's return from the East in 62 BC (cf. **how true this is was soon shown by events**).

Chapter 24

The power of the pirates had been a thorn in Rome's side since 102 BC, when the praetor M. Antonius received a command against them in **Cilicia**. Although he **celebrated a triumph** in 100 BC, he failed to check the menace, which worsened after the outbreak of the **Mithridatic war** in 88 BC when the pirates received **subsidies from the King** (App. *Mith.* 63). Their confidence and **arrogance** increased as Rome was convulsed by the Sullan **civil wars**; and Antonius' son (pr. 74 BC) and P. Servilius Vatia (procos. in Cilicia 78-4 BC) also failed to clear the Mediterranean. The pirates pillaged famous **sanctuaries** in Greece and Asia Minor and even Italy itself, where they captured the **praetors, Sextilius and Bellinus** (Cic. *Leg. Man.* 32-3; App. id. 93; 68 BC in Broughton ii.138). Apart from **the daughter of Antonius** the pirates also captured Caesar (*Caesar* 1.8-2) and P. Clodius (Dio 36.17.3).

Note Plutarch's very historical analysis here of pirate power, which is followed at the end of the chapter by fine narrative. This helps underline the strong moral note, that pirates are examples of just that type of character which is to be avoided.

The cult of the Persian deity **Mithras**, which promised immortality, was **still celebrated** in Plutarch's day and became very popular in the age of Antoninus Pius.

Chapter 25

By 67 BC the pirates' activities were disrupting **commerce** and threatening Rome's corn supply. Gabinius proposed **a law** giving one of the ex-consuls a command against all the pirates for three years, with powers detailed here by Plutarch (cf. Vell. 2.31.2; App. *Mith.* 94; **the sea** included the Black Sea). Plutarch's version of the events, however, is confused, and a clearer picture emerges from Dio (36.23-37), though the exact order remains uncertain. Gabinius may have taken his bill directly **to the assembly**, and although Pompey was not in fact named, it was obvious who the intended beneficiary was. **The most important and influential** senators were united in opposing the bill, but **Caesar**, who had suffered at the pirates' hands, **spoke in favour** of it (Caesar 5n.; his inclusion amongst the leading senators at this time is an anachronism; N.B. **all the other senators** should in fact read 'the others', i.e. of this leading group). The consul Piso was nearly **torn to pieces** when the mob stormed the senate on being informed of his remark about **Romulus** (who in one version was torn to pieces by senators, Livy 1.16.4); he was saved by Gabinius himself. Hortensius also spoke against the bill, and the senate found two tribunes willing to use their veto, L. Trebellius and L. **Roscius** Otho. At a second meeting of the assembly Pompey adopted his regular method of feigning reluctance, leaving Gabinius to beg him to put his country first. Trebellius, shouted down when he tried to speak, now vetoed the bill, and Gabinius was forced to use the tactic of Tiberius Gracchus in 133 BC, proposing Trebellius be deposed from office. When seventeen tribes had voted against him, Trebellius withdrew his veto, and it was now that **Roscius came forward to speak**, also to be shouted down. Gabinius then turned to **Catulus**, hoping he would avert the danger threatening the tribunes by supporting the bill. He refused to relent, but the law was passed, either now or at a further meeting (cf. **the assembly was adjourned**, ch. 26).

The end of this chapter reflects Plutarch's love of anecdotal material, which in this case is a scientific digression (cf. *Flaminius* 10.6; Livy 29.25.4; Val. Max. 4.8.5).

Chapter 26

Plutarch maintains that Pompey was absent on the day of the vote, in line with his pretended reluctance. At least one more law was passed, appointing him commander and giving him the **still greater powers** listed by Plutarch (it remains unclear whether Pompey's *imperium** was equal or superior to that of the other proconsuls; see Seager 35-6). So, by what bears all the hallmarks of a carefully planned operation, Pompey received the command of a force far greater than was necessary, and **the prices of foodstuffs** immediately dropped.

Further on Pompey's tactics cf. App. *Mith.* 95-6 (N.B. the Greek says Pompey **divided** the seas and the extent of the Mediterranean, not **the adjacent coasts**). His choice of legates (listed in Broughton ii.147-9) shows Pompey extending his patronage, as it significantly excludes his most faithful adherents (though rewarding his old friends Lentulus and Gellius). Several were to become consuls, and Pompey was forming links with important families such as the Metelli. His forces cleared the Mediterranean from west to east, firstly ensuring the corn supply from **Sardinia, Sicily** and Africa and within **forty days** the pirates were forced back to **their hive in Cilicia**.

Chapter 27

The only serious problem Pompey faced was the hostility of **Piso**, who was **discharging the crews of his ships** enlisted in Italy and his province of Transalpine Gaul. Pompey was forced to return **to Rome**, where he checked Piso before hastening to Cilicia via **Brundisium, Athens** and Rhodes. He was already showing mercy to those who surrendered as the pirates' plight worsened, and thus gained information on **those who were still in hiding**.

The escort scene again reflects Pompey's popularity (ch. 13n.). Plutarch also emphasises that Pompey was a philhellene (**Athens...he could not pass by**). This is typical of leading Roman figures but foreshadows Pompey's reflections in ch. 28.

Chapter 28

Details of the final campaign are lacking. Pompey probably captured several **castles and fortresses** (App. *Mith.* 96), before securing an easy victory in the bay of **Coracesium** (Flor. 1.41.12-14) and the capture of the stronghold. The war was brought to an end within **three months**, and Pompey was again hailed as 'Imperator'* (*SIG*^{3} 749A/B [A = Sherk 75B]; cf. ch. 12).

Pompey's humane treatment of **the prisoners** is remarkable and stands in stark contrast to his earlier 'teenage butcher' reputation. It also had the practical object of repopulating areas of southern Asia Minor devastated by the Mithridatic war, including the abandoned **city of Soli** in Cilicia which was renamed Pompeiopolis (on **Tigranes** see ch. 30n.). The largest of the settlements was **Dyme in Achaea.**

The reflection attributed to Pompey that man is **by nature** meant to live in a civilised community was in fact one of the tenets of Plutarch's own philosophy. The pirates were therefore acting 'against nature' in attacking such communities. Plutarch also believed that it is man's nature to aim at virtue, which is permanent. Therefore **vice** could be cured, and a man's character could change from bad to good, but not from good to bad (see Wardman 132-40). So Pompey's resettlement of the pirates would help to make them **civilized again**; and his humane actions were an example for others to follow, in accordance with the moral purpose of the *Lives* (Intro. 1). That Pompey was himself interested in philosophy is shown by his stays in Athens (chs 27, 42) and friendship with Theophanes (ch. 32n.).

Chapter 29

Pompey did not completely eradicate piracy from the Mediterranean, but his actions fully vindicated the terms of Gabinius' law, which in turn justified his actions **in Crete**. Nevertheless, he acted tactlessly in his treatment of Q. Caecilius **Metellus** Creticus (cos. 69 BC), who **had been sent out as governor** to deal with the pirate problem there. Pompey's leniency contrasted with Metellus' harshness, and the Cretan pirates appealed to Pompey. He sent his legate **Lucius Octavius** to receive their surrender, but Metellus ignored the instruction **to cease hostilities**. Another legate, the historian L. Cornelius Sisenna, unsuccessfully tried to persuade Metellus to cooperate, and on his death Octavius actually started to oppose Metellus, thus making Pompey **look ridiculous**. Further problems were averted by Pompey's appointment to the command against Mithridates, but Pompey's hostility resurfaced at Metellus' triumph in 62 BC (Dio 36.19.3).

Plutarch's account of Pompey's behaviour here contrasts strongly with that of his actions earlier in the pirate campaign. Pompey had previously acted with **tireless energy and the enthusiastic support** of his legates (ch. 26), behaved **with the greatest moderation** and treated the prisoners **very humanely** (ch. 27). Now he is criticised by **even his best friends** and has an **envious desire to outshine Metellus**, recalling his behaviour towards Metellus Pius and Crassus (ch. 21n.) and foreshadowing that towards Lucullus (chs 30-1). Plutarch brings out Pompey's obsession with glory by comparing him to **Achilles**, quoting Hom.

Iliad 22.207 (the plot of the *Iliad* turns on Achilles' uncontrollable anger: as a result of his feud with Agamemnon he refuses to fight the Trojans until **Hector** kills his close friend Patroclus; then in furious revenge Achilles kills Hector and maltreats his body).

Chapter 30

King **Mithridates** VI Eupator of Pontus began his attempt at an Anatolian empire in the late second century, and in 90 BC temporarily seized Bithynia and Cappadocia with the help of his son-in-law King **Tigranes** of Armenia. Further expansion was checked by Sulla, but in the early seventies Mithridates supported Tigranes, who built a new capital at Tigranocerta (moving the inhabitants of Soli; see ch. 28n.). War broke out when Nicomedes IV bequeathed Bithynia to Rome (75/4 BC), and Mithridates invaded the new province. In a series of campaigns down to 70 BC L. **Lucullus** (cos. 74 BC) drove Mithridates back to Armenia; but his financial settlement of Asia alienated the equites*, who in 69 BC began a campaign to have him replaced. Lucullus correctly decided that only Mithridates' capture would bring peace, and when Tigranes refused to hand him over, Lucullus invaded Armenia. His troops, however, mutinied in 69 and 68 BC, encouraged by his own brother-in-law P. Clodius. At Rome L. Quinctius (pr. 68 BC) was active in agitating against him, and Cilicia was assigned to the consul Q. Marcius Rex; then in 67 BC Gabinius transferred Bithynia and Pontus to M'. Acilius **Glabrio**.

By the end of 67 BC, therefore, Lucullus' position had become untenable, and the tribune C. **Manilius** introduced a law transferring Cilicia, Bithynia and Pontus to Pompey and giving him the command against Mithridates and Tigranes (Plutarch is technically wrong to say that **Pompey should be given...under the command of Lucullus**, since he had already been superseded; Plutarch also calls the proposer 'Mallius'). This was in addition to his powers under the Gabinian law, which **he was still to retain**, and immediately Pompey's enemies in the aristocratic party, again led by Catulus and Hortensius, objected to **so much power being given to** one man. They also felt that **Lucullus...was being robbed of the glory which he had earned**, and some preferred Marcius Rex and Acilius Glabrio. Unlike Gabinius' law, however, Manilius' had strong support in the senate. As well as Caesar (Dio 36.43.2) there were the ex-consuls C. Curio, C. Cassius, Cn. Lentulus and the former proconsul of Cilicia, Servilius Isauricus; and the praetor M. Tullius Cicero, who delivered the *Pro Lege Manilia* (60-3 for his reply to the **long speech of Catulus**). So **the law was passed**, and Pompey received the news of his command before setting out for Crete (cf. Dio 36.45.1-2 on his pretended reluctance). It is again unclear whether Pompey's *imperium** was equal to or greater than that of the other proconsuls; but both Plutarch and Appian (*Mith*. 97) exaggerate the extent of Pompey's powers, which were restricted to Anatolia, and Plutarch inaccurately includes **Upper Colchis** and **Armenia** as transferred provinces. Among Pompey's additional legates were Gabinius and L. Afranius (ch. 34).

Plutarch's account of the passing of the law has parallels with chs 25-6, such as the attitude of **the aristocratic party** and their objection to **so much power being given to Pompey,** Catulus' **long speech** and Pompey's absence from Rome. This time, however, Catulus is the only senator to oppose the bill, suggesting an increase in Pompey's power and validating the fears of ch. 25. Catulus' urging of the senators **to act as their forefathers had done** alludes to the secessions of the *plebeians** during the early Republican period, especially the one to the Mons Sacer (*Coriolanus* 6). Hence there is marked irony in this exhortation. Finally, the comparison with the power of **Sulla** is a gross exaggeration, but it links back to ch. 21 and makes the point that Pompey achieved the supreme power he wanted without recourse to Sullan methods (**force of arms**).

Chapter 31

Like Lucullus Pompey knew that the war would only end with Mithridates' death or capture. His large forces included the three legions of Marcius Rex in Cilicia, most of Lucullus' army, his own remaining forces and levies from **the subject kings and princes** (especially the Galatian cavalry), a total of c. 50,000 men (see Sherwin-White 192 n. 19). Preliminary diplomacy with Mithridates came to nothing, but Pompey had resumed the talks with Phraates III of Parthia begun by Lucullus: they agreed that the King would attack Tigranes, in return for the restoration of Mesopotamia, Adiabene and the 'Great Valleys' of Gordyene (Plutarch does not record contact between Pompey and Phraates until after the defeat of Tigranes in ch. 33). Pompey then marched north to Galatia, and on the way **he altered every single arrangement that had been made by Lucullus** and by a senatorial commission prematurely sent to settle the East, issuing his own edicts. Lucullus' **friends** therefore organised a **meeting,** which after initial politeness degenerated into a slanging match. Either at the meeting or afterwards Pompey called Lucullus 'a Xerxes in a toga' (Vell. 2.33.4), while Lucullus likened Pompey to **some crazy carrion bird**.

Seager (p. 46) strangely inverts the story of the **laurels**. Laurel wreaths adorned the fasces of generals who had been saluted as 'Imperator'* (further on **lictors** and **their rods** see ch. 19n.). Pompey himself seems to have been influenced by such omens (Cic. *Div*. 2.53; chs 42, 68nn.), but the story also encompasses two other themes: he is again robbing another of his glory (ch. 21n.), and once more he is the younger man superseding the older (ch. 14). On Pompey's **two triumphs** see chs 14, 22nn.; and for **Sertorius, Lepidus, and the followers of Spartacus** chs 16-21 with nn.

Chapter 32

While **Lucullus** returned to Rome, Pompey blockaded Asia Minor **between Phoenicia and the Bosporus** and turned eastwards after Mithridates. It becomes difficult to keep track of the campaign due to the vague geographical details in Plutarch, Dio and Appian, whose accounts probably go back through Livy and Strabo to the contemporary Theophanes and Poseidonius (see Sherwin-White 191 n. 15). On Theophanes, who was Pompey's adjutant (*praefectus fabrum*), see Intro. 4., chs 37, 42, 49, 76, *Cicero* 38.4; Gold, B.K., 'Pompey and Theophanes of Mytilene' *AJP* 106 (1985) pp. 312-27.

Pompey clearly faced a difficult task. Although he could pursue his favourite policy of fighting with **the advantage of numbers**, he immediately came up against the problem Lucullus had faced, Mithridates' harassing tactics with his superior cavalry. Pompey in truth was no more successful than his predecessor in his attempt to catch the King, who twice escaped investments. The first time was from a **mountain** area probably near the River Halys, the second from a **camp** on a hill called Dasteira. Pompey finally **caught up with him near the River Euphrates**, and the battle described by Plutarch was probably an ambush in a narrow pass. Mithridates was heavily defeated, but again he escaped and with his **three companions**, 3,000 infantry and some cavalry made for **Sinora** (or Sinoria, probably on the upper Euphrates). He then sent messengers to **Tigranes**, but he was facing a rebellion by his son (ch. 33) and perhaps realised the folly of continuing to support Mithridates. Mithridates was therefore forced to flee northwards to Dioscurias in **Colchis** and then the Bosporus – and Pompey again failed to catch him (Dio 36.48-50).

On the (otherwise unattested) **dream** of Mithridates and other dreams in Plutarch (cf. ch. 68; *Caesar* 32.9; *Cicero* 44.3-7) see Brenk, F.E., 'The Dreams of Plutarch's Lives' *Latomus* 34 (1975) pp. 336-49.

Chapter 33

Pompey settled some of his veterans in the new city of Nicopolis, then crossed into **Armenia**. He was met by the **young Tigranes**, who had joined his father-in-law Phraates' invasion and been defeated by his father at Artaxata. He led Pompey along the **River Araxes** towards Artaxata, and King Tigranes hastened to **surrender** in a staged meeting (he **was ready** to perform the Persian act of obeisance, *proskynesis*). Pompey, who was intent on using Armenia as a buffer state between the Roman and Parthian empires, referred to the great victory of **Lucullus** at Tigranocerta and accepted his submission on the terms related by Plutarch (N.B. Tigranes never held **Galatia**). Plutarch then abbreviates the outcome): while **Tigranes was perfectly satisfied,** his son was not. Pompey gave the prince **Sophene,** where several royal treasuries were located, but the young Tigranes refused to hand over funds Pompey needed and tried to escape. He was arrested and sent to Rome to **appear in Pompey's triumph** (Clodius arranged his escape in 58 BC, ch. 48). The King acquired the money and gave Pompey more than requested, for which he was made a friend and ally of the Roman people and given back Sophene (App. *Mith*. 104-5; Dio 36.53.5-6).

Pompey's sinister reply to Phraates shows that with the threat of Mithridates removed he was not in the mood to make further deals with Parthia. The suggestion (a demand in Dio 37.6.3) that **the Euphrates** should be **the boundary between** the empires should probably be placed in the context of ch. 38 (see n. there).

Chapter 34

Pompey still had not captured Mithridates, who was in **hiding among the tribes living about the Bosporus and the Maeotic Sea** (ch. 35). According to Plutarch and the other sources he **now went after** him, leaving his most loyal legate, L. **Afranius, in charge of Armenia.** The tribal wars then were fought because Pompey was not **allowed to pass through their land freely,** though they would also secure Rome's position in this area. It is clear, however, that Pompey was criticised for his failure to pursue Mithridates; and his wintering in primitive Albania suggests he was more interested in demonstrating Rome's power and winning glory for himself (see Sherwin-White 197-8).

Pompey firstly went north into the valley of the **River Cyrnus** (or Cyrus), which is joined by one branch of the **Araxes**. Here he was attacked by **the Albanians** under their king Oroeses but easily **routed** them (Dio 36.54, cf. 37.1-5.1). His once more lenient treatment of a defeated enemy helped to protect the eastern flank of Pontus, further ensured by the crushing defeat of **the Iberians** under Artoces near the River Pelorus. In these victories Pompey outdid even his hero **Alexander** (ch. 2n.), since Alexander's **empire** did not reach this far north (in 330/29 BC he made a **hurried** pursuit of Darius, then marched into **Hyrcania** at the southern end of the Caspian Sea; *Alexander* 42.5-44). Artoces escaped but later sent his children to Pompey as hostages; and Pompey finally marched through **Colchis**, which submitted, and reached the Black Sea at the mouth of the **River Phasis**. Here he **was** met by Servilius, the prefect of his fleet who was blockading the ports of the Euxine (Servilius' precise identity is unknown).

On **the Saturnalia**, a festival beginning on 17 December and in many ways resembling the modern Christmas, see Ogilvie, R.M., *The Romans and their Gods* (London, 1981) pp. 98-9.

Chapter 35

Plutarch emphasises the **great difficulty** Pompey faced in pursuing Mithridates in the north, and he gives as a reason for his second campaign against the Albanians **the news that** they had again revolted. Dio (37.3-4) states that Pompey invaded while there was still a truce, and he was perhaps trying to secure the Albanian interior (as Sherwin-White 200). The difficulties he faced in crossing the Cyrnus were caused not only by the **palisades** but also by the current (Dio), and he used his horses and pack animals to shield the infantry. His subsequent **march** through desert terrain was hampered by unreliable guides and illness caused by drinking the very cold water of the River Cambyses. Despite these problems Pompey eventually defeated the Albanians at the **River Abas**. Plutarch and Strabo (11.4.5) probably exaggerate the size of the Albanian forces, Strabo giving 22,000 cavalry and contradicting Plutarch's **badly armed**; and Dio more plausibly says that Pompey had to disguise his superior numbers to induce the Albanians to attack.

The Amazons were a mythical race of women warriors, situated on the edge of the known world (as the River Thermodon). They are a commonplace of Alexander-contexts (Alexander 46), and Pompey is again outdoing his hero. One of the Amazons' customs was to couple at certain times with men of other races (keep company with them for two months), only keeping the female offspring.

Chapter 36

For prestige purposes Pompey wanted to reach the **Caspian Sea** but **was forced to turn back**. His subsequent activities from 65 to the first half of 63 BC are obscure. Plutarch records that Pompey received **ambassadors**, including a delegation from Darius, the king of Media Atropatene. Velleius (2.40.1) turns this into an invasion of Media, while Appian talks of fighting and the inclusion of 'Darius the Mede' in the list of 'kings conquered' displayed at Pompey's triumph (*Mith.* 106, 117). This may stem from confusion with Gabinius' expedition to the Tigris (below). Another delegation came from the king of the **Elymaeans**, who lived northward of Media to the Araxes and the Caspian Sea.

Phraates, who had kept his side of the bargain with Pompey by invading Armenia, evidently expected the return of Gordyene, Adiabene and Mesopotamia and had taken the first two of these. He was, however, alarmed at Gabinius' expedition into Mesopotamia and sent an embassy to confirm the agreement. Pompey countered by demanding the return of **Gordyene** and **sent a force** under **Afranius** to effect this, reflecting both Pompey's contempt for Phraates and the strategic importance of Gordyene (Dio 37.5.2-4). He then spent the winter of 65/4 BC at the unidentified Aspis (probably in **Lesser Armenia**), captured some fortresses and received Mithridates' largest treasure-house from **Stratonice** (Strabo 12.3.38; App. *Mith*. 107; probably at the **Sinora** of ch. 32; Plutarch omits the vast treasury at Talaura, App. id. 115).

Pompey's sexual continence with regard to the **concubines** is clearly modelled on that of Alexander (*Alexander* 4.8, 21.5-11); while his probity in public finances is also stressed by other authors (e.g. Cic. *Flacc*. 67; Jos. *AJ* 14.105). The story of Stratonice's **father** again reflects Plutarch's love of anecdote (ch. 11n.). On Pompey's **triumph** see ch. 45n.

Chapter 37

One of the fortresses Pompey captured was **Caenum** (Strabo 12.3.31). Here was found Mithridates' biological collection, which fired the imagination of Pliny (*NH* 25.5-7). For **Theophanes** see ch. 32n. In 92 BC P. **Rutilius** Rufus, whose name became synonymous with incorruptibility, was scandalously condemned for extortion in Asia by a panel of equestrian* jurors. He had in fact protected the provincials from the exactions of the Roman tax-collectors, who thus enjoyed their revenge. Rutilius then went to live in exile among his supposed victims and compose **his histories**. It need hardly be added that no credence is to be placed on his alleged incitement of Mithridates **to the massacre of the Romans in Asia** (88 BC). On Pompey's **father** see ch. 1n.

Chapter 38

At **Amisus** Pompey reorganised Pontus as a province, confirming the positions of **local monarchs** and writing to the **King of Parthia**, significantly without addressing **him by his usual title** (Dio 37.6.2). The letter was in response to Phraates' protest against the campaign of Afranius (ch. 36) and demand that Roman troops should not cross the Euphrates (Plutarch puts this episode in ch. 33); and an angry Phraates then attacked Gordyene (ch. 39n.). Pompey was facing criticism because **the enemy was still alive** (though not with **a considerable force**); but instead of chasing him Pompey turned his attention to Syria. As Syria weakened its strategic position was becoming increasingly important; but for Plutarch Pompey is once more **led by his passion for glory** (ch. 21n.). Here he acts **as if bringing a punishment on himself** – the tragic sentiment is an important pointer to the general 'tragedy' of Pompey to come (ch. 9n.). Pompey is still acting very much like Alexander (cf. his reply to Darius' letter, *Alexander* 29.7-9, and desire for conquest) and in his passion envisaged a march **to the Red Sea** (i.e. Persian Gulf. His previous victories are exaggerated – the first two of them were in civil wars and in Africa he had not reached **the Outer Sea**, i.e. the Atlantic).

Chapter 39

Despite Servilius' **blockade** of the Crimean **Bosporus**, the claim that Mithridates was facing **famine** seems nonsensical in one of the richest grain-producing areas of the ancient world. Added to Cicero's defence of Pompey's actions in *Mur.* 34 and Dio's remark that the seas were harbourless and inhospitable (37.3.2), this seems like a reaction to the criticism of Pompey in Rome for his failure to capture Mithridates (sim. ch. 41). Pompey was no more able to achieve this than Lucullus had been, and Lucullus and his supporters doubtless made the most of it.

Pompey next marched into northern Syria, reaching Antioch late in 64 BC. **On his way** he buried the troops of Lucullus' legate Triarius which had been slaughtered at Zela in 67 BC, thus contrasting his pious actions with those of Lucullus. According to Appian (*Mith.* 106, 117) Pompey also conquered Antiochus of Commagene, who furnished hostages later to be featured in his triumph (ch. 45), but actual fighting has been doubted by modern scholars. Meanwhile **Afranius** had moved east of the Tigris to Arbela (ch. 36) and then back westwards to the **Amanus** range between Cilicia and northern Syria, where he joined Pompey in summer 64 BC.

The winter of 64/3 BC saw Pompey involved in much diplomatic business. Stung by Pompey's insult (ch. 38), Phraates invaded Gordyene in 64 BC; Tigranes appealed for help, but Pompey was now reluctant to get involved, though he **sent three judges to arbitrate**. The unnamed Romans decided in favour of Tigranes' retention of Gordyene, and Phraates moved instead to regain Mesopotamia. Pompey then concentrated on Syria, where the Seleucid monarchy had broken down. Antiochus XIII had been recognised as king by Lucullus in 69/8 BC, but in 67 BC Marcius Rex transferred the kingship to Antiochus' cousin Philip, while Antiochus himself was held captive by Sampsiceramus, the Arab lord of Emesa. By the time of Pompey's arrival Antiochus had somehow regained his throne, but Pompey decided neither man was competent to rule and annexed northern Syria as a Roman province. So the reason for the annexation was not that the **country had no legitimate kings**, but that Antiochus could not control the internal disorders and 'Pompey would not let Syria fall prey to the raids of Arabs and Jews' (Justin 40.2.3-5). There was also the threat of Parthia.

More problems had been caused in southern Syria by the rise of the Maccabean state of **Judaea**. The rival claimants to the throne were the brothers Hyrcanus, supported by the powerful Nabatean leader Aretas, and **Aristobulus**, who was favoured by Pompey's representative M. Aemilius Scaurus amid rumours of bribery. Both now appealed to Pompey, who summoned a conference at Damascus in spring 63 BC and marched from Antioch. Prior to the meeting he planned an attack on Aretas at Petra, but this was interrupted by Aristobulus' occupation of Alexandrion. He was forced into submission and retired to Jerusalem, but continued his intrigues until captured by Pompey (for this order of events see Sherwin-White 215). Plutarch records the Aretas episode in chs 41-2, during which Pompey receives the news of Mithridates' death in 63 BC and **immediately** withdraws. A better version is Josephus', that Pompey received the news at Jericho after Aristobulus' surrender at Alexandrion (*BJ* 1.138, *AJ* 14.48-53).

Pompey was faced with fanatical resistance by Aristobulus' followers in the fortified temple precinct at Jerusalem, and they held out for three months. Pompey then restored the government to Hyrcanus as high priest and imposed tribute; and on hearing of Mithridates' death, he returned to Amisus for the winter of 63/2 BC, leaving Scaurus in charge of Syria.

In this chapter Plutarch typically emphasises Pompey's humane provincial government, recalling his treatment of the pirates (ch. 28). On the other hand, Pompey is unable to control his unworthy subordinates, and this is to become a theme of the second half of the *Life* (esp. ch. 67, also his inability to control Clodius).

Chapter 40

Before leaving Syria Pompey began the reconstruction of Gadara in Judaea. This was the birthplace of his freedman **Demetrius** (ch. 2), a forerunner of the wealthy freedmen of the first century AD. Invaluable as an adviser on the East Demetrius was well rewarded, as Plutarch relates here. The story about M. Porcius **Cato** recurs in *Cato* 13. Its main point is to introduce Cato as a sage, philosopher and commentator figure, who will intervene when glory is going to Pompey's head (chs 44, 47, 48, 52); he will also provide stubborn opposition to him (chs 44, 46-8, 52, 54-6). According to id. 12.2 Cato's second trip to Asia, on which he visited **Antioch**, took place before he returned to stand for the quaestorship, probably in 65 for 64 BC (see Broughton ii.165 n.5; Pompey sent Demetrius to Antioch in 66 BC). Although only reaching the praetorship (54 BC), Cato was one of the leading Optimates* and was renowned for his strict adherence to Stoic and Republican **ideals**. In line with these he committed suicide after Caesar's victory at Thapsus (*Caesar* 54n.).

On **Pompey's** triumph see ch. 45n. His **theatre**, based on the one at Mytilene (ch. 42), was Rome's first stone theatre and was dedicated in August 55 BC (ch. 52n.; see Leach 146-7). Adjacent to the theatre were Pompey's Portico and his new senate house (Curia Pompeii), in which was placed the statue of Pompey at whose feet Caesar was to fall (*Caesar* 66.13). Of more immediate importance was the fact that the hall was outside the city boundary (*pomerium*), hence proconsuls like Pompey who had *imperium** could attend. Although his nearby house was **like a small boat attached to a big ship**, Pompey's main residence was his enormous Alban palace (see Leach 117).

On the toga and dinner parties see Carcopino, J., *Daily Life in Ancient Rome* (Harmondsworth, 1981) pp. 172-4, 287-300. Wearing the toga **with the hood...pulled down over his ears** was slovenly.

Chapter 41

On Pompey's march to **Petra** against Aretas see ch. 39n. A fuller account of Mithridates' **planning to lead an army...against Italy** is given by Appian (*Mith*. 101-2), but the likelihood of such an enterprise is rightly doubted by Sherwin-White (203-6) and McGing (165), and Plutarch himself only says it **was reported**. Mithridates was probably more concerned with strengthening his power in the Crimean region against Pompey's fleet, and this 'attack' may be part of the anti-Pompeian propaganda of the time (ch. 39n.). Pompey's problems with Mithridates were then solved for him by the death of Rome's **inveterate enemy** (ch. 20n.) after the revolt of **his son Pharnaces** in spring 63 BC.

Chapter 42

This chapter is pivotal between Pompey's success when away from Rome and at war, and failure in Rome and the political arena. Whereas **fortune** had favoured Pompey against Mithridates (ch. 41), it now turns against him; and the disappointment of his hopes on his return foreshadows the more important troubles he will face in ch. 46. This is part of Plutarch's characterisation of Pompey (ch. 13n.), but there is another element here, the tragic pattern of *hubris* and *nemesis* (insolence leading to divine retribution). Pompey's *hubris* is evident on his return journey, when he travels **with much more pomp and ceremony than before**, and **that divine power** is already **secretly at work** against him (N.B. the 'theological' insertion, which clearly alludes to Zeus' dispensation of good and evil in Hom. *Iliad* 24.527-33). So although the superstitious Pompey had tried **to propitiate the jealousy of heaven** in the matter of Mithridates' **corpse**, this was to prove unsuccessful.

For the moment, however, Pompey's career was reaching its peak. He was hailed as 'Imperator'* by his troops (*SIG* ^{3} 751 [= Sherk 75A], 752) and the report of Mithridates' death led to ten days' thanksgiving to the gods (*supplicatio*) in Pompey's honour, voted by the senate on Cicero's motion. More importantly his wealth now surpassed Crassus', and he had an unprecedented number of clients, including cities and whole kingdoms, which would support him in the civil war. Pompey did not **immediately** withdraw **from Arabia** but captured Jerusalem before hastening back to Amisus, where he found Mithridates' **body**. This he sent to the Pontic kings' burial site at **Sinope** for proper interment.The identities of **Publius** and **Ariarathes** are unclear. **Faustus** Cornelius Sulla, later engaged to Pompey's daughter (ch. 47), was the first over the wall in the siege of the Temple at Jerusalem. On **Mithridates' foster-brother Gaius** (*syntrophos*) see McGing 91, 93 n. 28.

On Pompey's settlement of **the affairs of the east** see Sherwin-White 226-34. Many areas were left under the control of loyal local dynasts and kings, such as Ariobarzanes in Cappadocia and Deiotarus in parts of Pontus and Lesser Armenia. Pompey's administrative skill is reflected in the elaborate organisation of Pontus, which was divided into eleven civic states on the model of Greek local government.

In spring 62 BC Pompey rewarded his troops on a lavish scale (16,000 talents, or 384 million HS) and **started on his journey home**. The leisurely trip included a visit to **Mitylene**, birthplace of his historian Theophanes (ch. 32n.), which was given back the **freedom** it had lost in supporting Mithridates. Its **theatre** was used as a model for Pompey's own stone theatre (ch. 40n.). At **Rhodes** he listened to a speech by his old friend, the philosopher **Poseidonius**, who agreed to write a history of Pompey's exploits; and at **Athens** his gift of **fifty talents** would help the **restoration** of the city after the damage inflicted by Sulla's siege of 87/6 BC. Further on Pompey's interest in philosophy see ch. 28n.

Pompey's first act as he approached Italy was to divorce **Mucia** for adultery. **The reason is** not in fact **stated** in the surviving Ciceronian reference (*Att.* 1.12.3) but is clear from a reference to her being one of Caesar's lovers (Suet. *Caesar* 50.1). The divorce was politically unwise for Pompey since he risked alienating the Metelli, though he supported Mucia's half-brother Metellus Celer for the consulship of 60 BC. His error was then compounded when he tried unsuccessfully to marry himself and his elder son to two Iuniae, daughters of D. Iunius Silanus and Cato's half-sister Servilia (ch. 44, *Cato* 30.2-4). As Plutarch sees, Pompey may have wished to neutralise the threat of Cato, which revealed itself when Pompey sent a request to the senate that the consular elections for 61 BC be postponed until he returned. This would have enabled him to canvass for his legate M. Pupius Piso, but its rejection was largely due to Cato (ch.44, Cato 30.1-2).

During Pompey's absence his supporter Cornelius was prosecuted for treason (*maiestas*), but the charge was dropped (66 BC); Manilius, however, was condemned for *maiestas* in 65 BC (Cicero 9n.). Cornelius was then prosecuted again for maiestas by the leading Optimates* and successfully defended by Cicero, which won him popular favour and Pompey's backing of his candidature for the consulship of 63 BC. Crassus, meanwhile, attempted to increase his *clientela** in 65 BC by enfranchising the Transpadanes but was blocked by his fellow censor Catulus, as he was also over the annexation of Egypt.

As consul Cicero faced the dilemma of supporting Pompey's interests while not alienating those of the Optimates* who had helped secure his election instead of Catiline's. Thus the agrarian bill of P. Servilius Rullus (tr. 63 BC) would provide land for Pompey's veterans but was successfully opposed by Cicero in his speeches *De Lege Agraria*. Cicero argued that the bill was against Pompey's interests, but Rullus and his colleagues were almost certainly acting on Pompey's behalf, as Sumner, G.V., 'Cicero, Pompeius, and Rullus' *TAPA* 97 (1966) pp. 569-82 (*contra* Ward 154-7). See further Seager 62-4; *Cicero* 12n. Cicero nevertheless felt that he had done enough for Pompey to write him a high-handed letter in 62 BC concerning the events of his consulship, and despite Pompey's cool reply a second letter came from Cicero hinting at an alliance (*Fam.* 5.7).

Caesar, meanwhile, seems to have been attempting to renew his relationship with Pompey after being connected with Crassus (see further *Caesar* 7n.). In 63 BC he took part in the farcical trial of C. Rabirius, initiated by the tribune T. Labienus, who would later desert Caesar for Pompey (ch. 64). He also supported the law of Labienus and T. Ampius Balbus permitting Pompey to wear triumphal dress at the games; and backed Pompey's legate Metellus Nepos, who as tribune in 62 BC proposed that Pompey be recalled against Catiline and be allowed to stand for the consulship *in absentia* (*Cicero* 23n.). He then interfered in the restoration of the Capitoline temple of Jupiter, proposing the transfer of the completion of the task from Catulus to Pompey. Opposition to Nepos and Caesar came from Cato, tribune this year, and things got out of hand. The senate passed its ultimate decree*, and Nepos and Caesar were suspended from office: Caesar temporarily returned to private life, but Nepos fled back to Pompey (*Cicero* 26.10, *Cato* 29.1). Would Nepos' treatment be used as an excuse by Pompey to invade Italy?

Chapter 43

Pompey was no Caesar, however (*Caesar* 31.2-3), and the fears and **rumours** proved groundless as he ordered his men **to disperse**. He had indeed already written to guarantee this, which pleased Cicero (*Fam.* 5.7.1), but there was still alarm at the prospect of his return. Plutarch's reasons for Crassus' departure are unconvincing, since he went to Asia and could well have met Pompey (see Ward 193-8; that Crassus took **his money** is an example of implausible detail in Plutarch). Whether in relief or as a genuine welcome Pompey was met everywhere by large crowds – but note that his third 'return' to Italy is very similar to those from Africa and Spain, with demonstrations of popular favour and an escort scene (ch. 13n.), and suspicions that he would act like Sulla (ch. 21n.).

Chapter 44

As a holder of imperium* Pompey could not *enter the city* of Rome proper, hence his **message to the senate**: his great power of ch. 43 is reversed, and he at once comes up against the problems and frustrations which will be a feature of the 50s narrative (on the message and his **proposed marriage alliance** with Cato see ch. 42n.). Similarly, the criticisms he faces, especially of abusing his position of power, are an important anticipation of criticisms in the second half of the *Life* (chs 46, 49, 53, 55, 67).

Pompey reached Rome at the time of the Bona Dea scandal (*Caesar* 9-10nn.) and was questioned about this on his first appearance at a public meeting (*contio*) held outside the city. Pompey merely praised the authority of the senate, and his speech in Cicero's view 'fell flat' (*Att.* 1.14.1-3). At a meeting of the senate Pompey was again non-committal, and Crassus took the opportunity to praise Cicero extravagantly, thus annoying Pompey. Pompey was in a dilemma over Clodius: he had helped him secure the Eastern command (ch. 30n.), but Pompey did not want to alienate Clodius' powerful enemies in the senate before his Eastern settlement was ratified. His actions in fact alienated Clodius, and Pompey turned to Cicero's oratory for support. He also turned to bribery to ensure at least one friendly consul in 60 BC: it was because the trusty **Afranius** was a 'new man'* that the large-scale bribery described by Plutarch was necessary. Equally important, L. Flavius was elected tribune with Pompey's support.

Cato's remark to **the women** is repeated in *Cato* 30.5.

Chapter 45

Pompey's third **triumph** on 28-9 September 61 BC (the second day was his forty-fifth birthday) was a propaganda masterpiece – he was from now on remembered as the general who conquered the three known continents (see Greenhalgh [1] 168-76). All the hostages, except the kings, were afterwards sent home, and only **Aristobulus** was executed (App. *Mith*. 117). For Tigranes' fate see ch. 48.

The triumph marks the acme of Pompey's career and the end of the first part of the *Life* (cf. ch. 46, **it would have been well...at this point**). His exploits put him on a par with Alexander, and there are clear parallels between the two, e.g. the enormous amounts of **money** (*Alexander* 36.1) and conquest of **Asia** (id. 34.1). The formal parallel follows in ch. 46.

Chapter 46

At his triumph Pompey supposedly wore the cloak of Alexander himself (App. *Mith*. 117). Nevertheless, the **parallel between** the two men in times ancient and modern is in many ways forced, as here with their respective ages (**he was nearly forty** is an error; see ch. 45n.). Despite the exaggerated claims of his triumph Pompey's military exploits hardly bear comparison with Alexander's, and a happier parallel to Alexander is Caesar, as Plutarch himself decided. The statement that **it was through Pompey's power and influence that Caesar was able to challenge Rome** is equally an oversimplification.

Prominent among the opposition to Pompey was Lucullus, who had returned from Asia to **a magnificent reception by the senate** but also to the attacks of the tribune C. Memmius. He finally celebrated his triumph in 63 BC and went into semi-retirement by his fishponds, until 60 BC. Flavius introduced an agrarian law, which was opposed by Cato, the now hostile consul Celer, Crassus and Lucullus, and Cicero proposed modifications, though these were designed not to alienate Pompey (*Att*. 1.19.4). Flavius finally arrested Celer, who summoned a meeting of the senate in prison, forcing Pompey to order Flavius to free him. Then, when Pompey asked for his Eastern acts to be ratified *en bloc*, Lucullus insisted on discussion of each item, and no conclusion was reached.

A humiliated Pompey now began to look for new avenues of support. Plutarch jumps to the tribunate of P. **Clodius** Pulcher in 58 BC, and he plays an important role in the characterisation of Pompey. Not only does Pompey fail to become a successful politician (ch. 13n.), but he is even used in turn by Clodius, who by ch. 48 is independent and uncontrollable. In the *Cato* Clodius is a far more subservient figure, and at

Caesar 14.16-17 it is Caesar as much as Clodius who is responsible for Cicero's exile (and he encourages Clodius in *Cicero* 30.5). Nevertheless Pompey eventually regains control over Clodius (ch. 49) – but a similar course of events with Caesar will not have the same result. The portrayal of Clodius in the *Pompey* also helps to indicate Pompey's passivity, especially during the 50s BC. See further Pelling [2] 132-4; ch. 47n. This chapter, then, marks a clear division in Pompey's life, from his being the popular hero to being the tool of the demagogues Clodius and Caesar (see Pelling [3] 162 with n. 11).

On the exile of Cicero see *Cicero* 30-3nn. Of more immediate interest to Pompey was the return of Caesar.

Chapter 47

Caesar arrived back **from his province** of Further Spain and was forced by Cato's shortsighted policy to forego his triumph so that he could stand for **his first consulship** (*Caesar* 13n.). He turned for support to Pompey and Crassus: Pompey needed help to secure the passage of the legislation concerning his Eastern affairs, while Crassus was facing problems over the Asian taxes. The tax-farmers (*publicani*) could not cover the costs of their normally highly lucrative contract to collect the taxes there, and late in 61 BC they asked the senate for a rebate. In this they were supported by both Crassus and Cicero, but Celer spoke against the request, and Cato prevented any decision. So Caesar won the backing of Pompey and Crassus, and secured his election.

Caesar's **reconciliation** of Pompey and Crassus, who had never been on the best of terms, was achieved by pointing out that the three working together could control Rome (*Crassus* 14.1-2). Their political alliance (*amicitia*), misleadingly called the 'First Triumvirate' by modern historians, certainly was not fully implemented until after Caesar's election, and possibly not until 59 BC. Cicero, whose oratory could be a useful weapon, was invited to join by the agent of Pompey and Caesar, L. Balbus, but declined (Cic. *Att.* 2.3.3-4). For an analysis of Plutarch's different accounts of the pact see Pelling [1] 76-7.

Cato's assessment of the later **quarrel** between Pompey and Caesar (cf. *Caesar* 13.5-6) overlooks the fact that his own intractable hostility was to a large extent responsible for the alliance between them. His judgment was appropriated by Pollio, and Cato's role in the narrative as the true seer is again evident (cf. ch. 48, 40n.). For Plutarch, Pompey's alliance with Caesar reflects his political weakness (ch. 13n.).

On Caesar's consulship see *Caesar* 14n. His first agrarian bill met determined opposition in the senate, led by **Cato** and M. Calpurnius **Bibulus**. Caesar was therefore forced to take it to the people. The continuing resistance of Bibulus then obliged him to call on Pompey and Crassus, who had hitherto remained behind the scenes. Pompey's speech supporting the bill (*Caesar* 14.4-6; App. *BC* 2.10; Dio 38.4.4-5.4) shocked **even his friends**, perhaps still not fully aware of the extent of Pompey's commitment to Caesar. This was clear, however, long before April, when Pompey **married Caesar's daughter, Julia** (*Caesar* 14.7, *Cato* 31.4; Cic. *Att.* 2.17.1; Suet. *Caesar* 21). By then Pompey was becoming increasingly unhappy with their alliance, and Caesar evidently acted quickly, since Julia was engaged to Q. Servilius **Caepio** (probably the adoptive father of Caesar's assassin M. Brutus). In return Caepio was betrothed to Pompey's **daughter**, Pompeia, though she was engaged to **Faustus** Sulla (on whom see ch. 42n.). Caesar himself married into the distinguished family of L. Calpurnius **Piso**, who was standing for the consulship of 58 BC.

Unlike many political marriages and despite a thirty-year age difference, Pompey's marriage to Julia was to be a happy one (e.g. chs 48, 53). Caesar also made Pompey his heir about this time (Suet. *Caesar* 83.1) and honoured him by asking for his opinion first in the senate, instead of Crassus (id. 21).

Note that Pompey is excused by **his friends**, and friends and advisors play a prominent role in the following chapters (49, 54, 57). This reflects Pompey's passivity, other aspects of which include: the voting of commands to him, sometimes against his wishes (chs 26, 30, 49, 54, 55, 61); his passivity in the political arena, in contrast to his military decisiveness (ch. 23n.); and his portrayal at the beginning of the civil war (ch. 61). He is only really himself when on campaign (ch. 13n.) or with his wife (e.g. ch. 53). See further Pelling [2] 133-4.

Chapter 48

Plutarch returns to the agrarian bill and the day of the voting, on which Bibulus suffered his indignities (*Cato* 32.2; Dio 38.6.1-3; on **fasces** and **lictors** see ch. 19n.). The violence secured the passing of the bill, and **Bibulus shut himself up in his house** to watch the sky for omens (*Caesar* 14n.). Pompey's Eastern **settlements** were then **ratified** in March, probably along with a one-third rebate on the purchase price of the Asian taxes and perhaps the recognition of Ptolemy XIII Auletes as King of Egypt (App. *BC* 2.13; Dio 38.7.4-6). On Caesar's provinces see *Caesar* 14n. The delayed elections naturally resulted in the victory of the candidates of Caesar (his **father-in-law** L. Calpurnius Piso) and Pompey (his old ally Gabinius).

The triumvirs' violent methods had cowed even Cato, who continued to act **like an inspired man...prophecy**, and Lucullus, who was still active in 56 BC in the continuing saga of Ptolemy Auletes (the luxury of Sybaris on the Gulf of Tarentum was proverbial). They also made the dynasts very unpopular, which upset Pompey, for whom another concern was the attempt of **Clodius** to give up his patrician* status to become a plebeian* (*transitio ad plebem*). As a tribune he would be able to exact revenge on Cicero for his part in the *Bona Dea* affair (*Cicero* 30-1). When Cicero attacked the triumvirs at the trial of C. Antonius, their immediate reaction was to carry out Clodius' adoption, Caesar presiding as the chief priest of Rome (*pontifex maximus*) and Pompey acting as augur (Cic. *Att.* 8.3.3). Pompey evidently regretted this and probably tried to have Clodius sent on an embassy to Armenia, so that he would be away from Rome at the time of the tribunician elections. Clodius responded by declaring that he would rescind Caesar's legislation. Meanwhile, Pompey's unpopularity increased, fuelled by Clodius' friend C. Scribonius Curio, and he was probably happy to be out of Rome serving on the commission set up to administer the distribution of land under Caesar's law. He assured Cicero of his support against Clodius, but Clodius had no intention of giving in to Pompey. It is questionable whether he was involved in an alleged plot to assassinate Pompey (see Seager 99-100); but the implication of Cicero in the plot seems to have been at least partly responsible for Pompey's change of feelings towards him. As the constant rumours and messages warning Pompey against Cicero took effect, Clodius' attack on Cicero in 58 BC met no opposition from Pompey. Cicero therefore went **into exile**, and Caesar left for **Gaul.**

Clodius, to whom **the people were devoted** mainly because of his law providing free corn distributions (*Cicero* 30n.), now turned his attentions to **Cato**, getting him **sent to Cyprus** on a special command as quaestor with praetorian power and to restore some exiles to Byzantium (*Caesar* 21.8, *Cato* 34.2-4). Cato would no longer be able to speak out against such extraordinary commands or attack Clodius' legislation (*Cicero* 34n.), but the annexation of Cyprus interfered with Pompey's Eastern settlement. Clodius then deprived Deiotarus of Galatia of his position as high priest of the Magna Mater at Pessinus, given to him by Pompey, and transferred it to his rival Brogitarus; but more importantly Clodius **rescued...Tigranes** from the house of Flavius, and Flavius' attempt to recover him led to a battle on the Appian Way and the death of another of Pompey's friends, M. Papirius. His gang then attacked Gabinius, and Plutarch jumps to Clodius' prosecution of T. Annius Milo in 56 BC for a further illustration of the uses made by Clodius of this gang (ch. 49n.; see Lintott 77-83). For the chronological displacement in this chapter see Pelling [2] 129 n. 9.

Chapter 49

It was probably in response to the Tigranes affair that Pompey began to work for Cicero's **recall**. With Clodius rivalling him for popular favour and trying to humiliate him politically, and with his enemies in the senate **delighted to see him being insulted**, Pompey supported the unsuccessful proposal of the tribune L. Ninnius to this effect. Clodius' reply was to threaten Caesar's legislation and then Pompey himself, with an apparent assassination attempt by **one of Clodius's servants** on 11 August (Cic. *Mil.* 18-19; Ascon. 46C). Terrified by a second plot against his life, **for the rest of** the year Pompey **stayed at home** and concentrated on Cicero's recall. He refused **to break off relations with Caesar** by divorcing Julia on the suggestion of the tribune Q. Terentius **Culleo**, but secured his reluctant backing for the recall and then rallied further support in Italy with **Cicero's brother** Quintus. The consuls' motion was passed in June (*Cicero* 33n.).

Cicero repaid Pompey **as soon as he returned** (7 September) by successfully proposing that he be given a commission to organise **the corn supply** (*cura annonae*). Bad harvests and transport difficulties, as well as the influx of Pompey's clients* to vote for the recall, had caused a food shortage and riots in Rome, the latter instigated by Clodius. Pompey requested fifteen legates, the first named being Cicero, and received control of the corn supply of the empire for five years as proconsul. Plutarch exaggerates his powers, which would have been far greater if the proposal of the tribune C. Messius had been adopted (Cic. *Att.* 4.1.7). Pompey doubtless preferred Messius' proposal, but the opposition to it was too strong.

The restoration of **Ptolemy** Auletes in 59 BC (ch. 48n.) proved unpopular and short-lived, and **the consul Spinther** proposed a motion in the senate that he be re-established by the next governor of Cilicia, who was to be Spinther himself (Cic. *Fam.* 1.1, *Pis.* 50; Dio 39.12-16). **Ptolemy's own wish** was to be restored by Pompey, and he came to Rome to use bribery to this end, staying at Pompey's Alban villa. The Alexandrians also sent envoys to oppose Ptolemy, some of whom he had murdered. Most of the senate was hostile to Ptolemy, and Cicero, whose recall owed much to Spinther, urged Pompey not to get involved. Various proposals were put to the senate, including one by Servilius Isauricus that Ptolemy should not be restored at all, which goaded Pompey's supporters into action. Among these were the tribunes of 56 BC, P. Rutilius Lupus and L. Caninius Gallus (Plutarch's **Cassidius**). After a series of debates in the senate Pompey suffered abuse at the trial of Milo (ch. 48), Cicero's version indicating that Clodius incited his supporters to shout for Crassus to go to Alexandria (*QF* 2.3.2). Pompey believed that Crassus was plotting to murder him, and he therefore thought it best to drop the Ptolemy matter.

Timagenes of Alexandria wrote a *History of Kings*, probably the source of much gossip about Augustus, with whom he fell out of favour. He also stayed with Asinius Pollio, one of Plutarch's sources. On **Theo-**

phanes see ch. 32n. Plutarch's confidence in **Pompey's...nature** concerning the Ptolemy affair was hardly shared by Cicero (*QF* 2.2.3).

Chapter 50

Plutarch returns to Pompey's *cura annonae*, which he conducted along similar lines to his campaign against the pirates by dividing up the relevant areas of the Mediterranean among his fifteen legates (we know only the names of Cicero and his brother Quintus). Pompey was actively involved, as Plutarch indicates, though he was keen to keep up with events in Rome and was given special dispensations allowing him to enter the city. The command suited Pompey's organisational skills, and soon his actions led to **a surplus** of food. This went some way to restoring Pompey's popularity, and at Clodius' expense. See further on Pompey's methods, and in general on the corn supply, Garnsey, P., *Famine and Food Supply in the Graeco-Roman World* (Cambridge, 1988) pp. 216-17. On Pompey's departure in the **storm** and his **good fortune** see Weinstock 121-3.

Chapter 51

Nevertheless, Pompey's backing of Milo and Sestius against Clodius lost him much popular favour, and his relationship with Crassus was at a low ebb. Cicero, who saw an opportunity to reconcile Pompey with the Optimates*, revived the question of Caesar's Campanian law, which was a drain on Rome's finances; at the same time the money Pompey needed to buy corn was granted. If Cicero thought, however, that he would thereby break up the coalition, he was sadly mistaken, as Crassus left for Ravenna to inform Caesar of what had happened (on Caesar's campaign **in Gaul** so far, which Plutarch turns into a **training** exercise for the civil war, see *Caesar* 18-21, 28nn.; for the athletic imagery see ch. 8n.). Caesar therefore hastened across Italy to **Luca** to meet Pompey before he left for Sardinia. On the so-called 'Conference of Luca' cf. *Caesar* 21.5-6, *Crassus* 14.4-6, *Cato* 41.1; Suet. *Caesar* 24.1; App. *BC* 2.17; Luibheid, C., 'The Luca Conference' *CP* 65 (1970) pp. 88-94. The picture in the sources seems to a large extent invention – it is by no means certain that Crassus was even there, let alone all the magistrates and senators, and Cicero implies he was not (on the **fasces** see ch.19n.). See Jackson, J., 'Cicero, *Fam.* 1.9.9, and the Conference of Luca' *LCM* 3 (1978) pp. 175-7; *contra* Ward, A.M., 'The Conference of Luca: Did It Happen?' *AJAH* 5 (1980) pp. 48-63. Nevertheless, the main result of the meeting is clear, with Pompey and Crassus to be reconciled in a second joint consulship for 55 BC (below) and, probably, the allocation of **provinces** arranged. Additionally Pompey would ensure via Quintus that Cicero dropped his attack on the Campanian land allotments, and Crassus would end his support of Clodius. Clodius and Pompey were reconciled, but Cicero's position had been compromised. Betrayed by the Optimates*, he began supporting Caesar and, along with Pompey and Crassus, spoke in defence of Balbus' citizenship (on Balbus see ch. 21n.).

This chapter is the beginning of a complex characterisation of Pompey during the 50s BC which is analysed by Pelling [2] 131-2. A vital moment comes when Pompey abandons his usual caution (*eulabeia*) in ch. 57, which lays him open to the workings of Fate (*Tyche*), itself a major theme of the *Life* (chs 21, 41-2, 46, 50, 53, 57, 73-5). This in turn paves the way for Pompey's tragic demise at the end of the *Life*. Pompey's character is also strongly contrasted with that of Caesar in the *Pompey* but not in the *Caesar* (see Pelling [2] 134).

Chapter 52

Pompey and Crassus had to use violence to overcome the opposition to their candidatures from Cato's brother-in-law L. **Domitius** Ahenobarbus, who was encouraged by Cato after his return from Cyprus (*Crassus* 15, *Cato* 41.2-42.1; Cato is again prominent as the standard of moral correctness). Bribery was then added to violence to prevent Cato's election **to the praetorship**, while the Caesarian tribune of 59 BC, P. **Vatinius**, was elected (*Cato* 42.4; Dio 39.32.1-2); and the violence continued at the election of the aediles (ch. 53). To end these disorders Pompey passed a law on bribery at elections, and other legislation included Crassus' curbing of guilds in canvassing (on the *collegia* see Lintott 78-83, and for their restoration see *Cicero* 30n.). The most important laws, however, were those giving new five-year provincial commands to Pompey and Crassus and a five-year extension to Caesar's command in Gaul. The former was certainly passed by C. **Trebonius**, the latter in the other sources is passed by Pompey and Crassus – Plutarch in fact knew this (*Cato* 43), and he conflates the measures here (see Pelling [2] 127). Crassus, eager for military glory, was to replace Gabinius in Syria with the chance to invade Parthia; Pompey had no need of further military success, but the two Spains and the one legion which **he lent to Caesar** (not **two**, as also *Caesar* 25.2; cf. *Cato* 45.3; Caes. *BG* 6.1.2) would later strengthen his position against him (ch. 57n.). Note that Pompey did not receive **the whole of Libya** (i.e. Africa), an error also made in *Caesar* 28.8, *Cato* 43.1; App. *BC* 2.18.

In 55 BC Pompey dedicated his stone **theatre**, which was not pleasing to all, his Portico and temple of Venus Victrix (see further ch. 40n.).

Cicero thought the scale of the programme excessive (*Off.* 2.60, cf. 57), and the crowd sided with the elephants.

Chapter 53

In this chapter we reach another important turning-point in Pompey's career, with the contrast between **popularity** and **resentment** which was foreshadowed in ch. 21. Additionally, Plutarch again reveals his love of anecdotal material; and Pompey's **constancy as a husband** is reiterated (ch. 36n.). The chapter ends with an analysis of the breakdown of the triumvirate, which clearly comes straight from Pollio and in which undue prominence is given to **fear of Crassus** and the role of **fortune** (below).

While the building programme **increased his popularity**, Pompey saw his supporters attacked in the courts. In addition Domitius and M. Cato this time secured their magistracies, and Domitius at once attacked Caesar, Crassus and Gabinius. Pompey therefore needed to be near Rome, and so for the first time a province was governed through **subordinate commanders** (Vell. 2.48.1; Dio 39.39.4). Plutarch adds the motive that he wished to spend time with Julia, who had a **miscarriage** on seeing his **blood-stained garments** after the aedilician elections (Dio 39.32.2; further on **Flora** cf. ch. 2). Julia's death in childbirth in August 54 BC threatened the coalition between Pompey and Caesar (*Caesar* 23.5-7); but Pompey's attitude did not **immediately** change then or even after the death of Crassus at Carrhae on 9 June 53 BC, whom the sources see as a balancing factor. Against this view of the role of **fortune** in the build-up to the civil war see the analysis of Gruen [2] 450-97, who traces political cooperation between the two down to 50 BC. Plutarch interprets this as Pompey giving Caesar an **impression...of goodwill** (ch. 56). Further on Plutarch's analysis of the origins of the civil war see *Caesar* 28; Pelling [3] 164.

The quote of the **comic poet** is frg. 401K; and for the division of the universe into three by Zeus, Poseidon and Pluto cf. Hom. *Iliad* 15.187-9.

Chapter 54

Pompey, who had not always **disbanded his armies** quickly enough to prevent suspicion of his motives (cf. chs 13, 21), now became concerned with the consular elections for 53 BC. These were postponed due to bribery and intrigue, and meanwhile Gabinius returned from Syria. He was prosecuted for treason (*maiestas*) but acquitted, largely through the efforts of Pompey, who it was feared might otherwise aim at **a dictatorship** (Cic. *Att.* 4.18.3, *QF* 3.4.1). Gabinius was then condemned for extortion despite the efforts of Pompey, who forced Cicero to defend his enemy. By now all the consular candidates were also being prosecuted, and no elections were in fact held in 54 BC. As the rumours of dictatorship increased, Pompey had to deny any such ambitions, but his real feelings were as usual unclear. His cousin C. **Lucilius** Hirrus (tr. 53 BC) increased the doubts by declaring himself ready to bring in a bill to this effect, but there was strong opposition, including Milo. Pompey was then absent for the first half of 53 BC but finally held the elections on the senate's request.

The elections for 52 BC were again postponed due to bribery and violence. The latter was inevitable with Milo standing for consul and Clodius for praetor, and Clodius supporting Milo's rivals P. Plautius Hypsaeus and Q. Caecilius Metellus Scipio (the father of Pompey's fifth wife, ch. 55). The violence reached a peak on 18 January 52 BC, when Clodius was killed on Milo's orders after a brawl on the Appian Way. Clodius' body was cremated in the senate house, which then burned down, and the mob shouted for Pompey to be made consul or dictator, prompting the senate to pass its ultimate decree*. Agitation for Pompey to be made dictator continued, and to prevent this **Bibulus,** supported by **Cato and his party,** made the counter-proposal that Pompey be appointed to the lesser position of **sole consul** (*Caesar* 28.7, *Cato* 47.2-3; Ascon. 36C; App. *BC* 2.23; Dio 40.50.4). He was so proclaimed by the interrex Ser. Sulpicius Rufus on 24 Interc. (an intercalary **interim period** between February and March).

Note that Pompey **allowed a state of affairs to come into existence where there was no government at all.** Plutarch does not suggest here that Pompey was plotting to become dictator, which would be out of step with the characterisation of him in this *Life* as a man to whom things happened (ch. 47n.). At *Caesar* 28.7, however, Pompey actually works **to get himself made dictator** (see Pelling [2] 134). For the remark **typical of Cato** cf. *Cato* 48.1-4.

Chapter 55

According to Plutarch **Pompey now...married Cornelia** (Dio 40.51.3). Caesar had offered him the hand of his great-niece Octavia, and suggested that he himself should divorce Calpurnia and marry Pompey's daughter; but Pompey declined and instead chose **Cornelia, a daughter of Q.** Caecilius **Metellus** Pius **Scipio** Nasica and like Julia significantly younger than himself. For her continuing devotion see ch. 74n. The **criticism for neglecting his responsibilities** seems, however, like a doublet on ch. 53, here leading to the **physician** motif which recurs in ch. 67 and *Caesar* 28.6 (cf. the sickness imagery in *Cicero* 10.5 with n.). This motif is important in Augustan ideology (e.g. the *Preface* of Livy). Pompey in fact, as Plutarch indicates, reformed court procedure and passed legislation against **bribery** and violence (App. *BC* 2.23). He was clearly attacking Milo, who was supported by M. Caelius Rufus, Cato and Cicero. Disturbances on the first day of his trial led Pompey to appear in person on the next two days **with an armed force**. On the final day he also filled the forum with troops, but the continuing threats of Clodius' supporters unnerved Cicero, and Milo was condemned (*Cicero* 35n.). Pompey's influence over this and subsequent trials is evident: both of the consular candidates Scipio and **Hypsaeus** (who was not, therefore, **of consular rank**) were prosecuted for bribery, and while his old friend Hypsaeus was contemptuously abandoned by Pompey and condemned, his new father-in-law Scipio was supported and acquitted. Whether he went as far as summoning **the jury to his own house** is uncertain, since he had already decided to choose Scipio **to be his colleague**. Finally, T. Munatius **Plancus** was prosecuted by Cicero as soon as he laid down his tribunate (Cato 48.4-5; Cic. Fam. 7.2.2-3). Contrary to one of his own **laws regulating the procedure**, which abolished character testimonials, Pompey sent a letter which Cato refused to admit (the version in the *Cato*, rather than making a **speech**).

On the extension of Pompey's command for in fact five years and the **1,000 talents each year** (= 24 million. HS) cf. *Caesar* 28.8; Dio 40.44.2.

Chapter 56

Pompey's other major concern in 52 BC was the position of **Caesar**, on which see *Caesar* 26, 29nn. Caesar needed dispensation to stand for the consulship in absence, and he persuaded all ten tribunes of 52 BC to propose this. Pompey supported them, **Cato** opposed, and the law was passed. Plutarch notes Pompey's insincerity, in line with the idea that their alliance had ended in 53 BC (ch. 53n.), but Pompey as yet had no intention of breaking with Caesar. Nevertheless, his law on provinicial government was seen as being aimed against Caesar – Pompey confirmed a decree of the senate in 53 BC that there should be a five-year gap between office and provincial command. Ex-consuls and ex-praetors who had not governed a province were to be used during the transitional period (*Cicero* 36n.), and Caesar might suddenly be replaced in Gaul. Suspicions were increased when Pompey passed a law requiring candidates for office to hand in their nominations in person. This conflicted with the tribunes' law above, and Pompey was forced to add a rider exempting Caesar which was not authorised by the senate or people. In these measures Pompey may have been flexing his political muscles, demonstrating his supreme authority (*auctoritas*) to both Caesar and the Optimates* (as Seager 148-50). In support of Suetonius' explanation (*Caesar* 28.3) that Pompey simply 'had omitted to make a special exception for Caesar' see Stockton, D.L., 'Quis iustius induit arma?' *Historia* 24 (1975) pp. 249-50.

Pompey did not request **the return of the troops** he had lent Caesar (ch. 52) until the summer of 50 BC (ch. 57n.).

Chapter 57

Pompey's **serious illness** also occurred in the summer of 50 BC (below); and Plutarch omits the important developments of 51 BC, when opposition to Caesar's command in Gaul was led by the consul M. Claudius Marcellus (*Caesar* 29n.). Caesar's recall in 51 BC, however, would be against the terms of the law of Pompey and Crassus in 55 BC (ch. 52), and along with the other consul, Ser. Sulpicius Rufus, Pompey opposed Marcellus, who backed down. Then on 22 July Pompey agreed to withdraw the legion he had lent Caesar, though not immediately; and on 1 September he declared that the senate should make no decision on Caesar's provinces for the time being, Metellus Scipio proposing they be discussed on 1 March 50 BC. If he were replaced at that time, Caesar might retain his *imperium** outside Rome pending a triumph but would be heavily dependent on Pompey's influence to be allowed to stand for the consulship in absence. This suited Pompey's desire to be without equal in Rome, and on 29 September the senate voted for such a debate on 1 March 50 BC with Pompey's approval, though his remarks on this occasion gave rise to the suspicion that he had come to some arrangement with Caesar. By October there was also the prospect of a command against the Parthians, and when the Parthian threat persisted into the summer of 50 BC, the senate decreed that Pompey and Caesar should each send one legion to Syria (Hirtius in Caes. *BG* 8.54.1-55.1). It was now that Pompey cleverly **asked for the return of the troops which he had lent** Caesar (ch. 56, cf. 52), who therefore lost two legions – and they were never sent to the East. Their loyalty to Pompey, however, was undermined by Caesar's **very generous rewards** of 1,000 HS per man (*Caesar* 29.4). Pompey remained in Italy, where pressure on him began to mount in 50 BC (ch. 58).

During the political struggle of 50 BC Pompey suffered a bad attack of a recurring fever, possibly malaria contracted during his Eastern command. On his recovery there was rejoicing **through the whole of Italy** (Vell. 2.48.2; Dio 41.6.3-4; but cf. Cic. *Att.* 8.16.1; on the escort scene see ch. 13n.). This display, while not in itself **one of the main causes** of the civil war, certainly prompted Pompey to believe mistakenly that all Italy would support him in a war against Caesar. In addition **Appius** Claudius Pulcher arrived with **the troops Pompey had lent to Caesar**. The **damaging stories**, which included officers' reports of low morale and the troops being ready to mutiny (*Caesar* 29.4-6; App. *BC* 2.30), helped to **put Pompey into a state of exaltation**, but he presumably did not know of Caesar's payment (above; the implication of the *Caesar* version is that the officers were acting on Caesar's behalf). Pompey's **calm** belief in his ability to raise troops was to be sadly exposed (ch. 60), and his delusion is an important element of Plutarch's characterisation. This is brought out by the highly tragic quality of Plutarch's analysis: Pompey abandons his usual **caution** for **unlimited confidence** and **contempt**. The tragic sequence of *hubris* and *nemesis* which began in ch. 42 is now fully in motion. See further ch. 51n.

Chapter 58

The pressure on Pompey stemmed mainly from the tribune C. Scribonius Curio, previously anti-Caesar but **hopelessly in debt** to him, though Caelius tells Cicero that Curio changed sides because his proposal as a pontiff to intercalate a month was rejected (Caelius in Cic. *Fam.* 8.6.5). He was now working on Caesar's behalf, along with **the consul Paulus** (L. Aemilius Paullus), whom Caesar had **won over** by supporting his building scheme (*Caesar* 29n.), and **Mark Antony**, whom Caesar was backing for the tribunate of 49 BC. When C. Marcellus initiated the debate on Caesar's provinces on 1 March, Curio countered with the proposal, which **looked fair enough**, that Caesar and Pompey should both lay down their commands (*Caesar* 30.1-2, *Cato* 51.5; App. *BC* 2.27; Dio 40.62.3). This turned the tables on Pompey, whose next move may have been to propose that Caesar leave his province on 13 November. Pompey claimed he was being fair, but Caelius saw this as an attack on Caesar and Curio rejected the proposal. After his illness Pompey returned to Rome to offer his resignation from his command, promising Caesar would do likewise. Caesar no longer trusted him, however, and Curio insisted that Pompey lay down his command first, proposing that both should be declared public enemies if they refused. Finally, on 1 December, Curio again proposed that Pompey and Caesar should resign their powers, but **the consul Marcellus** (not Curio) divided this into two motions (App. id. 2.30). The first, that Caesar should resign alone, was passed; the second, that Pompey be deprived of his command, was not, and Curio, supported by **Antony and Piso**, Caesar's father-in-law, then had his proposal passed by 370 votes to 22. This vote in fact revealed the extent of the opposition to Caesar, but **Curio rushed off** seeing it as a victory. Marcellus dismissed the senate, and making full use of the rumour that Caesar was **marching on Rome, went to see Pompey** (ch. 59; **Pompey had not been present at the meeting** because of his *imperium**).

For an analysis of chs 58-9 and the parallel *Caesar* 30-1 and *Antony* 5 see Pelling [2] 139-40. Note that *Pompey* has the debate of 1 December 50 BC, while *Caesar* and *Antony* have that of 1 January 49 BC; Curio's reception by the people and Antony's production of the letter come after the debate in *Pompey* but before that in *Caesar*; *Pompey* simplifies the voting sequence and omits the role of the consuls; the remarks are given to Marcellus in *Pompey*, to Lentulus in *Caesar*, where they are conflated (see id. 30n.). On the centurion's remark see *Caesar* 29n.; for those of Marcellus see id. 30n.; and for the **ten legions** Marcellus visualised **marching on Rome** see id. 33n.

Chapter 59

Marcellus on his own responsibility ordered Pompey to defend Rome, using **the forces** at Capua (the two legions sent by Caesar) and elsewhere in Italy and raising others. He was supported by both the consuls-designate for 49 BC, L. Cornelius **Lentulus** Crus and C. Claudius Marcellus (Dio 40.66.2). Pompey accepted with his usual reluctance, and Curio joined Caesar (*Caesar* 30n.).

Pompey may still have been hoping for a peaceful settlement, and this was also **the general demand**, especially when Curio brought **a letter from Caesar** on 1 January 49 BC. Antony, who was responsible for disrupting Pompey's levy, had attacked Pompey's career on 21 December and issued threats of force (it may be this meeting of the assembly to which Plutarch refers here). Now, on 1 January, Antony and another tribune, Q. Cassius Longinus, succeeded in getting the consuls to read Caesar's letter in the senate, but no vote was allowed (*Caesar* 30.3, *Antony* 5.3; Caes. *BC* 1.1.1). In the letter Caesar again **suggested that both he and Pompey should give up their provinces** but now threatened war if Pompey would not agree. Many senators were in favour of peace, but Metellus Scipio had a motion carried **that Caesar should be declared a public enemy if he had not laid down his arms before a certain date** (*Caesar* 30.4; cf. Caes. id. 1.2.2-6). That evening Pompey summoned the senators to his house to firm their resolve, but some were still in favour of sending envoys to Caesar. Then, on 4 January Cicero **returned from Cilicia**, where he had been governor since 51 BC (*Cicero* 36), and revived Caesar's proposal that he **should retain Illyricum** and Cisalpine Gaul (the latter omitted by Plutarch) with **two legions** (*Caesar* 31.1; Suet. *Caesar* 29.2). Either **Pompey objected to this plan and insisted that Caesar's soldiers should be taken from him** (*Caesar* ibid.) or, less likely, he accepted but the consuls objected (App. *BC* 2.32). Cicero then proposed that Caesar keep **Illyricum** and one legion (as Suetonius), but Lentulus, Cato and Scipio prevented Pompey's acceptance. On 7 January the senate passed its ultimate decree*, and the

Caesarian tribunes **fled from Rome in hired carts and dressed as slaves** (*Caesar* 31.3). Pompey was optimistic, and the senate decreed him money and provinces.

Chapter 60

With his accustomed swiftness of action (*celeritas*) Caesar soon **reached the River Rubicon** and came to **Ariminum** (*Caesar* 32n.). The tragic quality of the Rubicon scene, although not as marked as that of the longer version in the *Caesar*, is still evident: N.B. Caesar's hesitation before rushing into precipitate action. The scene sets up the tragedy of Caesar, which is separate from that of Pompey but at the same time interlocking with it.

Pompey was surprised by the speed and timing of Caesar's actions, and Rome **was filled with...terror**, believing Caesar would perpetrate massacres. Pompey's lack of readiness was exposed by L. Volcacius **Tullus**, who **advised sending a deputation to Caesar** unaware that Pompey had secretly done just that (Caes. *BC* 1.8.2, 4; Dio 41.5.2). The praetor M. **Favonius** recalled Pompey's boast of 50 BC (ch. 57), and Pompey replied with a warning that Italy might have to be abandoned (App. *BC* 2.37).

For Cato's prophecy cf. ch. 48, *Cato* 52.1-2.

Chapter 61

Cato's advice that Pompey be given supreme command **with unlimited powers** was not taken (for his remark cf. *Cato* 52.2). With people **pouring into Rome from all directions** Pompey could not **get accurate information about the enemy**. The speed of Caesar's advance upset his plans and left him unprepared; and with insufficient troops to defend Rome and with the war and the levy unpopular Pompey had little choice but to declare **a state of civil war** (*tumultus*) and order the evacuation of the city (ch.59; Cic. *Att.* 7.11.3). He left on 17 January, followed by the consuls and most senators (*Caesar* 33.6; Caes. *BC* 1.14.3). Cicero, although realising the possibility of an evacuation existed, had nevertheless expected Pompey to defend Rome. He therefore condemns Pompey's action as a panic measure and underlines the disadvantages (e.g. *Att.* 7.11.3-4). The loss of Rome was a great pyschological blow, and moreover Caesar secured the treasury. Despite all this, however, Pompey maintained his popularity, and many **could not bear to forsake him** (cf. *Caesar* 34.4).

Pompey's plan may have been to try to cut Caesar off from his army in Gaul, but he was hampered by a shortage of reliable troops. Then on 22 January Labienus arrived at Teanum Sidicinum after deserting Caesar (ch. 64; *Caesar* 34n.), and next day L. Caesar brought peace proposals from Caesar in response to Pompey's secret initiative. These, however, proved fruitless.

Labienus' reports encouraged Pompey, but by early February Picenum was lost. The only chance of stopping Caesar's march on Rome now rested with L. Domitius Ahenobarbus at Corfinium, but Pompey urged Domitius to link up with him at Luceria, to prevent their being cut off from one another. He had by then decided not to fight Caesar in Italy, but Domitius would not cooperate (and Pompey could not order him to do so, as he was not yet the supreme commander). Caesar soon took Corfinium, and on 19 February Pompey left for **Brundisium**, requesting the consuls to join him there (*Caesar* 35.2; Pompey in Cic. *Att.* 8.12a.1-2, 4).

Plutarch contrasts Pompey's withdrawal with Agesilaus' refusal to abandon Sparta to Epameinondas (*Comp. Ages. Pomp.* 3.3-4). Hence Pompey failed in his duty as a statesman to save Rome from civil war. See Wardman 235.

Caesar's clemency (*clementia*) after capturing Corfinium went some way **to calm people's fears**. **He then set out in pursuit of Pompey**, before he **occupied Rome** (Plutarch inverts the order of events), and tried to trap him in Brundisium, where Pompey was in the process of sending his troops across the Adriatic **to Dyrrhachium** (on the **thirty cohorts** see *Caesar* 33n.). His plan now was to use forces from the East to blockade Italy, hence **he sent his father-in-law, Scipio, and his son, Gnaeus, to Syria to raise a fleet**. He would need to cut off Italy's corn supply, and to prevent this Caesar sent legates to Sardinia, Sicily and Africa. Finally, on 17 March Pompey himself embarked for Greece.

For the warning given by **the people of Brundisium** about Pompey's **ditches and stakes** cf. Caes. *BC* 1.28.

Caesar did not have the fleet to follow Pompey, and so he returned to Rome (ch. 63; on the chronological displacement see Pelling [2] 128). Despite his clash with the tribune L. Caecilius **Metellus** (*Caesar* 35n.) Caesar's clemency was gradually allaying **people's fears**, while there was increasing alarm about Pompey's intentions if victorious. Cicero connected the planned blockade with desire for a personal rule (*regnum*) in the mode of Sulla (Cic. *Att.* 8.11.2), and Caesar was not slow to recall Pompey's youthful cruelties (id. 9.14.2).

Chapter 63

On his way to Brundisium Caesar **had captured Numerius** Magius, one of Pompey's prefects of engineers, and he twice sent him to Pompey in the vain hope of arranging an interview. He was followed by Caesar's legate Caninius Rebilus (a friend of Pompey's adviser Scribonius Libo), also to no avail. Caesar would have known that Pompey's use of the resources of the East might mean **a long war** which he would be hard pressed to win. For Pompey, on the other hand, peace would now seem like a surrender, and he used the excuse that he could not enter into discussions in the consuls' absence. Caesar, in sum, was more frustrated by, than **astonished** at, Pompey's departure, which was facilitated by Pompey's **complete control of the seas** and his own lack of ships.

Cicero for his part continued to criticise Pompey's strategy, which he likened to that **of Themistocles** (*Comp. Ages. Pomp.* 4.3, *Mor.* 205C-D; Cic.*Att.* 7.11.3). Plutarch, on the other hand, strongly defends Pompey's policy and goes on to note the strength of his forces and their admiration for him (ch. 64), his success at Dyrrhachium (ch. 65) and the correctness of his delaying tactics (ch. 66, cf. *Comp. Ages. Pomp.* 4.6). It is then Pompey's lack of political ability which resurfaces and, unable to control his senatorial subordinates, he fatefully changes his strategy (ch. 67). See further Pelling [2] 134-5.

Themistocles had been responsible for the abandonment of Athens and reliance on the fleet in the face of Xerxes' invasion (480 BC). The strategy of **Pericles** in the Peloponnesian War, however, was to retire behind Athens' walls in the face of the annual Peloponnesian invasions of Attica, with the food supply, brought in via Piraeus and the connecting Long Walls, ensured by Athens' naval supremacy.

Chapter 64

While Caesar went to Spain (ch. 63, *Caesar* 36n.), Pompey had the time to gather **a very great force** in the East (Dio 41.10.3-4). **His navy** came from Greece, Asia Minor and Egypt and was divided into five flotillas under the supreme command of Bibulus (**500 warships** is probably an exaggeration). Their main task was to prevent corn reaching Italy and protect Pompey's supply routes. Many of the **cavalry** in fact came from the East, with in addition herdsmen and slaves from Pompey's estates (**in the flower of Rome and of Italy** Plutarch anticipates ch. 69). **His infantry** consisted of nine legions: five from Italy, one from veterans in Crete and Macedonia, one from the remnants of the two legions from Cilicia and two from Asia levied by Lentulus; additionally there were two of Crassus' Syrian legions under Scipio. Further on these figures see *Caesar* 33n. This **mixed lot** was trained **at Beroea** in Macedonia under Pompey's direction (he was 57 on 29 September 49 BC; Plutarch's description attributes to him the characteristics of a typical Xenophontic 'ideal general'). Among the **kings and rulers** providing auxiliaries were Deiotarus of Galatia and Ariobarzanes of Cappadocia. Money came from Greece, Asia, Syria and the kings, and corn from Thessaly, Asia, Egypt, Crete and Cyrene.

Pompey also had the backing **of the leading men of Rome**, including both consuls of 49 BC, though some senators remained in the city. There the praetor M. Aemilius Lepidus proclaimed Caesar dictator, and Caesar held the consular elections for 48 BC at which he was returned with P. Servilius Isauricus (*Caesar* 37n.).

Plutarch names among Pompey's supporters **Labienus** (see Pelling [2] 129 n. 9; *Caesar* 34n.); M. Iunius **Brutus**, Caesar's assassin whose father **had been put to death by Pompey** (ch. 16n.); and **Cicero** (*Cicero* 38-9).

Chapter 65

With his **senate** Pompey could claim to be fighting **for the cause of justice** and was at last given the supreme command. **Cato** had joined him, having left Sicily on the approach of Asinius Pollio and Curio (*Cato* 53.1-3; Caes. *BC* 1.30.2, 4-5). Caesar, meanwhile, quickly defeated **the forces of Pompey in Spain** (by September 49 BC) and once more showed his clemency by allowing Pompey's legates Afranius and Petreius to join him (*Caesar* 36n.; the **soldiers** were demobilised). Hastening via Rome to **Brundisium**, he crossed on 4 January to Palaeste, near **Oricum**. He then sent L. **Vibullius** Rufus to Pompey with another peace proposal. Meanwhile Oricum and Apollonia went over to Caesar; Pompey **marched quickly** to Dyrrhachium and retook Oricum; and Caesar waited south of the river Apsus for reinforcements from Antony. This led to stalemate as Pompey refused to engage him, even with superior numbers, until Scipio's two legions arrived from Pergamum. He concentrated instead on cutting Caesar's supply lines, but bad weather hindered his fleet. Libo and Bibulus therefore opened unsuccessful delaying talks with Caesar, and at last Vibullius tried to discuss Caesar's earlier proposal. Pompey refused even to let him speak, for an agreement now would be tantamount to a Caesarian victory. Finally, in March/April Antony broke Pompey's blockade, and after a series of manoeuvres Caesar managed to get between Pompey and his base at Dyrrhachium. There followed an attempt by Caesar in turn to blockade Pompey's position, Pompey replied with an inner ring of **fortifications** and frequent **irregular engagements** took place. In one of these, on the hill of Paliama, Pompey in fact **had the better of things** (Caes. id.3.45.2-6). By about the end of June Caesar had completed the circumvallation, and Pompey himself began to suffer a shortage of supplies. After an unsuccessful attack in which he lost 2,000 men and with Caesar daily **challenging him to come out in the open**, Pompey finally received information from two deserters about Caesar's unprotected southern flank by the sea. This time Pompey's attack was successful, but earthworks which hindered Caesar's right wing during a counter-attack in turn hampered Pompey's forces, and **he was unable** to press home his assault. Also Caesar's troops rapidly withdrew, and Caesar thought Pompey **feared to push on** perhaps into an ambush, but that if he had done so he might have destroyed Caesar's whole army. Hence Caesar's damning verdict on Pompey's generalship, **'Today...winner'** (*Caesar* 39n.). Caesar put his losses at about 1,000, the figure also given in *Caesar* 41.1. Cf. Caes. id. 3.59-71; Fuller 210-27.

Chapter 66

After this victory Pompey was hailed once more as 'Imperator'*, though he refrained from using the title as **he wrote** victory letters. Caesar headed south to **Thessaly** with six legions, where he could link up with Domitius Calvinus against Scipio.

Pompey now had the options of invading Italy, fighting **a battle that would decide the whole issue** or delaying matters with a war of attrition. **Afranius** proposed the first of these, but Pompey did not wish to alienate public opinion by invading or lose face by running **away from Caesar for a second time**, and besides it would be disastrous militarily to **abandon Scipio and others of consular rank** (App. *BC* 2.65; Dio 41.52.3). See further Greenhalgh [2] 232-6, who rightly emphasises Pompey's dependence on the East. Others **were full of confidence** that they would win a battle (ch. 67, cf. 72) and were assuming that they would soon be returning to Rome to stand **for election to the various magistracies** (Caes. *BC* 3.96.1). Pompey himself preferred the idea of wearing Caesar down (*Caesar* 40.2-4).

In the Greek **what they were fighting for** is *to megiston athlon* ('the greatest prize'), another example of athletic imagery (ch. 8n.).

Chapter 67

Having reached this decision Pompey went after Caesar, leaving **Cato** with a garrison of fifteen cohorts at Dyrrhachium, which was interpreted by some **because he was afraid** (*Cato* 54.3-55.2) – this is one of the few occasions on which Plutarch seems aware of Pompey's relationship with the Optimates* and how they were using him to get rid of Caesar. His subordinates too were no longer happy with his leadership;

and Pompey was **criticized from all sides**, accused of prolonging the war in order to keep **himself perpetually in power** and order proconsuls about as if they were his **servants** (*Caesar* 41.2-5; Caes. *BC* 3.82.2; App. *BC* 2.67; Dio 42.5.5 for **'Agamemnon'**). To make things worse there was dissent amongst his officers, some charging **Afranius** with betraying his army **in Spain** for a bribe (*Caesar* 41.4; hence Afranius' gibe) and others **quarrelling** as to who **should succeed Caesar as Chief Pontiff** (*Caesar* 42.2; Caes. id. 3.82.3, 83.1). Pompey was clearly beginning to lose control, and he weakly **abandoned his own best-laid plans** for a single battle (Caes. id. 3.86.1).

This chapter contains an important analysis of Pompey's motivation and sees the culmination of his various weaknesses. He has so far avoided a decisive battle (ch. 66), and Plutarch defends his strategy (ch. 63n.). In this Pompey is acting true to his great military capabilities, but already he is being **influenced by...the common talk among the cavalry**: he is **a slave to his own idea of glory** and cannot tolerate criticism. The old tension between his military strength and political weakness has also resurfaced, and he is unable to control his unruly senatorial subordinates. Still concerned with his personal popularity, Pompey is **frightened of taking** the necessary **measures** and fails in his role as Rome's doctor (ch. 55n.). As in a tragedy, Pompey has reached a big moment of decision, and he weakly changes his mind; and from being in control of the situation, he is now carried along helplessly to his fate.

On **Tigranes** and the **Nabataeans** see chs 33, 39nn.; and for the figures relating to Caesar's successes (**800 cities** in *Caesar* 15.5) see *Caesar* 27n.

Chapter 68

Pompey marched to Larissa in Thessaly, where he joined Scipio; Caesar, meanwhile, advanced to **the plain of Pharsalia** south of Larissa. The details of the battle on 9 August remain problematic, Caesar's oversimplified account frequently differing from those in the later sources which probably derive from Caesar's officer Asinius Pollio (ch. 72). See Fuller 231-9; Pelling, C.B.R, 'Pharsalus' *Historia* 22 (1973) pp. 249-59; Leach 201-7; Greenhalgh [2] 248-54.

Like Alexander at the Hydaspes (*Alexander* 60) Pompey relied on his cavalry, assured of their superiority by **Labienus** (Caes. *BC* 3.86-7). On three successive days Caesar drew up his line, but Pompey, who had a strategic advantage on a hillside, refused battle. Caesar was then **intending to break camp and march towards Scotussa** (*Caesar* 43.7; Caes. id. 3.85.2), when his **scouts...reported that** Pompey was drawing up his army on the plain. He was thus conceding his strategic advantage, and the decision to fight was perhaps prompted by pressure from his subordinates (and Caesar's move might be designed to cut his supply-line).

The night before the battle Pompey made a sacrifice at which some of the victims escaped (App. *BC* 2.68). This would have **had a depressing effect** on the superstitious Pompey, as well as his dream and the **flame like a torch** (i.e. a fireball; cf. *Caesar* 43.5; further on dreams in Plutarch see ch. 32n.). For Pompey's temple to **Venus the Victorious** see ch. 52n.; and on Caesar's descent **from Venus** see *Caesar* 5n.

Note that Plutarch likens Caesar's troops to members of a chorus and Pharsalus is 'the stadium and theatre for the contest' (*Comp. Ages. Pomp.* 4.4). Plutarch's imagery reflects the tragedy of Pompey's fate (see Pelling [2] 134-5; ch. 9n.). Compare the frequent athletic imagery in the *Pompey* (ch. 8n.).

Chapter 69

For the initial distribution of forces cf. *Caesar* 44.2-6; Caes. *BC* 3.88-9; App. *BC* 2.76; Leach 205. L. Lentulus probably commanded Pompey's right wing (as Appian), while Caesar's centre was commanded by Cn. (not **Lucius**) **Domitius** Calvinus. With the river Enipeus protecting his right, Pompey concentrated Labienus' cavalry on the left against Caesar's crack **tenth legion** under P. Cornelius Sulla, but Caesar's reserve infantry cohorts routed Labienus, using their **javelins** as stabbing spears (ch. 71, *Caesar* 45.1-6; there may have been eight, not **six** cohorts; see ch. 71n.). See further Fuller 231-9.

For Caesar's criticism that **Pompey made a mistake in adopting these** stationary infantry **tactics** cf. *BC* 3.92. The Pompeians withstood the first attack of Caesar's two lines of infantry (thus justifying Pompey's tactics) but were routed by his reserve third line.

Caesar's figure for Pompey's legionaries is 47,000 (*BC* 3.88), but it was probably nearer to the 38,000 of Appian (*BC* 2.70). Hence Caesar's ratio of 2:1 is a gross exaggeration, though Pompey's legionaries still outnumbered Caesar's by about 3:2. According to *Caesar* 42.3 Pompey's cavalry outnumbered Caesar's by 7,000 to 1,000, which again may be an exaggeration; the numbers of auxiliaries on both sides can only be guessed at. See Brunt [1] 691-2; Greenhalgh [2] 302.

Chapter 70

The reflections of the bystanders are given to Caesar and Pompey themselves by Appian (*BC* 77), and the basic analysis in this chapter is solidly Pollian. There is a clear 'tragic chorus' effect, especially with the non-combatant **Greeks**: note the reflections on **the causes**; the emphasis on Rome's **self-destruction**; the contrast between Romans and barbarians; and the tragedy of a **family relationship** which had been **deceptive** (Julia's **marriage to Pompey** had not turned out to be a merely political one; see ch. 47n.).

Further on Plutarch's view of the civil wars in relation to Rome's decline cf. ch. 75, *Caesar* 28.6, 57.1; Jones 100-2. Civil wars led to monarchy (ch. 5), and this time the only solution seemed to be a monarch sent by divine favour (*Cicero* 44.3-5).

Chapter 71

According to Appian (*BC* 2.78) it was Pompey who sounded **the signal** first. For **Crassianus** see *Caesar* 44n.; on the organisation of the Republican legion (**120 men** formed a maniple, which had two centurions) see Keppie, L., *The Making of the Roman Army* (London, 1984) pp. 33-5.

For **the cohorts** Caesar held hidden in reserve see ch. 69n. It is the figure of **3,000 men** which Plutarch takes to signify **six cohorts** (ch. 69), but his 500 men to a cohort seems too many, especially as Caesar claimed to have 22,000 men in 80 cohorts at Pharsalus (*BC* 3.89.2; i.e. an average of 275).

Pompey's cavalry supposedly covered **their faces** to protect their good looks (*Caesar* 45.3-4 and n.).

Chapter 72

Pompey himself seems to have lost his nerve in the heat of the battle and **half-crazed** abandoned the field, though Lucan may be right in seeing his withdrawal as an attempt to end the bloodshed (*Caesar* 45.7; Caes. *BC* 3.94.5-6, 96.3-4; Luc. 7.683-97). Caesar has Pompey fleeing after the rout of the cavalry, Plutarch and Appian (*BC* 2.81) after that of the infantry. **Homer's description of Ajax** is in *Iliad* 11.544-6.

When Caesar's **victorious troops** attacked his **camp**, Pompey fled towards Larissa with Lentulus Spinther, Lentulus Crus, Favonius and one other (perhaps Deiotarus; see ch. 73n.).

The casualty figures, like the figures for the size of the armies, are hard to assess. Caesar's figures, for example (he vaguely estimates 15,000 Pompeians killed and is surer on more than 24,000 surrendered, *BC* 3.99), hardly match his overall figure of 47,000. **Pollio** may be closer to the truth with **6,000** regular soldiers killed (cf. App. *BC* 2.82). These included Domitius Ahenobarbus. Caesar lost between 200 (his figure) and 1,200 legionaries (Appian). See further Greenhalgh [2] 302-3.

For the luxury of Pompey's camp cf. Caes. *BC* 3.96.1. This reflected their **senseless confidence** (ch. 66n.).

Chapter 73

Another 'tragic' chapter, as Plutarch imagines **what was in** Pompey's **mind** after the reversal of his fortunes (an example of invention of material). The great general is now in flight, reduced to drinking **out of the river**, spending the night **in a fisherman's hut** and dismissing even his slaves: what a change from the great escort scenes of the past (ch. 13n.). The story of the **dream** and the ministrations of **Favonius** add to the pathos, which is brought to a peak by the quote from (probably) Euripides (frg. 961N).

Despite Plutarch's brilliant picture of Pompey's plight all was not lost, since Pompey still had his superior naval forces (ch. 76n.). Nevertheless, he advised **Larissa** to surrender to Caesar (Dio 42.2.3) and fled to **Tempe** with the two **Lentuli and Favonius**. The loyal **Deiotarus** may have been the fourth member of the party that Appian says fled from Pharsalus (*BC* 2.81; further on Deiotarus see ch. 42n.).

Chapter 74

From Tempe Pompey sailed **to Amphipolis** and thence to **the island** of Lesbos, to join his wife **Cornelia and his son** Sextus. Another dramatisation of their meeting is given by Lucan (8.40-108), and both versions reflect Cornelia's devotion to Pompey (her first husband was **Publius** Crassus, ch. 55).

Chapter 75

Pompey's reply to Cornelia once again has a tragic quality, with the reference to his change of fortune, mortality and, as the reader knows, vain hope for a resurgence of his fortunes. It is also an example of Plutarch inserting material which in his view may or may not be true (we are told).

Although in flight Pompey supposedly had time at Mitylene to have a discussion on Providence with the philosopher Cratippus (on whom see Cicero 24n.). This gives Plutarch the chance once again to expound the view that monarchy was required to solve Rome's problems (ch. 70n.). Further on Plutarch and Providence see Barrow 95-102.

Chapter 76

While he was at Lesbos four triremes came to Pompey from Rhodes and Tyre. With these he sailed to **Attaleia in Pamphylia**, where more forces joined him, and thence to Syhedra in Cilicia. Other reasons for optimism were the news that **his navy was still intact** (App. *BC* 2.87; Dio 42.2.1) and **Cato...was crossing over to Libya** with his forces from Dyrrhachium (ch. 67, cf. *Cicero* 39.1, *Cato* 55-6). On the other hand this news served to underline the folly of fighting at Pharsalus.

So Pompey reverted to his plan of a naval blockade, for which he needed **money and...men to serve in his ships**. Speed was essential, and Pompey decided not to join up with Cato and **King Juba** of Numidia in Africa or his other forces which had met at Corcyra. Rather, he was persuaded by **Theophanes** to head for **Egypt (only three days' sail away)**. There the king was now the young son of Ptolemy Auletes, who had been restored by Gabinius in 55 BC. For Theophanes see ch. 32n.

Plutarch says that Pompey himself thought about going to Parthia, which seems incredible (cf. Dio 42.2.5-6). He had sent Lucilius Hirrus there before Pharsalus, perhaps to ensure Parthia's neutrality, but it is difficult to believe that Pompey seriously considered an alliance with Rome's old enemy against Caesar. Cf. Caes. *BC* 3.82.4; App. *BC* 2.83. The Parthian king was Orodes II of the Arsacid dynasty.

The reference to the **supernatural power...guiding** Pompey to his fate gives the end of this chapter's narrative in particular a tragic quality. It follows a typical, yet seemingly realistic, discussion scene between the subject of the *Life* and his advisers. On Cornelia's **family** see ch. 55n.

Chapter 77

The decision to **seek refuge in Egypt** may have been taken in **Cyprus** at Paphos, perhaps prompted by the news that Antioch and Rhodes had gone over to Caesar. When he arrived off Egypt Pompey discovered that Ptolemy was engaged in a civil **war against his sister** Cleopatra (Caes. *BC* 3.103). Ptolemy was in his early teens, so Pompey's request for **protection** was debated by his **council (Achillas** was the army commander).

Plutarch emphasises the irony of Pompey's situation as he **was awaiting** the **verdict**: he was forced to rely on the mercy of the young Ptolemy because he could not bring himself to beg Caesar's forgiveness – Caesar whom he had never accepted as an equal, let alone a superior to whom he owed a favour.

Chapter 78

The assassins included L. **Septimius**, a senior centurion from the pirate war who had been left by Gabinius in Alexandria (Caes. *BC* 3.104.3).

That **there were just a few** **men sailing towards** Pompey again reflects his change of fortune (ch. 13n.). Pompey boarded their boat quoting **Sophocles** (frg. 789N).

Chapter 79

For Pompey's murder cf. Caes. *BC* 3.104.3; Cic. *Div.* 2.22, *Tusc.* 3.66; App. *BC* 2.85; Dio 42.3-4. The date is variously given as the day before his fifty-*eighth* birthday (i.e. 28 September 48 BC, as Vell. 2.53.3), on his birthday (*Camillus* 19.7, *Mor.* 717C) and the **day after his birthday.**

Chapter 80

Next day the consular **Lucius Lentulus** Crus arrived to suffer the same fate as Pompey, and Caesar reached Alexandria **not long afterwards** to be presented with **Pompey's head** and **signet ring** (*Caesar* 48.2; App. *BC* 2.86; Dio 42.7-8). For subsequent events in Egypt and the civil war see *Caesar* 48-56; and the death of **Theodotus** (? 43/2 BC) cf. *Brutus* 33.2-4 (N.B. App. id. 2.90 says he was crucified by Cassius). Pompey's loyal freedman **Philip** cremated the body and gave **the ashes...to Cornelia** for **burial at his country house near Alba** (ch. 40n.).

The *Life* ends on a typical Plutarchean note of moral redress, with the motif of 'just revenge', as he records the fate of his subject's killers. The endings of both the *Caesar* and the *Cicero* are similar. See Pelling on *Antony* 87.

Caesar

Chapter 1

C. Iulius Caesar was born on 12 July 100 BC, the only son of C. Iulius and Aurelia. The Iulii were a patrician* family but of little distinction, and Caesar's father only reached the praetorship. His mother was a plebeian* noble*, perhaps the cousin of the three Cotta brothers (coss. 75, 74, 65 BC), and was renowned for being a traditional Roman matron figure (ch. 9). More importantly C. **Marius**, consul in the year of Caesar's birth, had married his father's sister Julia.

Few details are recorded of Caesar's early life, and the beginnings of the *Lives* of both Plutarch and Suetonius are lost (Plutarch's begins in 84 BC). See Pelling, C.B.R., 'Plutarch, *Alexander* and *Caesar*: Two New Fragments?' *CQ* 23 (1973) pp. 343-4, 'Notes on Plutarch's *Caesar*' *Rh. Mus.* 127 (1984) pp. 33-45, esp. 33. In 87 BC (not 84, as Plutarch implies here) his name was put forward for the vacant **priesthood** of Jupiter (*flamen Dialis*), but he was never inaugurated (Vell. 2.43.1). In 84 BC, perhaps as he reached manhood (i.e. assumed the *toga virilis*), Caesar married **Cornelia, the daughter of** the consul **Cinna**. He then remained in the background when **Sulla** returned in 83 BC, and despite the role played in the civil war by his **cousin**, the younger **Marius, Caesar was overlooked by Sulla** during the proscriptions. Sulla prevented his election to the priesthood, however, which was in fact advantageous to Caesar since its accompanying restrictions meant a political and military career was out of the question. Sulla also insisted on Caesar's **divorce** from Cornelia, and **confiscated her dowry** and other legacies when Caesar refused (Suet. *Caesar* 1.1-2). Having done so Caesar thought it wise to go **into hiding**. He was captured by **Sulla's soldiers**, but through the intercession of the Vestal Virgins and his relatives Mam. Aemilius Lepidus and C. Aurelius Cotta he was granted a pardon by Sulla.

It was at this point that Sulla supposedly made his **many Mariuses** remark and commented on Caesar's loose-fitting clothes (Suet. *Caesar* 45.3). There are many stories involving Sulla's prescience (e.g. *Pompey* 15.2); his prophecy here and Cicero's foresight in ch. 4 are part of Plutarch's 'long view' of Caesar (ch. 28n.).

Caesar had got his way over Cornelia, who remained his wife until her death in 69 BC (ch. 5; Suet. *Caesar* 6.1). She bore him a daughter, the Julia who was to marry Pompey (*Pompey* 47.6). Caesar, however, now sensibly left Rome and joined the staff of M. Minucius Thermus, propraetor of Asia (Suet. *Caesar* 2.1). Such military service was regular for young Roman nobles* (*Pompey* 3n.) and might include diplomatic missions. Caesar was instructed to bring a fleet from **King Nicomedes** IV of Bithynia to the siege of Mytilene, which was being punished for supporting Mithridates. His stay with the King gave rise to rumours of homosexual relations, especially when he made a second visit, but his military career began gloriously with the award of the civic crown (*corona civica*) of oak leaves for saving a colleague's life during the storming of Mytilene in 80 BC.

Caesar continued his military service in 78 BC under the proconsul of Cilicia, P. Servilius Vatia, who campaigned against the pirates (*Pompey* 24n.), but returned to Rome on hearing of Sulla's death. In 77 BC he prosecuted the leading Sullan Cn. Cornelius **Dolabella** for extortion and then C. **Antonius** (ch. 4, misplaced). Caesar followed this in 75 BC by travelling to **Rhodes to study under Apollonius** (ch. 3, again misplaced), and it was on his way there that he **was captured** by pirates off Pharmacussa (**Pharmacusa**). He may have intended to go on to Bithynia, where Nicomedes had died (see Grant 28; Bradford 15-16).

In chs 1-4 Plutarch groups together the trip to Nicomedes, the pirate adventure and the study in Rhodes, before returning to Rome and domestic politics. This is a more elegant sequence of events than the true one (which Plutarch will have known) and gives the impression that Caesar won a brilliant reputation and great popularity by an eloquence which he had learnt through his Greek training. See Pelling [2] 128-9.

Chapter 2

Caesar's character is reflected in his insouciant behaviour and raising of his own **ransom** from **twenty** to **fifty** talents (= 1,200,000 HS), but he in fact had nothing to lose since he forced the coastal cities of Asia Minor to find the money. They also provided a fleet, with which he **captured nearly all of** the pirates, and he imprisoned them at **Pergamum. The governor of Asia**, M. Iunius Iuncus, was away in Bithynia, organising the country as a province, and Caesar **went in person to** Iuncus for his sanction to execute the captives. Velleius (2.42.3) records a slightly different motive for Iuncus' delayed action, that out of jealousy he wanted to sell the captives as slaves. Either way, Caesar ignored him and on his own initiative **crucified the lot of them**, taking **their property**. See Ward, A.M., 'Caesar and the Pirates' I *CP* 70 (1975) pp. 267-8; II *AJAH* 2 (1977) pp. 26-36.

The accounts of Plutarch, Velleius and Suetonius (*Caesar* 4) may derive from the **friend** Caesar had with him (a physician in Suetonius). On Caesar's **speeches** see ch. 3n.

Chapter 3

Caesar now **set sail for Rhodes** to complete his education in **oratory** (**Cicero** had lessons from **Apollonius** at both Rome and Rhodes; see *Cicero* 4n.). Caesar, who also wrote verses (ch. 2), had a great talent **as a political speaker**, second only to Cicero (he used a **plain style**, Cic. *Brut.* 261-2). His *Anti-Cato* was a reply to Cicero's pamphlet *Cato* (*Cicero* 39n.).

While at Rhodes Caesar was informed that Mithridates' forces had invaded Asia, and again acting on his own initiative he raised a force and expelled them. Then in 74/3 BC he probably joined the staff of M. Antonius in his command against the pirates (*Pompey* 24n.), since a C. Iulius was one of Antonius' legates (*SIG*³ 748, l. 23 [= Sherk 74]). He soon returned to Rome, however, on his election to the college of pontiffs after the death of his mother's cousin C. Cotta.

Chapter 4

The prosecutions of **Dolabella** and **Antonius** took place before Caesar's trip to Rhodes (ch. 1n.). Such prosecutions were by this time regular features in the early career of those aspiring to public office. Dolabella (cos. 81 BC) was proconsul in Macedonia; defended by Caesar's cousin C. Cotta and Hortensius, **Dolabella was acquitted** (Cic. *Brut.* 317; Suet. *Caesar* 4.1). The publication of his speeches nevertheless helped win Caesar **a brilliant reputation**, as well as Greek clients who in 76 BC asked him to prosecute C. (not **Publius**) **Antonius** Hibrida (cos. 63 BC), notorious for his plundering of Greece while prefect of cavalry in c. 84 BC. The case was heard before **Marcus** Terentius Varro **Lucullus**, who was in fact peregrine **praetor**, but Antonius scandalously received tribunician protection.

There is no reason to doubt that **these trials** and Caesar's **whole way of life** contributed to his **great popularity** (ch. 5n.), but the implication that he **was aiming at absolute power** from the beginning carries little credence (ch. 28n.). Cicero's foresight is part of the 'long view' of Caesar (ch. 1n.), though his remark was made 'at a later date' (the Greek for this in the text is not translated in the Penguin).

Chapter 5

After his return to Rome in 73 BC Caesar was elected **military tribune** for 72 or 71 BC (as Broughton ii.125, who makes **Popilius** tribune in 68 BC; the Greek probably means not only that Caesar won the poll but also that he had had a quarrel with Popilius; see Pelling, *Rh. Mus.* 127 [1984] pp. 34-5). This is recorded by Plutarch since it was **the first proof** of Caesar's popular support, which was strengthened by his stance on the tribunate. In 73 BC Caesar backed the agitation in this matter by the tribune C. Macer and in 70 BC supported the restoration of the tribunes' powers by Pompey and Crassus (*Pompey* 22n.). In the same year he addressed the assembly for the first time in support of Plautius' bill of amnesty for followers of Lepidus and Sertorius, who included Caesar's brother-in-law L. Cinna. Apart from these actions, and a speech against M. Iuncus (? the governor of ch. 2), we know nothing of Caesar's activities in 72-70 BC. Much of the time may have been consumed in the luxurious lifestyle noted in ch. 4. This took the form of womanising and collecting gems and art treasures (Suet. *Caesar* 47, 50-3). Caesar also **spent money recklessly** in order to win more popularity, and it was believed that his debt of **thirteen hundred talents** (= 31,200,000 HS) would ruin him (though it is unlikely that it was this large at this stage; see Pelling, *Rh. Mus.* 127 [1984] pp. 35-6).

Plutarch jumps from Caesar's military tribunate to 69 BC, the year of his quaestorship. His **brilliant public speech** at the funeral of **Julia** and his provocative displaying of **images of Marius himself** underlined his political position, and in the speech Caesar claimed descent from Venus and King Ancus Marcius (Suet. *Caesar* 6.1; App. *BC* 2.68). This year also saw the death of **his own wife** Cornelia, and Caesar set a precedent with another popularly received speech in honour of the young woman. In this he would have referred to Cinna, Marius' ally. On his **daughter** see ch. 1n.

Caesar then went out to Further **Spain as quaestor** to C. Antistius **Vetus** (pr. 70 BC; Suet. *Caesar* 7; Vetus' son was q. 61 BC, tr. 56 BC). There he administered justice but was clearly unhappy to be so far from Rome at this time. In 68 BC he therefore left Spain before the governor and returned to Rome via Transpadane Gaul. The Transpadanes were agitating for Roman citizenship, and Caesar took this further chance of building up his *clientela** by supporting them, but the senate garrisoned the area with two legions recruited for the Mithridatic war.

Balked in this enterprise, Caesar arrived back in Rome and married his second rather than **third** wife **Pompeia** (Suet. *Caesar* 6.2). This was a change of tactic, since Pompeia was the granddaughter of Sulla and his fellow consul of 88 BC, Q. Pompeius Rufus, but she was also from a wealthy family. However, Caesar then confirmed his *popularis** stance by supporting Gabinius' law of 67 BC (*Pompey* 25n.; Caesar was said to have had an affair with Gabinius' wife Lollia, Suet. id. 50.1). His curatorship of the **Appian Way** was another office whose reward could be popular favour, hence **he spent vast sums of his own money** (the Via

Appia was the main road from Rome to Brundisium, originally built as far as Capua by the censor of 312 BC, Appius Claudius Caecus). Caesar next supported Manilius' law (*Pompey* 30n.) and was elected curule **aedile** for 65 BC. Again, this office offered the prospect of winning popularity by putting on **lavish...performances**, and Caesar grasped the opportunity eagerly (Pliny, *NH* 33.53; Suet. id. 10). He completely overshadowed his Optimate* colleague M. Bibulus, and so began the hostility which was to flare up in their joint consulship of 59 BC (Caes. *BC* 3.16.3; they were also praetors together in 62 BC). Plutarch refers to the **show...of gladiators** which Caesar put on in memory of his father (who died in 85 BC). Coming so soon after Spartacus' revolt, this alarmed the senate, which fixed a limit on numbers, but **320 pairs** still fought. Caesar also restored Marius' trophies (ch. 6; Vell. 2.43.4; Suet. id. 11) and supposedly supported Crassus' unsuccessful plan to annex Egypt. By now Caesar would have embarked on his alliance with the wealthy Crassus (and perhaps also his wife Tertulla; Suet. id. 50.1), and Crassus may well have financed the expenditures noted above (Plutarch omits Caesar's backing of Pompey's commands and his alliance with Crassus to emphasise his rise through popular support; see Pelling [3] 166). It is doubtful, however, whether Caesar and Crassus were involved in an alleged conspiracy with the two consuls-elect for 65 BC, P. Autronius Paetus and P. Cornelius Sulla (Sall. *BC* 18-19). The mentioning of Caesar's name clearly stems from later propaganda, and it is most unlikely that he would have wanted the murder of the consul L. Cotta, his mother's cousin. See further McGushin, P., *C. Sallustius Crispus: Bellum Catilinae - A Commentary* (Leiden, 1977) App. IV.

Chapter 6

Plutarch's talk of **two parties in Rome** is by this time meaningless, the remaining hard-core 'Sullans' being few in number. Caesar had shown on several occasions where his loyalties lay, and on the **images of Marius** see ch. 5n. For Plutarch Caesar is the military and political heir of Marius (cf. ch.19; see Pelling, C.B.R., 'Plutarch on the Gallic Wars' *CB* 60 [1984] p. 90). On Marius and **the Cimbri** cf. *Marius* 11-27. Again, the idea that Caesar already **was aiming at securing supreme power** is to be rejected (ch. 4n.). On Q. **Lutatius Catulus** see *Pompey* 15-16nn.

Chapter 7

In 64 BC Caesar probably backed Catiline's unsuccessful candidature for the consulship, which was financed by Crassus. Caesar also acted as a prosecutor of those who had received blood money for killing the men proscribed by Sulla. Amongst the condemned was Catiline's uncle, L. Bellienus, but Catiline himself was acquitted *(Cicero* 10n.).

In 63 BC Caesar supported a proposal to restore rights to the sons of the proscribed, which was blocked by Cicero *(Cicero* 12.2; ch. 37n.), and he and Crassus were implicated by Cicero in Rullus' agrarian proposal *(Pompey* 42n.). Other activities of Caesar included the prosecution of C. Calpurnius Piso for extortion, in which Caesar attacked the Optimate* for executing a Transpadane. This reflects Caesar's *popularis* * stance, which is emphasised by his prosecution with the tribune T. Labienus of C. Rabirius (see Gruen [2] 277-9). He also opposed the execution of the Catilinarian conspirators (below) and led the criticism of Cicero for authorising this *(Cicero* 23.1-2); and another *popularis* * measure, again with Labienus, was the change in the appointment of pontiffs from co-option to popular election.

The connection with Labienus indicates a further strand of Caesar's political activity, his working with Pompey and his associates. This had already manifested itself in his support of the restoration of the tribunes' powers and of the Gabinian and Manilian laws (ch. 5n.). Now, in 63 BC, he supported the proposal of Labienus and Balbus celebrating Pompey's Eastern victories, and in 62 BC made further proposals to Pompey's advantage *(Pompey* 42n.). Plutarch once again omits this side of Caesar's actions to focus attention on his popular backing.

Caesar's election as **chief pontiff** is also to be seen in connection with Pompey. Following the confrontation with Catulus over Marius' images (ch. 6), Caesar now stood against him in this election, which was necessitated by the death of **Metellus** Pius in 63 BC (another candidate for Rome's main **priesthood** was the **distinguished** Servilius Vatia **Isauricus**, on whom see *Pompey* 24n.). Pompey's supporters would have been canvassing on Caesar's behalf, for which he repaid Pompey in 62 BC (below). Caesar himself spent large sums of money and was in great debt, but was not put off when Catulus **tried to bribe him** and **came out on top** of the poll (Suet. *Caesar* 13). This in itself (not the fear that Caesar **would go on to...violent extremism**) led to deeper enmity with Catulus, who with Piso then unsuccessfully attempted to exact revenge by inculpating Caesar in **Catiline's conspiracy** *(Cicero* 10-23nn.). For Caesar's **long speech** cf. *Cicero* 21.1, *Cato* 22.4-5; Cic. *Cat.* 4.7-10; Sall. *BC* 51. Caesar, who had prosecuted Rabirius for the murder of Saturninus after the passing of the senate's ultimate decree*, could not easily now support the execution of the conspirators under another *s.c.u.* It seems that he was also known to have links with Catiline, but there was no question of Caesar defending the conspirators. Hence his proposal of life imprisonment (as Caesar and Sallust), rather than a postponement of the decision (see Stockton 342; *contra* McGushin on Sall. ibid.). The latter version probably stems from confusion with the proposal of Ti. Claudius Nero (Sall. id. 50.4).

Plutarch here implies that the exposure of the conspirators (3 December) and the decision on their punishment (5 December) were made at the same sitting of the senate, though *Cicero* 19-20 shows that he knew otherwise. In both accounts there is some conflation (see Pelling [2] 127).

After the executions Caesar led the attack on Cicero (*Cicero* 23.1-3), and during his praetorship in 62 BC repaid his debt to Pompey by proposing that he finish restoring the Capitol and be recalled to stamp out the remaining resistance (*Pompey* 42n.).

On **Caesar's mother** see ch. 1n.

Chapter 8

Caesar's speech was a masterpiece and dissociated him from the conspiracy. It also made others think about the consequences of the death penalty, and his fellow praetors-designate (including Q. Cicero) supported him. Ti. Claudius Nero proposed a fresh discussion, which was against the wishes of Cicero, and of the ex-consuls only **Catulus** spoke against Caesar (*Cicero* 21.4). He was followed by **Cato**, now tribune-designate, whose speech swung the debate (*Cato* 23.1-2; Cic. *Att.* 12.21.1; Sall. *BC* 52; N.B. Cato was the half-brother of Servilia, wife of D. Silanus who first proposed the death penalty, and she was the favourite amongst Caesar's lovers, Suet. *Caesar* 50.2). The speech also directed anger and suspicion against Caesar, and when he proposed separate votes on the death penalty and confiscation of property and appealed to the tribunes, Caesar was nearly killed by **Cicero's bodyguard** (*Cicero* 21.4-5; placed in a different context by Sall. id. 49.4). Caesar was saved by his later adherent C. Scribonius **Curio** and other friends, but seeing the hostility he had raised stayed away from the senate for the rest of the year. The demonstration by the **mob** which **surrounded the senate** seems then to be a confusion with the events of Caesar's praetorship in 62 BC (Suet. id. 16.2), in which year even **Cato** as tribune proposed a cheap **grain** distribution to outbid Caesar's popularity (*Cato* 26.1; $7\frac{1}{2}$ **million drachmas** = 30million HS).

Plutarch shows commendable source acumen when he doubts the truth of the Cicero **story**. Cicero's lost **book** *On His Consulship*, which was written originally in Greek, clearly was known to Plutarch (cf. *Crassus* 13.3; *Cicero* 30n.).

Chapter 9

Plutarch's opening remark is nonsense. Immediately on entering office Caesar attacked Catulus in the matter of the Capitoline temple and followed this by supporting Nepos' proposal to recall Pompey, which led to a riot and the suspension of Caesar and Nepos from office (*Pompey* 42n.). Caesar retired home, only to be recalled when the mob demanded his restoration (Suet. *Caesar* 16). When L. Vettius then named Caesar among those guilty of complicity in Catiline's conspiracy, Caesar showed that he had in fact passed on information voluntarily to Cicero, and had Vettius beaten up and imprisoned. The president of the investigating court, L. Novius Niger, was also imprisoned for allowing the case against the higher magistrate to be heard, an affront to the dignity (*dignitas*) which Caesar always held dear (Suet. id. 17).

It was at the end of 62 BC that Caesar was involved in the **somewhat unfortunate affair** of '**the Good Goddess**' (Bona Dea). **Clodius...was in love with Caesar's wife Pompeia**, but she was watched over by **Caesar's mother**. The Bona Dea festival this year was held at Caesar's house (since he held *imperium** as praetor), and Clodius saw the chance for a rendezvous.

Further on Clodius, who gave up his **patrician*** status, see *Pompey* 48n. **His powers as an orator** made him one of the most successful of all the demagogues of the late Republic. On the Roman version of the Bona Dea myth cf. *Mor.* 268D-E; Macrob.1.12.23-7. The goddess' proper name was Fauna, either the daughter or wife of **Faunus** (the Greek god Pan). Cicero noted that **her name must not be spoken** (*Har. Resp.* 37). Further on **Midas, Dionysus** and the **Orphics** see *OCD* s.v.

Chapter 10

Further on this episode, which reflects Plutarch's love of anecdote, and Caesar's divorce of Pompeia cf. Cic. *Att.* 1.12.3, 13.3; Suet. *Caesar* 6.2, 74.2; Dio 37.45.1-2. Note that Clodius should certainly have been able to grow a beard, since as quaestor in 61 BC he would be at least 30. Caesar as Chief Pontiff lived in the **large** official residence (*domus publica*). Finally, **Abra** (better Habra) in Greek means 'favourite slave girl', and she **was in the secret** – Cicero, indeed, says a slave girl helped Clodius escape.

The religious scandal turned into a political incident, and a court was set up especially to try **Clodius for sacrilege** by a law of the tribune Q. Fufius Calenus (Cic. *Att.* 1.14.1-2, 5, 16.1-5). Clodius was **officially indicted** by L. Cornelius Lentulus Crus (see Epstein 108; he was not **one of the tribunes**), and there seemed to be no doubt about his guilt – or indeed about his **adultery with his sister** Clodia, once **the wife of** L. **Lucullus** (all three sisters in *Cicero* 29.5; Cic. *Mil.* 73). The court, however, was allegedly bribed by Crassus to acquit Clodius (*contra* Gruen [2] 275 n. 58), despite the fact that Cicero destroyed his alibi that he was at Interamna at the time in question – and so won his lasting enmity

(*Cicero* 29n.). **The most influential members of the senate** are here Lucullus, Hortensius, C. Piso and the consul M. Valerius Messalla.

The **illegible writing** of the jurors' votes (cf. *Cicero* 29.6 with Moles) probably reflects that they rubbed out both sides of their voting tablets, one of which was marked 'A' (*absolvo*, 'I acquit'), the other 'C' (*condemno*). **Most** is an exaggeration, the voting being 31-25 for an acquittal, out of a maximum of 75.

Caesar's famous remark, '**Because...my wife ought not to be even suspected**', justified by his position as Chief Pontiff, was probably prompted by a desire not to alienate the popular Clodius and his supporters, who included Crassus. The Bona Dea affair also gave Caesar the chance to divorce a wife who had not produced a child.

Note that several of the details in the *Caesar* version of this incident do not appear in the account at *Cicero* 28 (**the door open; the maid then ran off to tell Pompeia; Clodius lacked the patience to stay where he had been left**; the servant **asked him to come and play with her**; Aurelia's acts, the wives' reports to their husbands and the outcome) - they may be genuine or products of Plutarch's imagination (see Pelling [2] 129).

Chapter 11

Caesar received Further **Spain as his province** not **directly** but in March, the allotment perhaps being delayed by the Clodius affair. He left quickly, before the senate confirmed his appointment and official funds, in order to escape **his creditors**. These were satisfied for the time being by Crassus' **personal guarantee for 830 talents** (= 19,920,000 HS; *Crassus* 7.6; Suet. *Caesar* 18.1; App. *BC* 2.8 puts Caesar's debts at 100 million HS).

The story about **Alexander** is part of Plutarch's 'long view' of Caesar (ch. 1n.) and links with ch. 13, where he produces what **was in effect a revolution**. It is placed during Caesar's quaestorship in Spain (69 BC) by Suet. *Caesar* 7.1 and Dio 37.52.2, and could hardly apply to 61 BC, when Caesar was 38/9, since Alexander died at 32 (see further Pelling [2] 129 n. 9).

Chapter 12

The land that is now western Spain and Portugal was potentially lucrative for Caesar both financially and in terms of the military glory he was lacking, and he soon overcame the mountain tribes, to be hailed as '**Imperator**'*. **His campaigns** brought him and his troops vast amounts of money, part of which he sent back to Rome. He followed them with sensible administrative settlements, including debt reforms; and he honoured Gades, hometown of L. Cornelius Balbus, one of Caesar's most loyal followers (Cic. *Balb.* 63). Thus Caesar greatly enlarged his *clientela**, though much of Spain remained loyal to Pompey in the civil war.

Chapter 13

Caesar...arrived at Rome in June 60 BC. He had been awarded a **triumph**, but did not have time to celebrate this and enter the city as a private citizen to stand for the consulship. Personal candidature had been **the law** since 63 BC , and so Caesar sent to the senate for special dispensation, but **Cato...opposed the request** (*Cato* 31.2-4; Suet. *Caesar* 18.2; App. *BC* 2.8). Cato's obstruction made up Caesar's mind **to forgo the triumph and to try for the consulship**. It also alienated him from the Optimate*cause, and Caesar turned for support firstly to L. Lucceius, a wealthy rival who agreed to finance their joint candidacy, then to **Pompey and Crassus** (*Pompey* 47.1-3, *Crassus* 14.1-3, *Cato* 31.2-3; Suet. id. 19.1-2; Dio 37.54), though the 'First Triumvirate' was not formed until after the election (*Pompey* 47n.).

Chapter 14

The other candidate was M. **Calpurnius Bibulus,** Cato's son-in-law and Caesar's bitter enemy (ch. 5n.). To prevent Lucceius' election with Caesar, Bibulus' friends formed an electoral bribery fund, of which even Cato approved 'in the interests of the Republic' (Suet. *Caesar* 19.1). The idea, however, that the Optimates* also tried to restrict Caesar's influence in advance by allotting 'the forests and cattle tracks' (*silvae callesque*) of Italy as the consular province is probably to be rejected (see Seager 83). Caesar **was triumphantly elected** with Bibulus.

   Backed by Pompey and Crassus, Caesar introduced his programme of legislation. He began **as soon as he entered upon his office** with the first of two agrarian laws, which may have been formally proposed by the **tribune** P. Vatinius (Plutarch was aware that there were two bills, cf. *Cato* 32.3, 33.1; see Pelling [1] 77). This was taken firstly to the senate, where it met with **stiff opposition** – especially from Cato, who was arrested by Caesar and nearly imprisoned (*Cato* 31.4-32.1). Caesar therefore took it to the people, and when Bibulus refused to withdraw his opposition, called on Pompey and Crassus for their support (*Pompey* 47n.). Bibulus still refused to back down, but on the day of the voting he suffered indignities and, with violence threatened, the bill was passed (*Pompey* 48n.). On the terms of the law and the commissions of twenty and five appointed to administer it see Seager 86-7. It benefited mainly Pompey's veterans but also the urban poor. Bibulus' reaction was to **shut himself up in his house** and watch the sky for unfavourable omens until the end of the year, in order technically to invalidate the rest of Caesar's legislation (Suet. *Caesar* 20.1; App. *BC* 2.12; Dio 38.6.5-6; see Seager 190 n. 1).

The other legislation included the ratification of Pompey's Eastern acts, a rebate on the price of the Asian taxes and the recognition of Ptolemy Auletes as King of Egypt (see Seager App. 1). There was also a second agrarian law concerning the allotment of the fertile Campanian land, which this time benefited the urban poor. Further, Caesar passed a comprehensive law on provincial government and extortion which met no opposition, and minor measures included the publication of the Acts of the senate. Vatinius, in addition, authorised the foundation of a colony at Novum Comum, and Caesar treated the 5,000 new citizens, as well as the other Transpadanes, as Romans (ch. 29; Cic. *Att.* 5.11.2; Suet. *Caesar* 28.3; App. *BC* 2.26). Finally, Vatinius proposed a law that Caesar be granted the governorship of Cisalpine Gaul and Illyricum for five years with three legions, to which the senate added Transalpine Gaul and a fourth legion on Pompey's motion (*Pompey* 48.3; Cic. id. 8.3.3; Suet. id. 22.1; Dio 38.8.5). Plutarch therefore conflates the law and senatorial decree.

The report of the opposition and imprisonment of **Cato** appears to be a doublet of the incident noted above. Caesar's consulship, however, is remarkable for the unpopularity which he and his colleagues increasingly faced and the steps he took to deal with it. The story of Q. **Considius** reflects this unpopularity (cf. Cic. *Att.* 2.24.4), which was all the time fuelled by Bibulus. While at home he issued edicts and pamphlets attacking Caesar, and he was backed up by the younger C. Curio, who focused his attentions on Pompey (e.g. id. 2.19.2-3; Suet. *Caesar* 49.2, cf. the joke in id. 20.2). Hostility to the triumvirs spread through Italy, and with the three themselves divided over who should stand for the consulship, Cicero saw a rift developing (id. 2.7.3). Further trouble came from **Clodius**, whose transition to plebeian* status was engineered by Caesar and Pompey and at once regretted (*Pompey* 48n.). Pompey for his part had little choice but to back Caesar at this point, but he disclaimed responsibility for Caesar's methods. Caesar acted quickly to prevent a breakdown of the coalition by betrothing Julia to Pompey and making him his heir (*Pompey* 47n.). He also offered Cicero a legateship in Gaul, which he eventually declined (Cic. id. 2.18.3, 19.5, *Prov. Cons.* 41-2; *Cicero* 30.3 may imply, with Moles, that Cicero then changed his mind when Clodius became a threat, and asked Caesar for a legateship in 58 BC; *contra* Seager, R. in his review of Moles, *CR* 40.2 [1990] p. 480). The situation then changed with the alleged plot to assassinate Pompey, in which Cicero was implicated (Cic. *Att.* 2.24.2-4). Its effect was to create sympathy for Pompey, sow the seeds of doubt in his mind as to the loyalty of Cicero and alienate him further from the Optimates*. Clodius would then be allowed in 58 BC to turn his attention to Cicero with no hindrance from Pompey. Before he left for his province, Caesar also clashed with the new praetors Memmius and L. Ahenobarbus over his acts as consul. Without waiting for the outcome of the three-day debate, Caesar joined the troops he had nearby and entered on his proconsulship.

On the antithesis between **the senate** and the **Assembly of the People** see *Cicero* 11n.

Chapter 15

Plutarch begins his narrative of Caesar's **Gallic campaigns** by employing the device of internal comparison, here with other leading Roman generals: Q. **Fabius** Maximus Verrucosus (cos. 233, 228, 215, 214, 209 BC), whose delaying tactics saved Rome from Hannibal after the disaster at Lake Trasimene in 217 BC; **Scipio** could be either P. Cornelius Scipio Africanus (cos. 205, 194 BC), who defeated Hannibal at Zama in 202 BC, or P. Cornelius Scipio Africanus Aemilianus (cos. 147, 134 BC), who destroyed Carthage in 146 BC and Numantia in 133 BC; **Metellus** is most probably Q. Caecilius Metellus Numidicus (cos. 109 BC), who fought Jugurtha; **the two Luculli** are L. Licinius Lucullus (cos. 74 BC) and his brother M. Terentius Varro Lucullus (cos. 73 BC). Attendant on these comparisons are distortions of **Caesar's achievements**: e.g. he hardly treated the **prisoners** of Uxellodunum in a **reasonable and considerate way** (on this and the figures given here see ch. 27n.). Note also other commonplaces such as the **savage treacherous character** of the Gallic tribes (e.g. ch. 24), Caesar's famed clemency (Suet. *Caesar* 75.1-4) and his treatment of his men (ch. 16n.).

For Plutarch the wars are **a new start** to Caesar's career, and some of the topics which he regularly includes in the opening chapters of his *Lives* are postponed to this point – Caesar's true personality is only revealed now in Gaul (see the analysis of Pelling in *CB* 60 [1984]). Some other points to be noted are as follows. Plutarch cites the '**Commentaries**' of Caesar (ch. 22) but probably knew them via Asinius Pollio. Hence many details which are not found in Caesar may be attributed to Pollio: the figures of men slain and tribes conquered (ch. 15); the story concerning the devotion of Caesar's troops (ch. 16); Caesar **reached the Rhône in seven days** (ch. 17); Labienus' victory (ch. 18); the number of Ariovistus' dead (ch. 19); details of Caesar's crossing of the Rhine and of Britain (chs 22-3), and of Alesia and the surrender of Vercingetorix (ch. 27).

For Caesar's treatment of his men cf. Suet. *Caesar* 65-70. The identity of C. **Acilius** is uncertain, and he is not mentioned during the battle of 49 BC described in Caes. *BC* 2.6-7. For the centurion **Cassius Scaeva** cf. Caes. id. 3.53.4-5 (he received on his shield 120 holes); and on **Dyrrhachium** see ch. 39n. Q. Caecilius Metellus Pius **Scipio** Nasica (cos. 52 BC) fled from Pharsalus to Africa (**Libya**) and committed suicide after his defeat at Thapsus (ch. 53n.). **Granius Petro** was probably quaestor-designate for 46 BC.

The four anecdotes here probably derive from Pollio: the first three are found in the same order in Val. Max. 3.2.22-3, while Suetonius (*Caesar* 68.4) has Acilius and Scaeva, and Appian (*BC* 2.60) has Scaeva.

Chapter 17

Caesar recognised the importance of his army and was careful to distribute rewards (e.g. Suet. *Caesar* 38.1). His own bravery, skills and powers of endurance are illustrated by Suetonius (id. 57-8), whose description of his physical appearance does not completely agree with Plutarch's (id. 45.1-2; Suetonius says he was tall and well-built). Plutarch's description is full of ideal characteristics (Caesar is generous, brave, hard-working, a man of **action** and **an expert rider**); and statues may have influenced this picture (see Pelling, *CB* 60 [1984] pp. 91-2). For his epileptic fits cf. App. *BC* 2.110; chs 53, 60nn. Caesar was also famed for his speed of action (*celeritas*; chs 18, 32nn.).

Caesar honoured **his horse** with a statue before the temple of Mother Venus (Suet. *Caesar* 61). On his dictation cf. Pliny, *NH* 7.91. The equestrian* C. **Oppius** and L. Balbus were Caesar's agents in Rome, and they acted as intermediaries with Cicero in Caesar's **conversations...by letters**, which included a letter from Britain. Oppius probably wrote a biography of Caesar, as well as a pamphlet denying Caesar's paternity of Cleopatra's son Caesarion (Suet. id. 52.2; see further ch. 49n.). At his end Caesar had Cn. Pompeius Trogus and later A. Hirtius.

The story of the **dinner at Milan** is presumably the same as that recorded by Suetonius and attributed by him to Oppius, though Suetonius says rancid oil was served (*Caesar* 53). Oppius was probably also the source for the story of the **one room**, which in Suetonius' version was given to Oppius because he was ill (id. 72; hence Caesar's remark that **necessities should go to the weakest**). See further on Oppius as a source Intro. 4.

Chapter 18

Conditions **in Gaul** had been unsettled since the Allobroges revolted in 62 BC. They were defeated by 60 BC, but the Sequani and Arverni, aided by the Suebian prince Ariovistus, attacked Rome's old allies the Aedui. Ariovistus then began establishing a German kingdom in the territory of the Sequani, which aroused the **Helvetii**. These and the **Tigurini** moved **into the Roman part of Gaul** in 60 BC, rekindling memories of **the Cimbri and Teutons** (Teutones; cf. *Marius* 11-27; on the Tigurini see Pelling, *Rh. Mus.* 127 [1984] pp. 37-8). In March the consuls Metellus Celer and Afranius drew lots for the Gallic provinces, but things improved by May, and Celer was prevented from leaving for Transalpine Gaul by the tribune L. Flavius and died before April 59 BC. Caesar took the chance to exploit the situation in Gaul for his own ends: Vatinius' bill gave Caesar Cisalpine Gaul (ch. 14n.), and Celer's death allowed the addition of Transalpine Gaul. Caesar also secured recognition of Ariovistus as king and friend of the Roman people – he therefore remained quiet until the summer of 58 BC, when Caesar was ready to attack him (ch. 19; Caes. *BG* 1.35.2; see Pelling, id. pp. 3-9).

According to Caesar (*BG* 1.29) the tribes numbered 368,000, with 92,000 fighting men (perhaps in truth nearer 150,000, with a quarter under arms). Caesar would not allow them to cross his province, and a pretext for war was presented by an appeal for help from the Aedui, Ambarri and Allobroges. Caesar (not **Labienus**) attacked the Tigurini on the Saône (**the River Arar**), then crossed the river to pursue the remaining Helvetii (the polemical version of Plutarch will derive from Pollio and perhaps ultimately from Labienus' propaganda once he had joined Pompey; see Pelling, *CB* 60 [1984] p. 92). During the pursuit Caesar's Aeduan cavalry were routed despite vastly superior numbers, and his promised corn deliveries were not forthcoming. Caesar discovered that their commander Dumnorix was behind this, and he was placed under guard. Caesar was then forced to head for the Aeduan capital city Bibracte for corn (**a friendly city**), and the Helvetii **unexpectedly attacked** (Labienus on **Caesar's instructions** had seized a hill overlooking the enemy, but due to a subordinate's blunder Caesar's original plan had to be abandoned). Caesar **drew up** his men on a hillside, dispatching his cavalry to check the Helvetian advance, then sent away all the remaining horses. The **long and hard struggle** lasted deep into the night (Caesar does not say until **midnight**), the **rampart of wagons** holding up the Roman attack, and Caesar says some 130,000 **survived the battle** (implying the incredible casualty figure of 238,000). Caesar then showed both his clemency and tactical awareness by demanding the surrender of hostages but ordering the rest to return **to the land which they had left** (Plutarch regularly records such settlements, as ch. 23; see Pelling, id. p. 93). This was an attempt to stop **the Ger-**

mans crossing the Rhine, and the Boii were settled on the Aeduan borders. Cf. Caes. *BG* 1.11-29, on whose account that of Plutarch is based; Dio 38.31.2-33; Fuller 100-6.

Chapter 19

Plutarch continues to follow Caesar's account closely (through Pollio), as is clear from the statement that the German campaign of 58 BC **was fought directly in the interests of the Gauls**, who requested help at an assembly of Celtic chiefs (Caes. *BG* 1.31-3). The recent alliance with **Ariovistus** (ch. 18n.) is the reason why Caesar goes to such lengths to justify his actions, and he had the pretexts that **the Germans** had attacked the Aedui and had to be kept away from the borders of the empire.

Ariovistus refused to meet Caesar and rejected his demands; and when news came from the Aedui and Treveri of more German hostility, Caesar hastened towards Vesontio (Besançon), the capital of the Sequani, to forestall him. It was here that stories about the Germans caused panic among Caesar's troops and **officers**, and he had to summon **a meeting** of the latter, threatening to advance only with **the tenth legion**. His speech had the desired effect, and on the seventh day of continuous marching he was **within twenty miles or so of the enemy**. Ariovistus now agreed to a meeting, but even during this his cavalry began attacking Caesar's troops. Ariovistus then marched southwards, followed by Caesar, and after delays caused by the lots and divinations of the Germans' **holy women**, Ariovistus attacked (cf. Tac. *Germ*. 8, 10 on the women's use of wooden lots, also *Hist*. 4.61; their use of hydromancy is less likely – see Pelling, *Rh. Mus*. 127 [1984] p. 39). He was heavily defeated and pursued to **the Rhine** (five, not **forty miles** away in Caesar's account, but the text is uncertain). He died soon afterwards, and most of the German tribes crossed back over the Rhine. Cf. Caes. *BG* 1.34-54; Dio 38.34-50; Fuller 106-10.

Note that Plutarch changes the emphasis of Caesar's speech from the Germans being reluctant to fight (Caesar) to a parallel with **the Cimbri**, which allows him to affirm Caesar's position as the heir of **Marius** (ch. 6n.). He also simplifies the battle itself, which from Caesar's account was a close-run affair, and concentrates on psychological detail. See further Pelling, *CB* 60 (1984) p. 93.

Chapter 20

Caesar left his army among the Sequani under Labienus to secure these gains and himself spent **the winter** of 58/7 BC in **Cisalpine Gaul**.

From there he could keep an eye on the situation in Rome, and when Clodius threatened his consular legislation, Caesar reluctantly supported Cicero's return from exile (*Pompey* 49n.; one of the **many people** who **came to see him** was Cicero's supporter Sestius). Note that Plutarch's political analysis of Caesar the corrupter parallels and anticipates the end of ch. 21 (**hopes for...the future**) and is also paralleled at *Pompey* 51.1-3. The analysis derives from Pollio, who put it before Luca (cf. Suet. *Caesar* 23.2; App. *BC* 2.17). See further Pelling, *CB* 60 (1984) pp. 93-4.

The wintering of Caesar's six legions among the Sequani roused **the Belgians** to resist further Roman advance, in the **enormous numbers** of some 306,000 men according to Caesar (they hardly **revolted**, since they were not Roman subjects). Caesar hastened northwards, and having received the submission of the Remi, he relieved one of their towns, Bibrax, which was under siege (i.e. the Belgians **were engaged in plundering** them). The Belgians then tried to cut off Caesar's communications but were **routed** and dispersed, with Caesar sending his cavalry against their rearguard (Plutarch apparently conflates – **the destruction...to the Romans** happened in the battle, and then Caesar massacred the Belgians as they withdrew, only offering **a feeble resistance**; see Pelling, id. p. 94). Caesar himself marched quickly against the Suessiones, Bellovaci and Ambiani, receiving **without any fighting** their unconditional surrender (*deditio*; only the Ambiani were properly-speaking a tribe **by the Ocean**). He then moved north-eastwards towards the Sabis (Sambre) **against the** feared **Nervii**, who had been reinforced by the Atrebates and Viromandui. Caesar sent six legions ahead who were **fortifying a camp**, when they were ambushed by the Belgians, who had hidden in the woods (**thickly wooded** may be a mistranslation, but the text is doubtful here; see Pelling, *Rh. Mus.* 127 [1984] pp. 39-40). **They routed Caesar's cavalry** and rushed uphill against his camp. The ninth and tenth legions on the left repelled the Atrebates, while the eighth and eleventh broke the Viromandui, but their pursuit of the Belgians to the Sambre exposed the right flank, manned by **the seventh and twelfth legions**. These and the camp were attacked by the Nervii themselves, and the allied cavalry of the Treveri fled. The **centurions** of the fourth cohort of the twelfth legion were killed, and most of the other cohorts lost their centurions killed or wounded, including the chief centurion (*primuspilus*) P. Sextius Baculus. Caesar says he **snatched up a shield** from a soldier in the rear ranks and went to the front, calling on the remaining centurions by name and thus renewing the spirits of his men. He then joined up with the seventh legion and was reinforced by two legions from the rear and by **the tenth legion.**This turned the tide, and the Nervii were slaughtered. Plutarch records the casualty figures given by Caesar, who says their senate was reduced from 600 to **only three**. The Nervii were allowed to continue living in their own territory, but when the town of the Aduatuci treacherously resisted, 53,000 were enslaved. Meanwhile, P. Crassus (the triumvir's son) received the surrender of the tribes **who lived by the Ocean** in Normandy and Brittany. Cf. Caes. *BG* 2, 3.1-6; Dio 39.1-5; Fuller 110-15.

Chapter 21

Caesar now thought that Gaul had been pacified and set out for Illyricum. His report **of these victories** to **the senate** led to an unprecedented period of thanksgiving of **fifteen days** (Caes. *BG* 2.35.4), surpassing Pompey's ten in 63 BC (*Pompey* 42n.).

Crucial to the political situation at Rome during **the winter** of 57/6 BC was the state of the coalition. In December the tribune Lupus attacked Caesar's second agrarian law, and Cicero tried to break up the alliance by reviving this matter on 5 April 56 BC (*Pompey* 51n.). Additionally, Pompey and Crassus were at odds over the restoration of Ptolemy Auletes (*Pompey* 49n.). Caesar for his part went to Aquileia and began using **the money** he had secured by his campaigns to back **candidates for office** (*Pompey* 51.2; Vatinius was still defeated at the delayed aedilician elections). Further, Domitius Ahenobarbus, a candidate for the consulship of 55 BC, took up the question of the legality of Caesar's command, backed by Cicero (*Cato* 41.2-3; Cic. *Vat.* 35-6). Caesar therefore moved on to Ravenna, where he met Crassus, and thence to **Luca** (*Pompey* 51-2nn.; further on the version here see Pelling, *CB* 60 [1984] p. 95). **Appius** Claudius Pulcher certainly visited Caesar in March, long before Caesar reached Luca (Cic. *QF* 2.4.6). **Nepos** was **proconsul of** Nearer **Spain**.

The senate's **decrees** were for the treasury to bear the cost of the extra four legions Caesar had raised and to give him ten legates, thus legitimising his actions in Gaul (Cic. *Fam.* 1.7.10, *Balb.* 61). In addition, his command was to be prolonged, against the wishes of Cicero, who nevertheless delivered his speech *On the Consular Provinces* in support of Caesar. On the controversial question of the expiry date of this command see Seager App. 2.

For **Cato** see *Pompey* 48, 52nn.; and on his relationship with M. **Favonius** cf. *Cato* 32.6. Plutarch knew that Cato had been sent **to Cyprus** in 58 BC; for the chronological compression see Pelling [2] 128.

Chapter 22

In 56 BC Caesar's campaigns included the defeat of the Veneti. Cf. Caes. *BG* 3.7-29; Dio 39.40-6; Fuller 115-18. Once again he crossed the

Alps. At Rome his agent Balbus won his trial concerning his citizenship (*Pompey* 51n.), then in January Pompey and Crassus were elected consuls, and Caesar's additional five years of command were voted (*Pompey* 52n.).

Plutarch omits all this and resumes with Caesar's campaign of 55 BC against **the Usipes and the Tenteritae** (Usipites and Tencteri; see Pelling, *CB* 60 [1984] p. 95). These tribes had crossed the Rhine under pressure from the Suebi, and **Caesar's own account** of the campaign is in *BG* 4.1-19 (cf. Dio 39.47-8; Fuller 118-21). Caesar offered the **ambassadors** the chance to settle among the Ubii on the right bank of the Rhine, but was suspicious of their first request for a **period of truce** of three days. So he advanced within twelve miles of the Germans, who again sent envoys to ask for a truce while they negotiated with the Ubii. Caesar ordered his cavalry not to provoke the enemy, but they were **attacked** and ignominiously **routed**. A third **deputation** was therefore arrested, and Caesar fell on the Germans off-guard in their camp. The survivors fled to the junction of the Meuse and Rhine, where they were cut down or drowned. Caesar implies that the German casualties approached 430,000, and asserts that no Romans were killed and only a few wounded. According to the hostile historian **Tanusius** Geminus (cf. App. *Celt.* 18) the massacre shocked even the Romans, especially **Cato** (*Cato* 51.1-2), and a commission was set up to investigate the situation in Gaul. A comparison of these accounts suggests transmission of the story through Asinius Pollio (see Pelling [1] 93).

The German cavalry, which had been away seeking corn, escaped to **the Sugambri**, and when they refused his demand to surrender the fugitives, Caesar determined to make a display of Roman power across the Rhine. He therefore built his famous Rhine bridge, declining an offer of boats made by the Ubii.

Chapter 23

Across the river Caesar **burned and ravaged the country** of the Sugambri, who with the Suebi (**Suevi**) had retreated into their forests. He returned to Gaul after **eighteen days**, breaking down the bridge.

In the autumn of 55 BC Caesar turned his attention to **Britain** and the prospect of more military glory. Britain was thought to be rich in corn, cattle and precious metals, and its mystique was irresistible, but a pretext was the help the Britons had furnished to the Gauls. After preliminary diplomacy Caesar sent Commius, king of the Atrebates, to the island, but he was arrested and only released after Caesar's landing. Unable to transport his cavalry across the Channel due to storms, in one of which he lost twelve ships, Caesar achieved no significant military success; but twenty days of thanksgiving were voted for his efforts, reflecting the impression this reconnaissance expedition made in Rome. Cf. Caes. *BG* 4.20-38; Dio 39.50-3; Fuller 121-3. (N.B. **the reported size...incredible** is a mistranslation; the Greek means rather 'the reported size of Britain was so great that men refused to believe in its existence', and Plutarch has evidently misunderstood his source; see Pelling, *Rh. Mus.* 127 [1984] pp. 41-2.)

Caesar's preparations for his second British expedition were more thorough and included a new fleet. He was also careful to keep a close eye on events in Rome through his agents Balbus and Oppius, and we are kept informed by Cicero's letters to his brother Quintus, Caesar's legate, and to C. Trebatius Testa (*Cicero* 37n.). At the beginning of 54 BC Caesar made Cicero a considerable loan, and Cicero was also bound to Caesar by his brother's legateship. Caesar then flattered Cicero by dedicating to him his work on grammar, and Cicero replied with an epic poem on the British expedition.

Caesar fared better on the second British expedition, crossing the Thames and capturing a citadel which may have been Verulamium (St Albans). He was faced, however, by the powerful Cassivellaunus, **the King** of the Catuvellauni, whose guerrilla tactics disconcerted the Romans, and the situation in Gaul was worsening (also his fleet was for a second time severely damaged by a storm). So Caesar hastily came to an agreement with Cassivellaunus, took **hostages** and **imposed a tribute**. The whole army was withdrawn, and the hoped-for riches had failed to materialise. Cf. Caes. *BG* 5.1-23; Dio 40.1-4.1; Fuller 123-6. Note that Plutarch again records the settlement (ch. 18n.). His account as usual derives from Pollio (see Pelling, *CB* 60 [1984] pp. 96-7).

On his return to Gaul Caesar **found letters**, which **informed him of the death of** Julia (*Pompey* 53n.). Despite the protests of the consul Domitius Ahenobarbus and **the tribunes** she was buried by the people on the **Field of Mars** (Campus Martius), in honour of Caesar (Dio 39.64). He in return and without precedent announced games and a banquet in her honour (ch. 55n.).

Chapter 24

In Gaul discontent and a poor harvest led to the Carnutes killing their king Tasgetius, who had been appointed by Caesar. Caesar was also short of food and therefore was **forced to quarter** his legions in **many different areas for the winter** of 54/3 BC. Before he could return to Italy **Gaul broke out into revolt.** Indutiomarus of the Treveri stirred up the Eburones under Ambiorix (**Abriorix**), who **wiped out** fifteen cohorts in the most easterly winter quarters under the command of L. Aurunculeius **Cotta** and M. **Titurius** Sabinus. The Aduatuci and Nervii then besieged Q. Cicero in his **camp** until relieved by Caesar with two under-strength legions (**7,000 men**). By making his men **act as though they were afraid** and compressing his camp by narrowing its roadways, Caesar tempted the Gauls into **a disorderly attack** on unfavourable ground and routed them. Cf. Caes. *BG* 5.24-52; Dio 40.4-10; Fuller 127-9.

Plutarch's account of Ambiorix' revolt introduces the theme of Caesar's struggles against the odds until he reaches safety, culminating in the surrender of Vercingetorix. Again, it derives from Pollio (see Pelling, *CB* 60 [1984] pp. 97-8).

Chapter 25

This victory caused Indutiomarus to abandon his planned attack on Labienus but not the complete **collapse of the** revolt. Caesar summoned the Gallic chiefs to Samarobriva (Amiens), but the Senones refused to come and expelled their king Cavarinus, another of Caesar's appointees; and Indutiomarus led his forces against Labienus but was killed in a surprise cavalry attack. Cf. Caes. *BG* 5.53-8; Dio 40.11.

Caesar now received an additional **three legions**. One (not **two**) **of these** was lent to him by Pompey (*Pompey* 52n.), two were **recruited** in Cisalpine **Gaul**, and he thereby replaced the fifteen cohorts he had lost with thirty new ones. Early in 53 BC he punished the Nervii and then transferred his headquarters to Lutetia (Paris) before attacking the Senones. They and the Carnutes immediately submitted, and while Labienus subdued the Treveri, Caesar attacked the Menapii and laid waste the territory of the Eburones (Ambiorix escaped). Retiring to Durocortorum (Reims), Caesar executed Acco, the leader of the Senones, and then left for Italy. Cf. Caes. *BG* 6.1-10, 29-44; Dio 40.31-2; Fuller 129-32.

For events in Rome during 54/2 BC see *Pompey* 53-4nn. Caesar went to Ravenna to recruit more troops, and his agents in Rome reacted to the proposal of a dictatorship for Pompey by demanding a joint consulship with Caesar (Suet. *Caesar* 26.1; Dio 40.50.3). With Rome at a crisis point the oppressed Gauls took the chance to make a final attempt at freedom, and so began the great **rebellion**, led by the Carnutes (**Carnuntini**) and the **Arverni** under their leader Vercingetorix (**Vergentorix**), son of Celtillus.

Chapter 26

Caesar did not **set out immediately** but was delayed for several weeks by his negotiations with Pompey (*Pompey* 55-6nn.). The deliberate telescoping serves to underline Caesar's speed of action and is part of another idealised characterisation of Caesar the general, **who more**

than any other man was gifted... Plutarch's narrative of the revolt is itself characterised by its speed (see Pelling, *CB* 60 [1984] pp. 98-9).

The **commanders** of the revolt, including the previously loyal Commius, had been granted favours by Caesar, which may explain how Vercingetorix **knew** of Caesar's problems **in Rome**. Soon after Clodius' murder the Carnutes massacred the Roman traders at Cenabum (Orleans), and the Senonian leader Drappes disrupted the food supply, thus neutralising the power of the six legions quartered among his people. Vercingetorix was proclaimed king of the Arverni, and he persuaded the neighbouring tribes up to the Saône (**Arar**) to join him. While he marched against the Bituriges, the Cadurcan Lucterius took the other part of the army south towards Narbo. Caesar, however, forestalled him and then made an astonishing march across the snow-covered Cevennes towards the Arverni. This drew off Vercingetorix, who returned northwards to besiege Gorgobina, the capital of the Boii. Caesar's entry into the territory of the Bituriges led Vercingetorix to abandon the siege and march towards Noviodunum, but Caesar captured this town and marched on Avaricum, the Bituriges' capital. Eventually the town was captured, and nearly the whole population was massacred. Far from breaking the Gauls, however, this spurred them on, and now even **the brothers of the Romans**, the Aedui, were beginning to waver. Caesar called a conference of their leaders at Decetia and ordered their cavalry and 10,000 infantry to join him; then he led six legions towards Gergovia, the stronghold of the Arverni. It was now that the Aedui changed sides, and the 10,000 infantry on their way to Gergovia massacred the Roman supply column. Caesar was forced to take four legions from Gergovia and march against the rebel infantry, which immediately surrendered and returned to Gergovia without punishment (their leader, Litaviccus, escaped to Vercingetorix). The rest of the Aedui also resumed their allegiance. In his absence the two legions at Gergovia had been attacked, and when Caesar mounted a surprise assault on the fortifications, he suffered a rare defeat. Litaviccus now took the Gallic cavalry to Bibracte, and the Aedui again defected. Caesar sent Eporedorix and Viridomarus with their Aeduan cavalry against him, but they heard the news of their tribe's defection at Noviodunum, massacred the Roman garrison and traders and burned the town. Cut off from his supplies, Caesar boldly marched northwards to the Loire and thence against the Senones, linking up with Labienus near Agedincum.

At a Gallic assembly in Bibracte, from which were absent the Remi, **Lingones** and Treveri, Vercingetorix was confirmed as the overall commander, and he then tried in vain to win over the Allobroges. Caesar marched towards **the Sequani**, while Vercingetorix established himself at Alesia, the stronghold of the Mandubii. Near Dijon Vercingetorix attacked with his cavalry, which were far superior in numbers, but was eventually **overpowered**. Cf. Caes. *BG* 7.1-67; Dio 40.33-9; Fuller 132-48. Plutarch exaggerates the battle, so too the extent of Vercingetorix' operations, as part of his build-up to the dramatic siege of ch. 27 (see Pelling ibid.).

The story of the **sword** seems to be an example of Plutarch using oral tradition (see Pelling [2] 130; Intro. 4). It is also a typical case of a victor's magnanimity after the event (sim. Augustus in *Cicero* 49.5).

Chapter 27

After this defeat Vercingetorix withdrew to **Alesia**, which **Caesar besieged**. On this **famous** episode and subsequent events in Gaul cf. Caes. *BG* 7.68-90, Book 8; Dio 40.40-3; Fuller 148-65. Caesar surrounded the stronghold with eleven miles of siegeworks, and meanwhile over several weeks forty-three states came together in the territory of the Aedui. Against these forces, which he puts at the incredible total of c. 250,000 infantry and 8,000 cavalry, Caesar was forced to build an outer line of defences, fourteen miles in circumference, and while the food ran out in Alesia, the Romans also began to grow short of supplies. Finally, after two attempts to relieve the town, the Romans won a total victory. Next day Vercingetorix surrendered, to be held captive for six years until Caesar's **triumph** in 46 BC (ch. 55n.). (The Gauls in Alesia were not **unaware of what was going on** but withdrew their force which was attacking **the interior line of fortifications**; and there is no horse riding in Caesar's account of the surrender of Vercingetorix – again, the extra details will derive from Pollio.)

Caesar sent his legions to winter quarters (52/1 BC) and himself went to Bibracte. Further campaigns followed, until Caesar captured Uxellodunum on the Dordogne, and the leader of the Senones, Drappes, committed suicide (Lucterius escaped but was captured and executed; as an example to further would-be rebels Caesar cut off the hands of the garrison). Commius surrendered to M. Antony, and Caesar wintered at Nemetocenna (Arras), from where he established the new Gallic constitution and tribute. According to ch. 15 (cf. *Pompey* 67.6) Caesar killed or captured two-thirds of the fighting population of **three million**, captured **800 cities** and subdued **300 nations** (i.e. cantons). Velleius (2.47.1) gives the more realistic figure of over 400,000 killed and a greater number captured. Whatever the true figures Gaul was quiet for more than a decade, except for the Bellovaci in 46 BC. Vast wealth also accrued to Caesar, and with this he paid off his debts and helped secure the loyalty of his officers, men and other political connections. This loyalty was vital as Caesar began to look again towards the political situation in Rome.

Chapter 28

Plutarch's analysis of the origins of the civil war derives from Asinius Pollio (see Pelling [3] 164). This chapter is a prime example of the insidious belief that Caesar planned to seize sole power **from the very beginning**, which leads Plutarch to exaggerate his earlier position and adhere to the theory that he withdrew **from the ring** of politics and used the Gallic wars as **a course of training** (sim. *Pompey* 51.2). See Intro. 3; ch. 1n.

On the situation in Rome after the death of **Crassus (the collapse of good government, Pompey as sole consul** in 52 BC and **his provinces,** which did not include **all Africa**) see *Pompey* 53-5nn. For the portrayal of Pompey as desiring the dictatorship see *Pompey* 54n.; and on the idea of **monarchy** as the only **remedy for the disease of the state** cf. ch. 57, *Pompey* 70n. (55n. for the physician motif).

Chapter 29

Caesar now was faced with a dilemma. If he returned to Rome and stood for the consulship, he would have to give up his *imperium**, which would render him liable to prosecution in the period before he entered office. Caesar therefore desired to retain his *imperium** whilst standing for the consulship in absence, and a law concerning the latter was passed in 52 BC (*Pompey* 56n.). He then had to be exempted by Pompey from his law concerning personal candidacy, but Pompey's law on provincial governorships meant that Caesar might be replaced in Gaul before taking up his consulship of 48 BC. Hence Caesar wanted his **provincial commands prolonged**, but this was opposed by the consul of 51 BC, M. Claudius Marcellus (Plutarch refers to the consuls of 49 BC, C. **Marcellus** and L. Cornelius **Lentulus** Crus). As a leading Optimate* Marcellus **hated Caesar**, and he used the report of the victory at Alesia to declare that the war was over; in his view the law allowing Caesar to stand in absence had been superseded by Pompey's law, and a successor should be appointed at once. Marcellus was opposed by his colleague Ser. Sulpicius Rufus, a number of tribunes and Pompey (*Pompey* 57n.), and the matter was allowed to drop. Marcellus consequently turned to the status of the Transpadanes, who were treated as Roman citizens by Caesar (ch. 14n.), and **had a senator from Novum Comum** flogged.

For his part Pompey agreed to recall the legion he had lent to Caesar (below), but over Caesar's provinces he refused to **declare himself either way**. Finally the senate passed Marcellus' motion that the question of the consular provinces should be discussed on 1 March 50 BC (*Pompey* 57n.). Before the appointed day a new Caesarian tribune had emerged, C. Scribonius **Curio**, and the consul L. Aemilius Paullus (**Paulus**) was also a supporter (Pompey 58n.; he built the **Basilica** Pauli Aemilii to replace the Basilica Aemilia et **Fulvia** of 179 BC). On Caesar's expenditure see Gelzer 177; ch. 27n. (**fifteen hundred talents** = 36 million HS).

During the debate on the provinces Curio proposed that both Caesar and Pompey give up their commands (ch. 30n.). **Pompey now...came into the open** and proposed that Caesar should leave his province on 13 November. This was rejected by Curio, who repeated his own proposal. Then in the summer the senate resolved that Pompey and Caesar should each send one legion to the East, and Pompey cleverly asked **for the return of the** legion **he had lent** Caesar in 53 BC (ch. 25).

On Pompey's **false hopes** see *Pompey* 57n.; the version here probably means that the officers were working for Caesar (a better translation than **about Caesar**; see Pelling [2] 131, *Rh. Mus.* 127 [1984] pp. 43-4). For the suspicion that Caesar was attempting to **seize supreme power for himself** see Intro. 3. The remark of the centurion (cf. *Pompey* 58.2) is attributed to Caesar by Appian (*BC* 2.25), who places it after M. Marcellus' opposition in 51 BC.

Chapter 30

The suggestion made by Curio **on Caesar's behalf** that both men **lay down** their arms reflects Caesar's confidence in his position as an equal of Pompey, though he claimed he was trying to reduce tension (for the accusation of **tyranny** made against him see Intro. 3). Pompey, however, would not tolerate any equal, and the reception he received after his serious illness and the return of the troops he had lent Caesar fuelled his own confidence (*Pompey* 57n.). On 1 December Curio repeated his proposal that Pompey and Caesar should resign their commands, to the delight of **the people**; but he was opposed by the consul C. Marcellus, who ordered Pompey to defend Rome (this was the meeting at which **the consuls put** their two questions to the vote, Plutarch's account being confused; note also that Lentulus' remark here is a conflation of the two remarks attributed to Marcellus at *Pompey* 58.4, 6; see Pelling [2] 127 n.3, 140; *Pompey* 58n.). Curio unsuccessfully tried to have the consuls issue a decree invalidating Pompey's levies, then joined Caesar. On 1 January Antony and his fellow tribune Q. Cassius with difficulty secured **the consuls'** permission to read the **letter...from Caesar** in the senate (the consuls were now C. Marcellus and **Lentulus** Crus). **Scipio**, acting for Pompey, and Lentulus urged resistance, and Scipio's **motion** was passed. For the **mourning** cf. *Pompey* 59.1.

Chapter 31

Further vain attempts at **a reconciliation** and **a compromise** were made by Caesar and **Cicero** over the next few days (*Pompey* 59n.). Cicero's efforts were opposed by **Lentulus**, Cato and Scipio, and on 7 January the senate passed its ultimate decree*. The tribunes were warned that the senate could not guarantee their safety, and Lentulus' insults of Antony and Curio, combined with the ignominy when they **fled from Rome**, furnished Caesar with **excellent material for propaganda among his troops** (Caes. *BC* 1.7, 22).

Chapter 32

Caesar, meanwhile, was at Ravenna with **no more than 300 cavalry and 5,000 legionary soldiers**. Pompey and the senate needed time for their levy and no doubt expected Caesar to await both the spring and the arrival of his legions from **the other side of the Alps**. Caesar, however, realised the need for the speed which was one of his trademarks (*Pompey* 60.1), and so he sent out an advance party **to occupy...Ariminum** (in fact the first town in Italy). This group, led by Q. **Hortensius** (pr. 45 BC), was to take the town by surprise, hence Caesar disarmed suspicion by **watching gladiators** and a theatrical performance. He himself left in the evening of 10 January and lost his way before coming to the **road** which brought him to **the Rubicon** (? Fiumicino). Crossing this **frontier** with his famous remark, he began the civil war. The quote, which Caesar made in Greek (*Pompey* 60.2), is from Menander (cf. Athen. 13.559E).

Much of the story in the sources will derive from **Asinius Pollio**. Caesar can in reality have had little or no hesitation as to his course of action, and in his own account he does not even mention the Rubicon. Plutarch, on the other hand, seizes the opportunity the story provides for dramatic effect. Caesar is like a tragic hero faced with a dilemma: he has **two alternatives** open to him, each of which could prove disastrous, and initial hesitation is followed by an unreasoning rush into action. Caesar also feels an intense moral ambiguity, but his desire for **fame** outweighs his concern for **sufferings**, and this flaw in his character (*hamartia*) precipitates a series of 'tragedies' which include both his own demise and that of Pompey (*Pompey* 60n.). See further Sirianni, F.A., 'Caesar's Decision to Cross the Rubicon' *Ant. Class*. 48 (1979) pp. 636-8; Tucker, R.A., 'What Actually Happened at the Rubicon?' *Historia* 37 (1988) pp. 245-8.

The Athenian tyrant Hippias also had a **dream** of **incest** on his return to Attica with the Persians in 490 BC, but the outcome was to be rather different (Hdt. 6.107). Suetonius (*Caesar* 7.2) and Dio (37.52.2,

41.24.2) put Caesar's dream during his quaestorship in Spain, and Plutarch deliberately reinterprets and displaces the dream for dramatic effect. Further on dreams see *Pompey* 32n.

Chapter 33

Ariminum was captured, and other towns in quick succession (Caes. *BC* 1.11). For Caesar's strategy see Hillman, T.P., 'Strategic Reality and the Movements of Caesar, January 49 BC' *Historia* 37 (1988) pp. 248-52; and on the reaction in **Rome** see *Pompey* 60-1nn. It is clear that Pompey did not **at this time** have **more troops available to him than Caesar,** hence he was forced to abandon the city. The exact number of Caesar's legions is unclear, since the sources variously give nine (Caes. *BG* 8.54), ten (*Pompey* 58.6) and eleven (Cic. *Att.* 7.7.6). The total was possibly nine, plus the unofficial Gallic 'Alauda' legion (Suet. *Caesar* 24.2). Caesar (*BC* 1.6.1) says Pompey had ten legions 'ready', but we know only of two in Italy (those recalled from Caesar in 50 BC) and seven in Spain (Caes. id. 1.38.1). The other would have comprised troops levied in 52 BC and late in 50 BC. By the time he left Italy Pompey had five legions, of which the consuls took thirty cohorts and Pompey twenty (*Pompey* 62.2; Caes. id. 1.25.2). More important than the number of legions is the total number of men. Pompey's legionaries at first numbered c. 25,000, less those captured by Caesar at Brundisium (Caes. id. 1.28.4). In the East he raised another four legions, giving a total of perhaps 45,000 legionaries, plus unknown numbers of auxiliaries and by the time of Pharsalus 7,000 cavalry. Caesar took seven legions to Greece totalling 15,000 legionaries (id. 3.2.2, 6.2), plus 500 or 600 cavalry. The discrepancy in numbers was made up by the additional four legions Antony took across in March or April (ch. 39), as well as by the greater experience of Caesar's men. He can have had few auxiliaries in the beginning, but with the addition of Antony's 800 Caesar had 1,300 or 1,400 cavalry. On these figures see Greenhalgh [2] 296-302.

Chapter 34

On the exodus from Rome and the people's continued support of Pompey **in exile** see *Pompey* 61n. **Labienus** deserted Caesar and arrived at Teanum Sidicinum on 22 January (*Pompey* 64.3; Cic. *Att.* 7.13.1). His reports encouraged Pompey to hope that he might hold Picenum, but this hope soon proved unfounded, and the only chance left for Pompey in north Italy lay in L. **Domitius** Ahenobarbus' army at **Corfinium** (which eventually numbered 33 **cohorts**). He, however, refused Pompey's repeated requests to join up with him at Luceria and was cut off in

Corfinium (*Pompey* 62n.). Caesar's clemency after the capture of the town, reflected in his freeing of Domitius, helped allay people's fears, especially in **Rome**, and many returned to the city. Domitius repaid Caesar by going **back to Pompey**, via Massilia (ch. 36n.). Further on this campaign see Fuller 183-9.

Chapter 35

As was his regular practice Caesar administered an oath of loyalty to Domitius' men and the other **troops which were being raised for Pompey** (Caes. *BC* 1.13). Having failed to prevent Pompey's escape **to Brundisium**, Caesar marched there and invested the town, but again failed to prevent Pompey's escape **to Dyrrhachium** (see Fuller 189-91; *Pompey* 62-3nn.; on the relative order of composition of the *Caesar* and *Pompey* see Intro. 4).

It had been a swift campaign (just over **sixty days**) and almost **without...bloodshed**. Unable **to pursue** Pompey through lack of ships, Caesar now ordered vessels to be assembled at Brundisium and sent legates to Sardinia, Sicily and Africa to secure Italy's corn supply. He next planned to subdue Spain but first marched **to Rome**.

Caesar had suffered a setback to his attempt to gain political legitimacy when both **consuls** crossed to Dyrrhachium. In addition to the tribunes Antony and Cassius there were several praetors in Rome and a number of senators, but he needed the backing of leading consulars. He met Cicero at Formiae, but Cicero refused to return to Rome (*Cicero* 37n.) and at the meeting of **the senate** on 1 April only Sulpicius Rufus and Volcacius Tullus of the consulars were in attendance. Caesar reiterated his desire for peace, inviting the senate **to send a deputation to Pompey**; then he made a similar speech to the people, promising a corn distribution and a donation of 300 HS to each citizen. No one was willing to go on the peace mission, and **the tribune** L. **Metellus** vetoed Caesar's use of the reserve **treasury**. Caesar overcame Metellus' opposition by threatening **to kill him** and secured the money he required, but in so doing he ruined his popular image as a defender of the tribunes' rights (*Pompey* 62.1; Caes. *BC* 1.32-3; App. *BC* 2.41; Dio 41.16-17; his words were those of a tyrant – see Intro. 3).

Chapter 36

In early April Caesar **marched into Spain**. On the way he besieged Massilia (Marseilles), where resistance was led by Domitius Ahenobarbus (despite Caesar's lenient treatment at Corfinium). He then joined his legate C. Fabius, who was near Ilerda with six legions, faced by five legions under the command of L. **Afranius** and M. Petreius. Here Caesar suffered a serious **lack of food** when the bridges over the Sicoris were destroyed by a flood. At Rome the news caused another flood of senators and citizens to Pompey, but Caesar managed to build a new bridge to secure his supplies. Several Spanish towns north of the Ebro went over to Caesar, and Afranius and Petreius decided to move south of the river into Celtiberia, the area of Pompey's influence. Caesar blocked the route and forced them to surrender, then ordered the army to be dismissed, while its commanders were allowed to return **to Pompey**. Cf. Caes. *BC* 1.34-87; Fuller 193-206.

Caesar next summoned the leading citizens of Further Spain to a meeting at Corduba. The Pompeian commander, the historian M. Terentius **Varro**, set out for Gades, but before he arrived the province went over to Caesar, and one of his legions mutinied. The other was handed over by Varro to one of Caesar's officers, Sex. Caesar, and Varro himself surrendered at Corduba. Gades was rewarded with the promise of Roman citizenship.

On his return to Italy Caesar received the surrender of Massilia after a year's siege (see Yavetz 73-4). It was here that Caesar learned he had been appointed **dictator** by the praetor Lepidus (not by **the senate**, ch. 37; Caes. *BC* 2.21.5).

Chapter 37

Having dealt with a mutiny at Placentia, **Caesar returned to Rome.** As **dictator** he could legitimately hold the elections, in which he was made consul with P. **Servilius Isauricus**, son of the consul of 79 BC (ch. 1n.). In his **eleven days** of office Caesar also passed measures to relieve **debts** and to restore **exiles** and the sons of those proscribed by **Sulla**; and he celebrated the Latin Festival, conferred citizenship on Cisalpine Gaul, confirmed that of Gades, distributed corn and arranged the provincial administration. See Yavetz 62-73, 133-7.

L. **Piso** brought up again the question of the **terms of peace**, but a confident Caesar had Isauricus speak **against this proposal** and **set out for the war.** He had already sent his twelve legions and cavalry to Brundisium, and he found his men **tired out** by the long march from Spain and the climate (Caes. *BC* 3.2.3). Caesar only had sufficient ships to transport seven (not **five**) **legions** and his cavalry, and with these he crossed on 4 January 48 BC to the Ceraunian Headlands of Epirus near **the Ionian Gulf**, unobserved by Pompey's fleet (Caes. id. 3.2.2-3, 3.6). On the size of his forces see ch. 33n. The men **left behind** were prevented from crossing by Bibulus' blockade until April.

Caesar immediately advanced northwards to Apollonia. As he was for the time being greatly outnumbered, he sent L. Vibullius Rufus,

whom he had twice captured (at Corfinium and in Spain), with an offer
of peace to Pompey (Caes. *BC* 3.10). While Vibullius was on this
mission, **Oricum and Apollonia** and the neighbouring towns went over
to Caesar (App. *BC* 2.54). Pompey re-took Oricum, reached Dyrrhachium before Caesar and then had no choice but to reject Vibullius'
proposal (*Pompey* 65n.). Caesar, meanwhile, camped at the river Apsus
and awaited Antony's reinforcements. He occupied the shore-line to
disrupt Bibulus' supplies, and eventually Bibulus fell ill and died. Pompey for his part hastened from Dyrrhachium and camped across the
river from Caesar. Cf. Caes. id. 3.11-18.

Chapter 38

Further on the story of Caesar's daring attempt to cross **to Brundisium**
(cf. Suet. *Caesar* 58.2; App. *BC* 2.57; Dio 41.46) and **Caesar's fortune** in
general see Weinstock 112-27. It fits well with the particular tragic
theme of the *Life*, which was highlighted by the Rubicon crossing (Caesar's **mind** is again **in a most disturbed state**); it also reflects Plutarch's
own interest in the role of fortune in men's lives, and its connection with
virtue (on which see Wardman 179-89). Although the story, which is not
in Caesar's account, may be apocryphal, it underlines the dire straits in
which Caesar found himself. In Rome, meanwhile, the praetor M. Caelius Rufus was also stirring up trouble over the debt problem and joined
with Milo in an uprising against Caesar, but both were killed. At length
Caesar managed to get a letter through to Antony, who with Fufius
Calenus finally landed at Lissus.

Chapter 39

While Pompey withdrew to Asparagium, Caesar sent C. Calvisius
Sabinus to Aetolia to secure his food supply. Sabinus was given the
legion of Acilius, who was at Oricum guarding Caesar's fleet. Pompey's
elder son Gnaeus therefore attacked the weakened Acilius, then
burned Antony's transport ships at Lissus, and so Caesar was now
completely cut off from Italy. He offered battle at Asparagium and in
turn cut off Pompey from his base at Dyrrhachium (Caes. *BC* 3.31-41).
On the subsequent blockade of Dyrrhachium see *Pompey* 65n.
   The situation concerning **supplies** naturally changed during the in-
vestment. From being **badly off**, Caesar got into **very serious difficulties**
(*BC* 3.47, 48 for the episode of the 'chara' **root**); but then the corn
began to ripen, and Caesar blocked Pompey's water supply and
prevented his cavalry from foraging. Pompey was eventually forced to
attempt a break-out: the first time he was unsuccessful (*Pompey* 65n.),

and it was on this occasion that the Cassius Scaeva episode occurred (ch. 16n.), but a second **attack** was a **great success**. During this Caesar tried to stop his men fleeing and **was very nearly killed** by a standard bearer (Caes. id. 59-71; App. *BC* 2.61-2).

It was a serious defeat for Caesar, who uttered his famous remark on Pompey's generalship (*Pompey* 65.5; Caes. *BC* 3.70; Suet. *Caesar* 36). While Pompey and his troops were exultant, Caesar had to encourage his men and alter his plans. If Pompey followed him to **Thessaly**, he would force a decisive battle; if Pompey returned to Italy, he would march there overland with Domitius Calvinus; if Pompey besieged Apollonia and Oricum, he would attack Metellus **Scipio** and draw Pompey into battle.

Chapter 40

The **confidence** of Pompey's army and his own caution are similarly recorded in *Pompey* 66.1-2 (see n.). The **effect** of their long campaigns on Caesar's troops seems to be a doublet of ch. 37, and Caesar had no difficulty in regrouping his men and escaping Pompey's pursuit (Caes. *BC* 3.75-7).

Chapter 41

Pompey was now pressed to fight a decisive battle (*Pompey* 67n.; also on the casualty figure **of a thousand**). On Cato's reaction to the war and this victory cf. *Cato* 53-4. Caesar stayed briefly at Apollonia, then marched into Thessaly. **After his recent defeat** the population was hostile, and Caesar was forced to storm **Gomphi**. Its speedy capture revitalised his men, and Caesar turned a blind eye to their misbehaviour (Suet. *Caesar* 67.1), but more importantly this deterred most of the other cities from opposition. Cf. Caes. *BC* 3.78-81.

Chapter 42

The positions of the rival camps in **the plain of Pharsalus** are uncertain. They were probably north of the river Enipeus and to the north-west of the town. Caesar does not even mention the name Pharsalus in his account – this is given by Plutarch (*Pompey* 68.1, *Cicero* 39.1), Suetonius (*Caesar* 35.1) and Appian (*BC* 2.82).

For Pompey's continuing reluctance to fight, his dream and the confidence of his staff see *Pompey* 67-8 with nn. The inequality of **the numbers of the infantry** and to a lesser extent the cavalry is exaggerated

(*Pompey* 69n.). **The personal beauty of the riders** was supposedly a critical factor in Pompey's defeat (ch. 45). Note that the supposed lacuna in the text of ch. 42 is rejected by Pelling, *Rh. Mus.* 127 (1984) pp. 44-5.

Chapter 43

For three days Caesar offered battle, and then he decided **to break camp** and march **to Scotussa** (*Pompey* 68n.). **Corfinius** is probably Caesar's quaestor in Illyricum, Q. Cornificius. After Caesar's legate Q. **Fufius Calenus** had brought the reinforcements with Antony, he was sent to Achaea but did not capture **Athens and Megara** until after Pharsalus (*Brutus* 8.3; Caes. *BC* 3.56). The **service of purification** is put on the eve of the battle by Appian (*BC* 2.68). On the **bright flaming light** see *Pompey* 68n. It should be noted that Caesar was no believer in religion (ch. 52n.).

Chapter 44

Pompey now decided to fight (*Pompey* 68n.). For the formation of the battle-lines and Caesar's criticism of **Pompey's generalship** see id. 69n. Caesar's **right** wing was in fact commanded by P. Cornelius Sulla, Pompey's probably by L. Lentulus.

The Homeric-style story of C. Crastinus (**Crassinus**) is related, with less gory detail, in Caes. *BC* 3.91, 99.2-3 (cf. Luc. 7.470-3). The Greek in fact reads 'Crassinius' (as App. *BC* 2.82; 'Crassianus' in *Pompey* 71.1-3).

Chapter 45

The vital role of the reserve **cohorts** is noted by Caesar without the embellishments of Plutarch and Appian (*Pompey* 71.4-5; Caes. *BC* 3.93.5, 94.1-4; App. *BC* 2.78). See further Fuller 237-8; *Pompey* 69n. The **good looks** of the cavalry are also remarked on by Plutarch in ch. 42. On Pompey's reaction to the defeat and **what happened to him later** see *Pompey* 72-80 with nn.

Chapter 46

Caesar had attempted to defend himself against charges of treason for his actions in Gaul by publishing the *Gallic War*, and it is to his precarious position after the war that his remark here alludes (cf. Suet.

Caesar 30.4). The source, **Asinius Pollio**, also gave the reasonable Pompeian casualty figure of **6,000** (*Pompey* 72n.). The survivors were, in Caesar's regular fashion, **incorporated in his own legions** (Caes. *BC* 3.98, 107.1), and among those pardoned was his future assassin M. Iunius **Brutus** (*Brutus* 5-6; Vell. 2.52.5). The object of the pardons **of prominent people** (cf. Cic. *Fam.* 15.15.3) was to win the cooperation of the leading senators, who had on the whole been opposed to Caesar. Those whom he had already spared, however, were mostly put to death.

Chapter 47

The story of the heavenly sign at **Tralles** in the Maeander valley is one of several recorded by Caesar (*BC* 3.105.3-6). The relevant Book of **Livy** (111) is lost, but this passage is important as an indication of one of Plutarch's sources (see Intro. 4).

Caesar remained at Pharsalus for two days, freed **Thessaly** and then **went in pursuit of Pompey**, via Amphipolis and the Hellespont to **Asia** (Caes. *BC* 3.102). There, in imitation of Alexander, Caesar visited and honoured Ilium, city of Aeneas, the son of Aphrodite (Venus) from whom his family claimed descent (ch. 5n.). The miracles in Asia reflected Caesar's divine lineage, and at Ephesus a monument was erected to the descendant of Ares and Aphrodite, 'god manifest and common saviour of mankind' (*SIG*[3] 760, = Sherk 79D; see Weinstock 128-32). Caesar in return saved the Ephesian treasury, reduced taxation **by a third** and freed **Cnidus** on behalf of **Theopompus**, to whom he later granted citizenship. See Yavetz 101-4.

Chapter 48

From Asia Caesar sailed to Rhodes and thence to **Alexandria**, arriving three days **after Pompey's death** (Caes. *BC* 3.106.1-3; Ep. Livy 112). Pompey's wife and **friends** had escaped, and it was Lentulus Crus who was **arrested** (Pompey had two centurions, a freedman and a slave with him, and the freedman at least was not arrested, *Pompey* 78.4, 80.2-3).

Caesar went to the palace and began to levy contributions, on the pretext that the Egyptian government had aided Pompey. He was also owed 17^1/2 **million drachmas** (= 70 million HS) in connection with the restoration of Ptolemy Auletes and the loan raised for him by C. Rabirius Postumus (Suet. *Caesar* 54.3). **The eunuch Pothinus** firstly obstructed the payment and then used the temple treasures and the royal **gold and silver** to make Caesar unpopular. Further on Pothinus see *Pompey* 77n. (Pompey had in fact been **killed** on the motion of Theodotus by Achillas). He **had driven out Cleopatra**, the King's sister-wife and joint ruler, and she was at Pelusium attempting to force her return. Caesar, seizing the opportunity to extend his patronage, invited Ptolemy and Cleopatra to appear before him.

Chapter 49

Cleopatra smuggled herself into the palace **inside a sleeping bag**, and soon **captivated Caesar** (Dio 42.34.2-35.1). Ptolemy in response incited the mob, and Caesar, outnumbered but with Ptolemy in his possession, agreed to concessions. He decided that, in line with their father's will, the two **should share the throne of Egypt**. While he awaited the arrival of Domitius Calvinus with reinforcements, Caesar then indulged in sightseeing and feasting with Cleopatra. For his part Pothinus continued **plotting** and summoned **the general Achillas** from Pelusium to attack the palace (Caes. *BC* 3.108.2). Ptolemy and Pothinus were arrested, and Caesar managed to defend the palace with his small force, but the famous **great library** was destroyed by **the fire** which he started to cripple the royal fleet (Dio 42.38.2). Caesar also occupied the wondrous **Pharos** lighthouse, to keep the sea open to his fleet, and summoned help from Syria and Asia Minor. Pothinus was now executed, and while Ptolemy was held captive, his sister Arsinoe escaped with the eunuch Ganymedes. Arsinoe was hailed as queen by the rebels, and having had Achillas executed, Ganymedes took over command. Several operations on land and sea followed, and eventually Caesar secured Pharos and the Heptastadion **mole** connecting the island to the city. He then suffered a serious defeat in which he had to **swim...to escape** (Hirtius in Caes. *BAlex*. 5-22; Suet. *Caesar* 64; Dio 42.40.2-5). Caesar maintained his position, however, and the Alexandrians **finally** asked for **the King** to be handed back, in order to negotiate peace terms. He became a puppet ruler, but the war continued until Caesar, reinforced by Mithridates of Pergamum, stormed the King's camp. Ptolemy drowned in the Nile, and Alexandria surrendered. Cf. Hirtius id. 25-32; Dio 42.41-3.

Caesar had already been in Egypt for six months, and he remained there until the beginning of June 47 BC. Political negotiations with Cleopatra were conducted on a Nile cruise, the first outcome of which was that Caesar recognised Egypt's independence under the rule of Cleopatra and her second brother-husband Ptolemy XIV. Caesar **then set out for Syria**. The second outcome of the cruise (it seems) was a baby, who was given the name Ptolemy Caesar and **whom the Alexandrians** mockingly **called Caesarion** ('Caesar's offspring'; see Gelzer 257 n. 1). Caesar's paternity was later denied by Oppius (ch. 17n.), and Caesarion was put to death by Octavian in 30 BC (*Antony* 82.1). Cf. Hirtius in Caes. *BAlex*. 33; Suet. *Caesar* 35.1; Dio 42.44; Fuller 240-57.

Chapter 50

Caesar's prolonged absence in Egypt allowed the Pompeians to recover from Pharsalus. In October 48 BC Cato, Labienus, Afranius and Petreius sailed to Cyrenaica in north Africa; by then Metellus Scipio had also reached Africa and was recognised as the overall commander of ten legions, four Numidian legions, cavalry and 120 elephants, with the governor Attius Varus and King Juba of Numidia subordinates. Meanwhile, in Asia Minor the king of the Cimmerian Bosporus, **Pharnaces, the son of Mithridates**, attempted to recover his father's empire in Galatia, **Cappadocia, Bithynia** and **Pontus. Domitius** Calvinus was defeated by Pharnaces near Nicopolis in **Lesser Armenia**, and had to retire to **Asia**. Pharnaces then seized Pontus and marched towards Asia, but was halted by a revolt in the Bosporus. Caesar went from Alexandria via Antioch to Tarsus, where he settled the affairs of Cilicia and received several Pompeians, including C. Cassius Longinus (ch. 62n.). In Galatia Caesar allowed Deiotarus, who had sided with Pompey (*Pompey* 73n.), to remain king but delayed settling his dispute with his fellow **tetrarchs** over the extent of his kingdom. Caesar also took Deiotarus' legion and cavalry to add to his own depleted forces and the two remaining legions of Calvinus, and then marched against Pharnaces, who was near **Zela** in Pontus. On 2 August Caesar camped close to the King, who attacked him and was **annihilated** (Pharnaces escaped but was soon killed). **Caesar wrote to** C. Matius (a better reading than **Amantius**) **in Rome** his famous words '*veni, vidi, vici*', which were later displayed on an inscription at his triumph, and hastened to the coast of Asia Minor, settling the affairs of the area: Mithridates of Pergamum received one of the Galatian tetrarchies and was made king of the Bosporus; and Deiotarus was only made to concede Lesser Armenia to Ariobarzanes of Cappadocia. Cf. Hirtius in Caes. *BAlex.* 65-78; Suet. *Caesar* 35.2, 37.2; Fuller 257-60.

Chapter 51

Caesar returned to Tarentum in September 47 BC. On his way to Brundisium he met Cicero and allayed his fears with a friendly reception, and finally in October **came to Rome** (*Cicero* 39n.).

Caesar's second dictatorship was **now a year** old, and he had been granted extraordinary honours, including control over the fate of the Pompeians and over peace and war; the right to hold the consulship for five successive years and to hold the elections; tribunician privileges; and the right to appoint praetorian governors. In Rome the tribune of 47 BC, Cicero's son-in-law P. Cornelius **Dolabella**, proposed to abolish debts and remit house-rents but was opposed by his fellow-tribunes C.

Asinius Pollio and L. Trebellius. In the end the senate passed its ultimate decree* giving full authority to Antony, Caesar's Master of the Horse. Discontent had spread through Italy, and the legions in Campania had to be calmed by Antony, in whose absence Rome fell into a state of anarchy due to the rivalry of Dolabella and Trebellius. Eventually Antony marched into the forum, and 800 citizens were killed. On his return Caesar dropped Antony for two years, but he was careful to stand by the popular Dolabella and reduced rents. He also auctioned his opponents' property, and Antony was forced to pay the full price for **Pompey's house**. Caesar then faced more problems with the veterans in Campania, and he sent the later historian C. Sallustius Crispus with a promise of **1,000 drachmas** (= 4,000 HS) per man. His mission was unsuccessful, **two men of praetorian rank** (C. **Cosconius**, ? tr. 48BC; **Galba** is unknown) were killed, and the veterans marched on Rome. Caesar confronted them in the Campus Martius, addressed them as 'Citizens' (Quirites), discharged them and promised rewards when he returned from Africa. The men pleaded to go with Caesar, and eventually lost one-third of their bounty and land. Cf. Suet. *Caesar* 70; App. *BC* 2.93; Dio 42.52-55.3.

Caesar took the consulship of 46 BC for himself with M. Lepidus, who was replacing Antony in his favour. Having augmented the senate with equites*, centurions and men of even lower status, he resigned the dictatorship and in December left Rome for **Sicily** (ch. 52). Cf. ps.-Caes. *BAfr.* 1-2; Dio 42.51.3-5.

On **Amantius** see ch. 50n.; and on **Corfinius** see ch. 43n.

Chapter 52

On **Cato and Scipio, King Juba** and their **considerable force** see ch. 50n. At Lilybaeum Caesar **pitched his own tent on the beach** to emphasise his readiness to attack (ps.-Caes. *BAfr.* 1.1); and he then headed towards Hadrumentum in the south of the African province, where **he landed** with only **3,000 infantry and** 150 **cavalry**, but also **without being observed**. He stumbled as he disembarked, and therefore clasped the ground and shouted, 'I hold you, Africa'; and he showed further disdain for religious scruples by his use of Scipio Salvito (**Sallustio**) to overcome the **ancient oracle** (Suet. *Caesar* 59; Dio 42.57.5-58.3; further on Caesar's lack of traditional religious beliefs cf. Cic. *Div.* 2.52; Polyaen. 8.23.32-3).

Unable to assault Hadrumentum with his small force, Caesar marched south to Leptis Minor to await the arrival of reinforcements. Some came on 1 January 46 BC, and the last part of the convoy landed on 4 January. Caesar's main problem was **food for his men** and **provisions for his horses** (they were in fact fed on **seaweed** after the first battle below, ps.-Caes. *BAfr.* 24.4); so he set out on a foraging expedition. On this he met a strong force under Labienus, which he eventually drove back, only to be attacked in the rear by a second force under Petreius. For a while **the enemy had got the better of things**, but Caesar managed to retire to his camp at Ruspina (id. 3-19; see Fuller 264-70). It was a close shave for Caesar, whose men were at first disorganised by Labienus' new tactics (cavalry interspersed with light-armed, **fast-moving Numidians**). The story of **the standard-bearer** and the episode with the off-duty cavalry presumably derive from **Asinius Pollio.**

Chapter 53

Caesar now began fortifying his camp and sent three cohorts to garrison Acylla in return for corn. At length the tide began to turn, as Caesar mounted a propaganda campaign against Scipio and promised deserters a welcome reception. Having received reinforcements Caesar left Ruspina and offered battle at Uzita, which Scipio refused. He then planned an attack on Uzita and fortified a camp close to the town, but a shortage of food eventually forced Caesar to march further south towards **Thapsus**. On the way he fought a risky engagement near Zeta, which prompted him to retrain his men, and this at once proved successful in an engagement near Sarsura. Cf. ps.-Caes. *BAfr.* 20-79.

With the sea on one side and a **lake** and marsh on the other, Caesar finally enticed Scipio into battle (ps.-Caes. *BAfr.* 80-86.1; Dio 43.7-9.1). **Afranius and Juba** blocked the southern exit of the isthmus with their camps, and while Scipio began the blockade of the northern exit, Caesar attacked. Scipio's camp was captured by one part of his force, the other captured the camps of Afranius and Juba. Caesar's veterans would accept no surrender, and over 10,000 were killed, with only **fifty** of Caesar's men lost (see further Fuller 271-81). Of the enemy leaders Scipio committed suicide during a sea-battle against P. Sittius, who also captured Faustus Sulla and Afranius (they were executed on Caesar's orders). Petreius and Juba fled to Taura, where they were refused entry: Juba then killed Petreius and was himself despatched by a slave. Labienus, Attius Varus and Pompey's sons Gnaeus and Sextus reached Spain. Most of those who begged for mercy were spared, but not L. Caesar.

Plutarch's alternative version of the battle may have been invented to account for the massacre of survivors by Caesar's troops, which the general failed to prevent. Suetonius notes, however, that Caesar 'twice had epileptic fits while on campaign' (*Caesar* 45.1; further on his **illness** see ch. 17n.).

Chapter 54

Caesar now marched to **Utica**, which was under the **command** of M. **Cato**. Cato helped those escaping from Thapsus but himself **committed suicide**, in line with his Stoic and Republican principles (*Cato* 58-72; Cic. *Att.* 12.4.2). His death served to increase his threat to Caesar: when Cicero wrote his pamphlet *Cato*, Caesar replied with an *Anti-Cato* which went too far, and Cato became a martyr to Republicanism (*Cicero* 39n.). Caesar spared Cato's son and settled the affairs of the old province, imposing fines; he also turned most of Juba's kingdom into the province of New Africa, then sailed via Sardinia to Rome.

Plutarch's typically indecisive discussion of Caesar's character here reflects the principle set out in *Cimon* 2.4-5.

Chapter 55

On his return Caesar was again voted unprecedented honours by the senate, including fifty days' thanksgiving; the dictatorship for ten years; a three-year censorship of morals; and the right of designating magistrates for election, sitting on the curule chair in the senate between the consuls and speaking first in all debates. Despite his acceptance of these honours Caesar was at pains to stress that he was not aiming at a tyranny but had only fought the civil war to protect his dignity. In his **speech to the people** he listed the benefits he had conferred on them (the **three million pounds of olive oil** is the fine he imposed on Leptis Magna in Africa), and he preceded this with a conciliatory speech to the senate (Dio 43.15-18). He especially cultivated Cicero, who taught Hirtius and Dolabella oratory and hoped for a restoration of the Republic. The other major figure was M. Marcellus, whom Cicero hoped Caesar would allow to return from exile: Caesar granted the recall, and Cicero thanked him in the *Pro Marcello* (Marcellus was murdered on his way home). In this speech he urges Caesar to re-establish the Republic, but Caesar had no intention of resigning his dictatorship as Sulla had (Suet. *Caesar* 77). Already there was dissent among some of his own followers at his conciliatory attitude, and an assassination was attempted for which it was rumoured Antony was responsible. Nevertheless, Caesar later recalled T. Ampius Balbus and Q. Ligarius (on whom see *Cicero* 39n.).

Caesar now began the difficult and lengthy task of providing land for his veterans (ch. 57) and started preparations for his four **triumphs** (Plutarch omits the Gallic triumph) between 20 September and 1 October. The number of enemy dead (excluding Roman citizens) was said to be 1,192,000 (Pliny, *NH* 7.92), and captives on display included Vercingetorix (who was afterwards executed), Arsinoe and the **son of** Juba who was four. The sight of Arsinoe and the representations of events in

Africa connected with Scipio, Petreius and Cato were not well received, and Pharsalus was not mentioned (Cic. *Phil.* 14.23). Caesar also felt obliged to deny the obscene allegations of his soldiers' songs about his relationship with Nicomedes (Suet. *Caesar* 49.4; Dio 43.20.2-4; ch. 1n.). The procession included a vast amount of precious metals, which was divided amongst **his soldiers** and the poor, who received in addition corn and oil. **He gave a feast** and gladiatorial games, and distributed meat to honour his promise on the death of **Julia** (Suet. id. 26.2; ch. 23n.). Finally, as part of these victory celebrations Caesar dedicated the Forum Iulium on 26 September (it had been built since 54 BC), in the middle of which was built the temple vowed before Pharsalus to Venus Genetrix. Cf. App. *BC* 2.102.

After the shows Caesar turned to the task of legislation and reform. His **census** of Rome enabled the reduction in the number of people entitled to free corn from **320,000** to **150,000**, and due to the depopulation **caused by the civil wars** privileges were granted to fathers of large families (Suet. *Caesar* 41.3; Dio 43.25.2). Other measures included the banning of political clubs; the establishment of colonies; grants of citizenship; and laws regulating criminal and civil procedure, allowing only senators and equites* to serve on juries (against Cotta's law of 70 BC; *Pompey* 22n.) and increasing penalties. Finally, Caesar introduced the new Julian calendar (ch. 59n.).

Caesar's treatment of the senate, however, caused great resentment, with his frequent refusal to allow discussion particularly of foreign affairs, and his creation of new senators from supposedly obscure and provincial origins was also unpopular amongst older members. Caesar was destroying what remained of the old-style politics, though we must remember that this reaction to the new senators is not surprising, and 'obscure origins' might still mean 'equestrian* rank' (see Yavetz 168-72).

Chapter 56

Caesar's stay in Rome was cut short by events in **Spain**. There the two Pompeian legions drove out the governor C. Trebonius and were soon joined by Sex. Pompey, Attius Varus and Labienus; then Cn. Pompey raised thirteen legions, and Caesar's generals Q. Fabius Maximus and Q. Pedius were forced to remain with their recruits in camp near Obulco (Porcuna), east of Corduba.

Caesar therefore **set out for Spain** and after his departure **was declared consul for the fourth time** for 45 BC without a colleague by Lepidus (cos. 46 BC and now Master of the Horse); he was also appointed dictator for a fourth time from April 45 BC. Caesar reached Obulco on the twenty-seventh day of his journey (Strabo 3.4.9; App. *BC*

2.103); overland this is more than 1,500 miles, which means he covered an astonishing 50-60 miles per day – small wonder he wrote a poem called *The Journey* (Suet. *Caesar* 56.5). Caesar immediately marched on Corduba, but Sex. Pompey prevented the capture of the city. Caesar then began to besiege Ategua with its abundant stock of corn, which Cn. Pompey failed to defend in time, and its fall led the Spanish communities to start deserting him. After further engagements and a defeat near Soricaria, Pompey determined to fight a decisive battle on favourable ground **near the city of Munda** (ps.-Caes. *BH* 23-7; Dio 43.35.2-4). On 17 March with 8 legions and 8,000 cavalry Caesar attacked the Pompeian force of 13 legions, cavalry and 6,000 light-armed troops; and after heavy fighting in which Caesar once more had to intervene personally to prevent disaster (Vell. 2.55.3; Suet. *Caesar* 36; Flor. 2.13.78-83), his superior cavalry turned the tide. Among the **30,000** Pompeian dead were Labienus and Attius Varus. Caesar returned to Corduba, executing all men under arms and fining the city heavily; he treated Hispalis (Seville) in the same way, before moving to Gades. Cn. Pompey had in the meantime been killed in flight by the men of C. Didius (**Deidius**), and his **head** was put on display in Hispalis (ps.-Caes. id. 32-9).

Caesar stayed in Spain until about June, punishing rebel Spanish communities, organising the administration and founding new citizen colonies. On his return to Italy, Caesar was reconciled with Antony in Narbo. He was promised a consulship for 44 BC but supposedly already knew of an assassination plot against Caesar (*Antony* 13.1 with Pelling).

Caesar did not return to Rome **to celebrate a triumph** until early October 45 BC. In September he was on his estate at Labicum, where he wrote his will. His heirs were his great-nephew L. Pinarius and nephew Q. Pedius (one quarter of the estate) and especially his great-nephew C. Octavius, whom he adopted (ch. 68n.). Caesar had received more extraordinary honours after Munda, including: fifty days' thanksgiving; the title 'Imperator'* as an hereditary name; the right always to appear at official occasions in triumphal dress and always to wear a laurel wreath; a temple to Freedom and a palace; control of the army and finance; and to a ten-year dictatorship was added a ten-year consulship. Additionally, ruler cult was initiated in Rome, with Caesar's ivory statue to be carried alongside images of the other gods and statues inscribed 'To the invincible god'. Not all of this was pleasing even to the people, however, and at the victory games on 20 July Caesar's statue received no applause; there was also talk of tyranny. Then the triumph itself **displeased the Romans** despite the official line that it celebrated victory over **foreign generals**, and Pontius Aquila remained seated as Caesar passed by the tribunes' bench. Caesar responded with further **public** feasts (ch. 57) and unprecedented triumphs for his legates Fabius and Pedius. Also in October Caesar resigned his consulship and arranged the elections (ch. 58n.) and he continued with his colonisation policy (ch. 57n.).

Chapter 57

Caesar was appointed **dictator for life** by 9 February 44 BC and had assumed the title *dictator perpetuus* by 15 February (on the theme of one-man rule giving **a respite** see Pompey 70n.). **This meant an undisguised tyranny** but avoided the hated title 'King' (*Rex*). Nevertheless, the acceptance of this title was a disastrous error, finally dashing hopes of a return to the Republic and arousing suspicions of Caesar's real intentions (ch. 60n.). These suspicions were fuelled by Caesar's acceptance of **extravagant additions** to his honours, which included: the title of Father of his Country (*pater patriae*); statues in the temples of Rome and Italy and two in the forum; the building of temples of Concordia and Felicitas (reflecting Caesar's **good fortune**) and a new senate house (Curia Iulia); the month of his birth (Quinctilis) to be renamed Iulius and a tribe to receive his name; censorial authority for life; and tribunician inviolability. A final set of honours was voted in Caesar's absence in late 45 or early 44 BC. In addition to a golden chair and golden wreath adorned with jewels, Caesar was to be honoured as Divus Iulius with a temple consecrated to him and his **Clemency**, and he was to be buried within the city boundary. For the idea that Caesar was voted excessive honours to provide a **pretext** for his murder cf. Nicol. Dam. frg. 130.67J; Dio 44.7.3.

Caesar had shown his clemency to **Brutus** after Pharsalus (ch. 46n.; he was urban praetor in 44 BC) and to **Cassius** in Cilicia (ch. 50n.; peregrine praetor 44 BC). Cassius was now one of the few to vote against Caesar's proposed new divine honours, which Caesar himself accepted ungraciously (ch. 60n.).

A vital part of Caesar's policy in Rome was conciliation (ch. 55n.), and he passed a general amnesty for all his political opponents (see Yavetz 96-7). This established peace, and Caesar emphasised this by re-erecting **statues** of Sulla and Pompey, giving rise to Cicero's remark (*Cicero* 40.4-5). He also dispensed with his **bodyguard** of armed Spaniards (Suet. *Caesar* 86.1; App. *BC* 2.107), though according to Dio (44.6.1) he was instead escorted by senators and equites*; further, senators swore an oath to protect him. Caesar clearly was warned of the plot to assassinate him, and this makes the refusal of a bodyguard all the more surprising. Ill-health (ch. 60) was thought to be a factor in his lack of precautions (Suetonius), but Caesar's attitude to **death** had previously upset Cicero after the plot on his return from Africa (Cic. *Marc.* 25; cf. ch. 63; Suet. id. 86-7; App. id. 2.109). If he was trusting to his famous luck (*fortuna*), he was indeed taking a huge risk – still, he would soon be in his more accustomed surroundings of a military camp. See further Gelzer 325-8.

For the **feasts** see ch. 56n.; and on his regulation of the **grain** dole see ch. 55n. Another essential element of Caesar's policy was the foundation of **new colonies**, for both **his soldiers** and the common people. These included settlements at **Carthage** (Colonia Iulia Concordia Carthago) and **Corinth** (Laus Iulia Corinthus, mainly for freedmen; Carthage and Corinth had been **captured** and destroyed in 146 BC by Scipio Aemilianus and L. Mummius respectively). See Yavetz 97-100. The spread of Romanisation and the citizenship, however, and the influx of foreigners into Rome and the senate (ch. 58n.) were unacceptable to the old Roman nobility*. See further on these policies Yavetz 137-50.

Chapter 58

Caesar's arrangements for the **praetorships and consulships** included the election of Q. Fabius **Maximus** and C. Trebonius for the last three months of 45 BC and the promise of consulships for Antony and Dolabella (Suet. *Caesar* 80.2; Dio 43.46.2). Caesar had made so many promises that he had to increase the number of posts, which were thereby devalued: fourteen praetors and forty quaestors were elected in 45 BC, and sixteen praetors in 44 BC. Caesar in fact rejected the right to designate the magistrates, and the tribune L. Antonius gave him the right to recommend half the candidates except for the consulships. Additionally, after he had been appointed to his command against the Parthians, Caesar was authorised to appoint officials for three years: these included A. Hirtius and C. Pansa as consuls for 43 BC, Decimus Brutus and L. Munatius Plancus for 42 BC (the details are doubted by Yavetz 129-30). The senate, meanwhile, was increased to 900, with new members including the sons of freedmen, centurions and Celts (see Yavetz 168-72); and Caesar also received the right to appoint patricians* (these included Octavius).

When the consul Maximus died Caesar revealed the contempt in which he now held the offices of Rome. The assembly met to elect quaestors on 31 December 45 BC, but on hearing the news of Maximus' death Caesar had C. **Caninius** Rebilus (**Rebilius**) elected consul after lunch, and although Cicero could jest, he was also greatly upset (Cic. *Fam.* 7.30.1-2 with different quips; Suet. *Caesar* 76.2; Dio 43.46.2-4).

Once again, the idea that **Caesar was born to do great things** should not be extended to suggest that he actually planned them from the start (ch. 28n.). It was clear, however, that he **had made his plans** for further enterprises before his assassination, including **an expedition against the Parthians** of which he had already been given the command. The excuse for the invasion was Parthian support of Q. Bassus in Apamea against Caesar's legate C. Vetus, but the Romans had a burning desire to avenge the defeat of Crassus in 53 BC. That Caesar was not attempting to conquer Parthia as a whole is suggested by his proposed subsequent **march** (via southern Russia, **the Caspian Sea, the Caucasus** and thence presumably along the Danube to Gaul) and the length of three years for the expedition. See further McDermott, W.C., 'Caesar's Projected Dacian-Parthian Expedition' *Anc. Soc.* 14 (1983) pp. 223-31. During his preparations the rumour spread of a prophecy **in the Sibylline books that Parthia could only be conquered...by a king** (ch. 60); and that L. Cotta, one of those responsible for oracles and a cousin of Caesar's mother, therefore intended to propose on 15 March that Caesar be declared king in the provinces (ch. 64; Cic. *Div.* 2.110; Suet. *Caesar* 79.4; App. *BC* 2.110; Dio 44.15.3-4). This and other false rumours increased suspicions of Caesar's monarchical intentions. See further ch. 60n.; Yavetz 201. On the Sibylline books see *OCD* s.v. Sibylla.

Other grandiose schemes (a clear parallel to Alexander's 'Last Plans') included **a canal through the isthmus of Corinth**, which would improve west-east trade and communications, and another from **the Tiber** to **Terracina**, which would drain the Pomptine **marshes**. The new waterway would also improve trade, and Caesar wished to extend the harbour **at Ostia** and build a road across the Apennines to the Adriatic. More arable land would be secured by draining the Fucine Lake. In the city, whose boundary (*pomerium*) he extended, Caesar planned to build up the Campus Martius with a huge temple to the god, erect an enormous theatre against the Tarpeian Rock and open the Vatican plain by diverting the Tiber. Finally, M. Varro was to assemble a collection of the whole of Greek and Latin literature, and the civil law was to be codified (see Yavetz 159-60).

Chapter 59

Caesar's **reform of the calendar** was long overdue, the discrepancy between the official and actual dates now being over two months. It was to last until AD 1582, when Pope Gregory XIII solved the problem of the gap of eleven days between the astronomical and Julian years. Caesar replaced the traditional **lunar** year from 1 January 45 BC with **the solar year** of 365¼ days, inserting sixty-seven days between November and December 46 BC (the calculations were made by the Greek Sosigenes). The reform also had political implications, since previously priests could vary the length of years at will (*Pompey* 58n.). Hence even this reform could be attacked. See further Yavetz 111-14. The invention of intercalation was attributed to **King Numa** (*Numa* 18.1-2) or Servius Tullius (Macrob. 1.13-14).

Chapter 60

If we can believe Suetonius and his (hostile) source T. Ampius Balbus,

Caesar said 'that the Republic was nothing – a mere name without form or substance' (Suet. *Caesar* 77). He would not tolerate opposition to his actions, and his long absences from Rome distanced him in more ways than one from Republican ideals (cf. ch. 47n.). So although Caesar was ready to be conciliatory to the senate, he equally had no intention of giving up his power, and as honours and powers were heaped on him, Caesar's position became increasingly isolated. The excesses of his triumphs and celebrations fuelled resentment, his treatment of the senate was deeply offensive, and his actions finally began to alienate even **the common people** (ch. 56n.).

After his final set of divine and **extravagant honours had been voted** (ch. 57n.), the senate went to inform Caesar of these in his new forum. Caesar remained seated, and his remark and whole **conduct** were badly received. He therefore **excused his behaviour** by saying that he had suffered another epileptic attack (this was probably genuine: Dio 44.8.3 says he was suffering from diarrhoea, which is consistent with epilepsy; for his fits see 17n.). The implication of **Balbus** (or C. Trebatius) in this is also found in Suetonius (*Caesar* 78.1). Further on Balbus see ch. 17n.; and on this episode Yavetz 197-8.

Dio's view (43.45.1) is that his extraordinary honours had virtually made Caesar a monarch. Caesar refused the proposal to grant him this title, which had been cursed, but there were contrary signs (e.g. Caesar sometimes wore tall red boots like the Alban kings, a right he claimed as the descendant of Aeneas' son Iulus). Then one of Caesar's statues on the rostra was found to have been **decorated with** a laurel wreath interwoven with a white fillet (ch. 61; App. *BC* 2.108; Dio 44.9). The tribunes L. Caesetius Flavus (**Flavius** ch. 61) and C. Epidius **Marullus** had the diadem removed and the culprit imprisoned, and although annoyed Caesar said nothing. Dio attributes this act to the conspirators, but it is possible that Caesar himself was responsible, testing the people's reaction. Next, when returning from the Alban Hill on 26 January, Caesar was greeted by some spectators as '**King**'. He replied **that his name was not King** (*Rex*, the cognomen or surname of one branch of the Marcii) **but Caesar**, and Flavus and Marullus again had the man responsible for the original utterance removed for prosecution (App. ibid.; Dio 44.10). At this point Caesar showed his disapproval of the tribunes, whom he thought to be behind these incidents, and when they issued an edict that they were unable properly to carry out their duties, Caesar had them removed from office and expelled from the senate, on the motion of Helvius Cinna (ch. 68n.). This act, however, only damaged Caesar's reputation further. On the false rumours of a prophecy **in the Sibylline books** see ch. 58n. For a discussion of whether Caesar really had a **passion to be made King** see Yavetz 201-12; and further on Plutarch's account of the assassination see Intro. 3.

Chapter 61

For Caesar's **insulting treatment of the tribunes** see ch. 60n. L. Iunius **Brutus** was traditionally the founder of the Republic in 509 BC (cf. *Publicola* 1-10). 'Brutus' in Latin meant 'stupid' (id. 3.4), and the **Cymaeans** of Asia Minor were celebrated for their stupidity (Strabo 13.3.6).

The tribunes episode had nothing to do with that on 15 February at **the Lupercalia**. Antony twice presented Caesar, now dictator for life, with **a diadem**, which he refused to accept and had **carried to the Capitol**, since Jupiter was the only king of the Romans. Caesar also had this recorded in the official records (*Fasti*; cf. *Antony* 12.1-3 with Pelling). The motive for Antony's action has been debated since antiquity. Was Caesar testing the people's reaction or showing that he did not want the kingship? Was Antony acting on Caesar's orders or to expose him or with a genuine wish for Caesar to be king? Plutarch's view in the *Caesar* is that Caesar wanted the title, and this was an **experiment** that **proved a failure** (and the initial **applause...was not spontaneous**), in the *Antony*, where Plutarch's purpose is different, Antony acts independently (see Pelling [2] 144-5). Dio's account (44.11.1-3) implies that Caesar was in fact wearing his regal dress rather than **a triumphal robe**, while Cicero says he was already wearing a crown (*Phil.* 2.85). The **golden throne** (ch. 57n.) was one of the honours which caused offence and may be represented on coins of 43 BC (but see Crawford, M.H., *Roman Republican Coinage* [Cambridge, 1974] no. 491).

The origins of **the Lupercalia** are obscure, in one version being founded by Romulus (*Romulus* 21.3-5; see Ogilvie on Livy 1.5.1-2). Plutarch often explains a Roman name (**the Arcadian Lycaea**) for his Greek readers (see Wardman 37-48).

Chapter 62

Those of the **people** who now looked to **Brutus** would have been clients of the old aristocrats, influenced by the anti-Caesarian propaganda (see Yavetz 200). For Brutus, supposedly **a descendant of the Brutus** of ch. 61, see The Family of Caesar Stemma on p. vi. Reconciled with Caesar after **Pharsalus** (ch. 46n.) he had helped secure the life of his brother-in-law Cassius (*Brutus* 6.3; Cassius married Iunia, Brutus' sister). Caesar then appointed him governor of Cisalpine Gaul, and promised him the urban praetorship of 44 BC and consulship of 41 BC (ch. 57, *Brutus* 6.6-7.3, 8.2 for the **skin** remark; App. *BC* 2.111-12). After his pardon Cassius became a legate of Caesar and peregrine praetor in 44 BC (*Brutus* 7.1-3, with Caesar's remark); but he voted against the last group of Caesar's honours (ch. 57n.), and hated and was suspected by Caesar

(*Brutus* 8, with the **fat, long-haired people** remark, cf. *Antony* 11.3 with Pelling). For **the messages** cf. *Brutus* 9.3; and on **Dolabella** see chs 51, 58nn.

The true motives for the plot have given rise to much speculation, but the portrayal of Caesar in Plutarch and other sources as the hated tyrant still provides the most convincing explanation. The origins of the plot, and its originators, are equally obscure, Plutarch suggesting that it was Cassius who urged on Brutus (*Brutus* 8.3). Nor did the 'Liberators' have clear plans for the future (see Yavetz 191-2).

Chapter 63

For the omens foreboding evil cf. Suet. Caesar 81.1-3; App. BC 2.115. The stories related by the historian, geographer and philosopher Strabo may come from his Historical Commentaries (Lucullus 28.7). The soothsayer who warned Caesar to beware the Ides (15 March) was named Spurinna.

For Caesar's views on death see ch. 57n. The dinner with Lepidus is also recorded by Suetonius (Caesar 87) and, with a different version, Appian (BC 2.115). On Caesar's marriage to Calpurnia see Pompey 47n. As for the gable-ornament, the relevant book of Livy (116) does not survive.

Chapter 64

Plutarch seems to be correct in suggesting that the conspirators feared **the whole plot would come to light** if they delayed, and they had to hurry because Caesar was about to leave for Parthia on 18 March. See Horsfall, N., 'The Ides of March: Some New Problems' *G&R* 21 (1974) pp. 191-9. It was probably late February or early March before the conspirators made the final decision to assassinate Caesar, prompted by his summoning of the senate on that day to discuss Dolabella's election to the consulship (cf. also the rumour that L. Cotta intended to propose Caesar **be declared King of all the provinces**, ch. 58n.).

For Caesar's **will** see ch. 56n. **Decimus Brutus** was heir in **the second** degree (Suet. *Caesar* 83.2). The **slave belonging to someone else** (in the Greek *oiketes allotrios*) is in Appian (*BC* 2.116) one of Caesar's intimates (*ton oikeion tis autoi*).

Chapter 65

For **Artemidorus** cf. Suet. *Caesar* 81.4; App. *BC* 2.116; Dio 44.18.3. This 'if only x had happened' type of story adds drama and suspense as events approach their climax.

Chapter 66

The drama of the assassination also afforded Plutarch the opportunity to comment on the role of daemons: **some heavenly power** was working to ensure that the murder **should take place** by **a statue of Pompey** (N.B. Plutarch twice gives an alternative to the role of **chance** in this chapter). The full dramatic irony of this is brought out near the end of the piece, as Caesar falls **against the pedestal** of the statue and Pompey receives **vengeance**.The tragic content and imagery of the chapter are indeed marked. Caesar loses his reason and is filled with **emotion that was...divinely inspired**, while Casca is **much disturbed in mind**; the non-conspirators are **horror-struck** and Caesar is **like a wild beast**, while the assassins are engaged in a **sacrifice**. Thus the tragedy begun by Caesar's *hamartia* at the Rubicon (ch. 32) reaches its fulfilment.

For Pompey's **statue**, his new senate **building** and **his theatre** see *Pompey* 40n. It is in fact Cassius (not **Caesar**) that Plutarch says **was a follower of the doctrines of Epicurus**, the famous Athenian philosopher (341-270 BC). One of these was the theory that the gods have no concern with man's affairs. On Plutarch's anti-Epicurean views see Russell 67-8.

It was also in fact C. Trebonius who **detained** Antony (as in *Brutus* 17.1): Plutarch has made an error, perhaps of memory (see Pelling [1] 79). Caesar, meanwhile, took the auspices, which were unfavourable, and entered the senate. Pretending **to support the petition** of L. **Tillius Cimber** (? pr. 45 BC) for the recall of his exiled **brother**, the conspirators crowded round Caesar and Tillius began **the attack (the signal** is similar to the one Caesar himself was to have given in the alleged conspiracy of 66 BC; see Weinstock 347). The tribune C. Servilius **Casca** struck **the first blow** and **called to his brother** P. Casca Longus **in Greek** (i.e. Greek and the tyrannicides conquer Latin and the tyrant); and Caesar gave up his struggle **when he saw that Brutus had drawn his dagger** (*Brutus* 17.2-4; Suet. *Caesar* 82.1-3 and Dio 44.19.2-5 have 'You too, my son'). See further Dubuisson, M., 'Toi aussi mon fils!' *Latomus* 39 (1980) pp. 881-90.

Chapter 67

The immediate result of the assassination was that terror gripped Rome, but the precise sequence of events is uncertain (cf. *Antony* 14 with Pelling). Plutarch here transfers Brutus' **speech** from 15 to 16 March, and omits a day by putting the meeting of **the senate** on the 16th instead of the 17th. A more likely order of events is as follows. The senators did not wait to hear Brutus but **fled**, so he and the other conspirators **marched...to the Capitol**, protected by D. Brutus' gladiators (on these see Horsfall, *G&R* 21 [1974] p. 195). The occupation of the Capitol had symbolic, anti-tyrannical significance, since there stood Jupiter's temple, traditionally dedicated in the first year of the Republic after the overthrow of the tyrannical Tarquinius Superbus. They were joined on the way by, among others, Dolabella, **Gaius Octavius** Balbus **and Lentulus Spinther** (on Balbus cf. Val. Max. 5.7.3; App. *BC* 4.21; Spinther probably died at Philippi; **young Caesar** is Octavian). Returning that day to the forum, **Brutus made a speech** to sound out the views of the people and was heard in **complete silence**, but when the praetor L. Cornelius Cinna attacked Caesar, the crowd were incensed. The 'Liberators' returned to the Capitol and in the evening began negotiating with **Antony and Lepidus**. In the hostile tradition Antony, saved by Brutus, had donned the dress of a slave and barricaded himself in his own house, while Lepidus rushed to the island in the Tiber, where he had a legion, and prepared to support Antony. During the night the troops occupied the forum, and Antony received Caesar's papers from Calpurnia; he then summoned the senate to meet on 17 March. Lepidus and Caesar's agent Balbus wanted to attack the Capitol, but Hirtius and Antony preferred conciliation. At the meeting of the senate Antony's speech for compromise was supported by Cicero and L. Munatius Plancus, and it was decided that Caesar's acts should be ratified but his assassins should be given an **amnesty** (according to *Cicero* 42.3 in imitation of the Athenians, who declared an amnesty after the overthrow of the Thirty Tyrants in 403 BC). Further, Caesar was to be given a public funeral, and his will was to be read (ch. 68). The conspirators then returned to the forum, accepting the sons of Antony and Lepidus as hostages.

It was not in fact **voted that Caesar should be worshipped as a god** until about 1 January 42 BC; nor were **provinces and appropriate honours** bestowed on the conspirators. Brutus and Cassius were not offered their provinces until August; and Caesar had already assigned Trebonius, Cimber and D. Brutus their provinces, which will have been confirmed with the rest of his acts (so too the consulship of Dolabella, which Antony had opposed but now permitted).

Chapter 68

Caesar's will was opened in Antony's house, and its main beneficiary was Caesar's great-nephew C. Octavius, who took the name Caesar (*Cicero* 44.6; Suet. *Caesar* 83; ch. 56n.). Antony was a second-degree heir. The **legacy** included 300 HS **to each Roman citizen** (120 HS, Dio 44.35.3). Caesar's funeral was probably held on the next day (20 March), and the ensuing violence was, according to Cicero (*Phil.* 2.91), caused by Antony's emotional speech (cf. *Cicero* 42.3-5; Suet. *Caesar*

84-5; Pelling [4] 153-4). C. Helvius **Cinna** (tr. 44 BC) was murdered by mistake for L. Cornelius Cinna, who had made an inflammatory speech after the assassination (ch. 67n.). Cf. *Brutus* 20.5-6; App. *BC* 2.147. Helvius had tabled the motion deposing Flavus and Marullus from their tribunates (ch. 60n.), and supposedly proposed that Caesar should be allowed to marry any women he pleased to procreate children.

Brutus and Cassius did not leave Rome for Latium until early April; for the story of **what happened to them** cf. *Brutus* 21.

Chapter 69

Plutarch ends the *Life* with notable tragic and theological elements. Caesar, like other Roman statesmen, clearly believed in the great power of fortune in men's affairs, which protected him in the fishing boat (ch. 38n.). Plutarch, who was interested in fortune for the light it shed on a man's character, here stresses the role of Caesar's guiding *daimon* (**genius**), which **helped him in his life** and avenged his **murder, visiting** the assassins with **retribution**. These spirits could also be malignant, however, as in ch. 66 (see Wardman 74); and Caesar's guardian *daimon* is then fused with Brutus' **evil genius**. In the *Brutus* version of the story (37.3) Cassius doubts the existence of *daimones*, and Russell concludes (p. 78) that Plutarch had no firm system of 'demonology'.

Despite Caesar's unpopularity the conspirators made a serious error in assuming that his murder would win popular favour. The events in 44/3 BC after the assassination are outlined in *Cicero* 43-9nn. Brutus and Cassius overran Asia Minor and reached the Hellespont by September 42 BC. Antony and Octavian went to meet them **at Philippi** in Macedonia, and **after his defeat** in the first battle there Cassius **killed himself**. Brutus was defeated three weeks later, and he too committed suicide. Cf. especially *Brutus* 41-2 (**the first battle**), 43 (the death of Cassius; cf. *Antony* 22.3), 36.3-4 (**the phantom** at Abydos), 48.1 (the second visit of **the same phantom**), 49-52 (**the second battle** and Brutus' suicide; cf. *Antony* 22.4). For this typical ending with moral redress see *Pompey* 80n.

Caesar was not quite **fifty-six...when he died** (ch. 1n.). **The great comet** appeared on the first day of the games given by Octavian to honour his apotheosis; it was therefore held to be Caesar's soul being elevated to heaven, and a star was placed on the head of his statues.

Cicero

Chapter 1

M. Tullius Cicero was born on 3 January 106 BC in Arpinum, birthplace
of C. Marius. Arpinum had been granted full Roman citizenship in 188
BC, and its local nobility, mainly the Gratidii, Marii and Tullii Cicerones, would have had equestrian* status at Rome (e.g. ch. 11).
Cicero's enemies alleged that **his father...was born and bred in a fuller's shop**, and a connection with the cloth business is suggested by *CIL*
10.5678. However, low birth was a common type of slur (ch. 26, *Demosthenes* 4.2; N.B. fullers used urine), and the family certainly was important by the time of Cicero's grandfather, who married into the Gratidii.
The derivation of '**Cicero**' from **the Latin word for a chick-pea** may
also, in fact, suggest a respectable agricultural ancestry; but little reliance can be placed on the connection with Attius Tullius (**Tullus
Attius**), who traditionally had aided Coriolanus in the early fifth century
(*Coriolanus* 22). Cicero himself jokes that he was related to King Servius Tullius (*Tusc.* 1.38). **Cicero's mother, Helvia**, is only referred to
once by him and again by his brother Quintus (*Att.* 11.9.3, *Fam.*
16.26.2). His father, also called M. Tullius Cicero, suffered from poor
health and spent most of his time studying in Arpinum (Cic. *De Leg.*
2.3). He was a client*of the Scauri and Catuli, hence Cicero's **spirited
reply** (also **Scaurus** = 'swollen-ankled', **Catulus** = 'puppy'). The reference is to M. Aemilius Scaurus (cos. 115 BC) and Q. Lutatius Catulus
(cos. 102 BC) or his son of the same name (cos. 78 BC). For Cicero's
quaestorship in Sicily see ch. 6n.

Note that Cicero is given advice by **his friends** (sim. chs 3, 4, 5, 20,
31, 33, 43, 46). These episodes are designed to reflect Cicero's moral
progress, and other themes of the *Cicero* are his lack of daring and
inordinate caution, boastfulness, wit and excessive ambition (see
Moles). His witty remarks and jokes (chs 5, 7, 9, 25-7, 38) will derive
from the collection of his freedman Tiro (Quint. 6.3.2-5).

Chapter 2

The ease of Cicero's **birth** was a good omen. Other allusions to **the**

present time occur in chs 13, 48, *Pompey* 24.5.

Unlike his Greek parallel (*Demosthenes* 8.3) Cicero possessed great **natural abilities**, even at **the age** of about seven. This applied to **poetry** as well as oratory (ch. 40, a prodigious **500 lines...in a night**), and an early influence on Cicero was the Greek poet Archias (ch. 24n.). His works included an heroic poem on Marius and the much derided epic on his consulship (chs 20, 30nn.). The *Pontius Glaucus* was the tale of a Boeotian fisherman who jumped into the sea and became a sea-god (Ovid, *Met.* 13.920-68). Despite Plutarch, the ancients' verdict on Cicero's poetry was generally hostile.

Plutarch's reference to Plato closely follows *Republic* 5.475B-C; Cicero's attitude to learning was similar (*Fam.* 4.4.4).

Chapter 3

When his school days were over, Cicero went to Rome to study rhetoric and law in **the circle of** Q. **Mucius Scaevola**, who was from 90 to c. 87 BC leader of **the senate** (*princeps senatus*; cos. 117 BC); and on his death in the circle of Scaevola's cousin, the Chief Pontiff of the same name (cos. 95 BC; Plutarch's main source in chs 3-4 is Cic. *Brutus* 303-22). This brought him into contact with two of Rome's leading orators, L. Licinius Crassus and M. Antonius; and other members of the circle were Q. Cicero, the sons of Crassus' intimate C. Visellius Aculeo, whose wife was the sister of Cicero's mother, and probably T. Pomponius, whose extended residence at Athens later earned him the name Atticus. It was in 88 BC at the start of the Mithridatic War that Philo (**Philon**), who had taken over the leadership of Plato's Academy from **Cleitomachus** in 110 BC, fled to Rome: on Plutarch's inversion of the temporal order see Moles.

During his apprenticeship the Social War broke out against Rome's Italian allies, and in 89 BC the seventeen-year-old Cicero began his **military service** under Pompey's father Strabo (Cic. *Phil.* 12.27). He thus met Pompey and probably Catiline, and then served **under Sulla** in Campania **against the Marsians**, the leaders of the revolt (Cic. *Div.* 1.72). In the civil war of 87-82BC, which ended in **the unlimited power** of Sulla, Cicero went back to **his studies**, significantly under the Stoic Diodotus, and learned dialectic (logical argument) and the rhetorical exercise declamation. The political situation in Rome at this time caused a delay in the beginning of Cicero's legal career, and so when he started he was already trained. In 81 BC Cicero began studying under the rhetorician Molon of Rhodes, and he had by then written his first rhetorical work, *On Invention*. The leading orator at Rome was now Q. Hortensius Hortalus, and he was Cicero's opponent when he defended P. Quinctius in 81 BC (*Pro Quinctio*). Cicero made his name, however, in 80 BC with his successful defence of Sex. **Roscius** of Ameria against a charge of parricide (*Pro Roscio Amerino*). Plutarch's account contains inaccuracies, in particular the implication that Sulla and Cicero were directly opposed (see Moles). It was in fact Erucius who **indicted Roscius for...murder** (*Rosc.* 35), and according to Cicero Sulla himself was completely free from guilt (id. 21, 25). Nevertheless, the involvement of his influential freedman L. Cornelius **Chrysogonus** in the conspiracy against Roscius was expected to deter any **lawyer** from taking on the case, and it was again **Cicero's friends** who emboldened him (ch. 1n.).

Sulla's lists of the condemned were the infamous proscriptions of 82-1 BC, by which the outlawed victim's property was **put up for auction** on public notices. Chrysogonus **bought the property** in fact for 2,000 HS (Cic. *Rosc.* 6, 21; i.e. 500 drachmas), when it was valued at 6 million HS (= **250 talents**). Cicero's willingness to **help** reflects his humanity (see Moles). He **was greatly admired for** his defence, but there is no evidence that the nobles* who were linked with Roscius therefore helped Cicero's career (see Rawson 23-4). Equally, we should not put much trust (if any) in Plutarch's contention that Cicero was now **afraid of Sulla** (see Moles). Cicero says he followed the defence of Roscius with 'many other cases', and **went abroad to Greece** in 79 BC **for the sake of his health** and oratorical studies (*Brut.* 312-14, simplified here by Plutarch).

Chapter 4

Cicero may by now have married the very young Terentia, but she would have been left behind as he spent six months **in Athens** with his brother, younger cousin L. Cicero and perhaps Ser. Sulpicius, studying under the leading Academic of the time, **Antiochus of Ascalon** in Palestine. The **position of the New Academy** was the impossibility of knowledge (scepticism; i.e. **sense perception is** *not* **reliable**), a doctrine expounded by **Carneades** of Cyrene (213-128 BC). This was challenged by Antiochus, who promoted the doctrines of the Old Academy but was influenced **in most respects** by Stoicism. He therefore **quarrelled with the disciples of Cleitomachus and** Philo, whose stance was that the New Academy was simply a continuation of the Old. Cicero himself **loved the doctrines of the New Academy** (e.g. *Acad.* 1.13), but there is no reason to believe that **he planned** to **retire to Athens** and pursue **philosophy**.

On his two-year trip abroad Cicero also attended lectures on Epicureanism and according to Plutarch **consulted the god at Delphi** (ch. 5), though this is doubtful since Cicero himself never mentions it. With Quintus he toured **Asia** Minor and **Rhodes** to study with **the best-known rhetoricians**; and at Smyrna he also met Rutilius Rufus (*Pompey*

37n.). In Rhodes Cicero met the Stoic **Poseidonius** (*Pompey* 42n.), but the purpose of this part of the trip was to resume his rhetorical studies under **Apollonius** Molon (ch. 3n.), who also taught Caesar (*Caesar* 3.1). It was he who ironed out the remaining faults in Cicero's style (for oratory likened to **equipment** cf. *Pericles* 8.1, *Cato* 4.2; see Moles); and Cicero was then ready to return to Rome, which had nothing to do with **Sulla's death** or the urging of **his friends** and of **Antiochus** (further on the role of Cicero's friends see ch. 1n.).

The names of Cicero's other teachers come from *Brut.* 315-16. **Xenocles of Adramyttium** in Mysia was a famous orator in the florid 'Asianist' style; **Dionysius of Magnesia** in Lydia is otherwise unknown; **Menippus** of Stratonicea was in Cicero's judgment 'the most eloquent man of all Asia in that time'.

The Apollonius story is also found in *De Vir. Ill.* 81.2. The foremost Greek teachers **did not understand Latin** (*Brut.* 310); for Rome's taking over of Greece's remaining glories cf. *Brut.* 254.

Chapter 5

For Cicero's visit to **Delphi** see ch. 4n. The **oracle** checked the excessive **eagerness** which for Plutarch was one of Cicero's traits (see Moles). Cicero's **own nature** was **ambitious**, and the point of the oracle is that he should avoid the corrupt ambition which comes with being guided by **popular opinion**. See Flaclière, R., 'Cicéron à Delphes?' *Bull. Corr. Hell.* suppl. 4 (Paris, 1977) pp. 159-60.

After he returned to **Rome** in 77 BC, Cicero did not remain quiet but put his oratorical training to further use, and his **caution** is a part of Plutarch's characterisation (see Moles; for the encouragement of **his father and...friends** see ch. 1n.). Cicero did not yet have any popular appeal, however, hence **people called him...names. Greek** here implies effete, and his reputation as a philhellene could be held against Cicero, since many Romans despised the Greeks.

Cicero did not **at once** reach **the top** in his **work as an advocate**, rivalled as he was by C. Aurelius Cotta and especially Hortensius, but he was learning fast and overcame his **elocution** problem in the manner of **Demosthenes** (*Demosthenes* 6-7; he was helped by the actor Satyrus). For the similarity between oratory and acting cf. Cic. *De Orat.* 1.128. **Roscius the comedian** (Q. Roscius Gallus) was a famous actor and friend of Cicero, and asked him to defend Quinctius (ch. 3n.). He was himself to be defended by Cicero (*Pro Roscio Comoedo*). On Claudius Aesopus (**Aesop**), another friend of Cicero, cf. Cic. *Sest.* 120-3, *Tusc.* 4.55 (on Accius' *Atreus*); Hor. *Ep.* 2.1.82 (Plutarch's story is not attested elsewhere). **Atreus** took his **revenge on Thyestes** (his brother, who had an affair with Atreus' wife Aerope and thereby secured the golden ram, the possession of which carried the kingship of Mycenae) by serving up at a banquet the flesh of Thyestes' own children.

For Cicero the effect of oratorical devices depends on **delivery** (*De Orat.* 3.213); his own was on the slow side. **Ready wit** was also important (id. 2.216-34; cf. the *Pro Murena*; ch. 17n.), and Cicero's was famous (ch. 1n.) – but he carried it too far (chs 25, 27nn.). For other criticisms of Cicero cf. chs 6, 24, 25, 27, 32, 38, 41, 46.

Chapter 6

Cicero **was appointed quaestor** for 75 BC at the age of thirty. His **province** was western **Sicily** under the propraetorian governor Sex. Peducaeus, who was based at Syracuse. Cicero himself was based at Lilybaeum as a virtual deputy-governor (he was not a **governor**), and from there he administered the **grain** supply. Cicero's **careful management of affairs** won him unprecedented honours, as he himself says (*Planc.* 64-5; cf. ch. 1, *Comp. Dem. Cic.* 3.3). While in Sicily Cicero proudly discovered the tomb of Archimedes and took the opportunity of establishing a *clientela** there. He also defended some well-born **young men from Rome** (this incident and **the war** are otherwise unknown).

Cicero's **amusing experience**, of which Plutarch gives a simplified account, happened at Puteoli (*Planc.* 65). Plutarch invents the **well-known man** (Cicero's version has two strangers), and Cicero himself was in fact asked about news **in Rome**. The moral Cicero drew was that he should take care to be seen everyday, but Plutarch takes the opportunity to criticise him again, reiterating the dangers of ambition (Cicero's concern with fame and reputation **very often** affected his **policies**; cf. chs 24, 25, 27, 28, 32, 37, 38, 45; see Moles).

Chapter 7

Cicero returned to Rome in 74 BC and later felt that his oratory had at this stage reached 'full development and a certain maturity' (*Brut.* 318). All the while he was training himself **to memorize** the **names** both of the **important** people whose influence he would need to further his political career and of his clients* (Roman politicians, including Cicero, used a nomenclator, a slave who would prompt his master on the names of people he met). Then in 70 BC Cicero stood for the plebeian aedileship, avoiding the tribunate.

Cicero's **fortune was** only **small** in comparison with those of the great capitalists (ch. 8, *Comp. Dem. Cic.* 3.3). He had inheritances worth more than 20 million HS (chs 8, 41; Cic. *Phil.* 2.40), his wife was wealthy and he owned houses in Rome and Arpinum, as well as several villas elsewhere (ch. 8n.). Nevertheless, he was often in debt (ch. 41). By the Cincian law of 204 BC **an advocate** was not allowed to take **fees**: rather he would accept **gifts** and inheritances, and would expect political support in return **for his services**; and Cicero himself took gifts (ch. 8).

The famous **prosecution against Verres** took place in August 70 BC. C. Verres was propraetor in **Sicily** from 73 to 71 BC, and his notorious exactions led to his trial for extortion. Although he was defended by **Hortensius**, Cicero produced so much damning evidence against him that he abandoned his defence before Cicero's second *Verrine* **speech** was delivered. Plutarch's version is confused. The presiding praetor in 70 BC, M'. Acilius Glabrio, was not **doing what** he **could for Verres** but was honest (*Verr.* 1.29), and the **various methods of postponement** were attempted by Verres' friends. The aim was to delay the trial until 69 BC, when one of these friends, M. Metellus, would be praetor and president of the court, and Hortensius and Q. Metellus would be consuls. Cicero therefore collected the evidence in Sicily in half the allotted time; and instead of a long opening speech he put forward the evidence in a brief introduction, then **called his witnesses** (id. 1.55). Verres was condemned on 14 August, two days before Pompey's Games began – and little judicial business would be conducted in the rest of the year due to festivals.

Cicero competed for the right to prosecute with Q. **Caecilius** Niger, who planned to collude with Verres (whose quaestor he had been; cf. the *Divinatio in Caecilium*). The point of the **Jew/pig** remark is simply that *verres* is Latin for a male pig (Plutarch in mentioning that the **boar** is **castrated** is thinking of circumcision). 'Soft' is a better rendering of the Greek *malakia* than **not a robust character** and brings out the idea of effeminacy. Hortensius withdrew his defence in the face of Cicero's devastating opening, and Plutarch exaggerates his venality (to contrast him with Cicero) by saying **the sphinx** was **made of ivory** (bronze in Quint. 6.3.98; the monstrous sphinx asked the Thebans the riddle about the three ages of man, and after each failed attempt to solve it devoured one of them, until the riddle was solved by Oedipus). Further on this trial see Stockton 43-9; Rawson 40-3; *Pompey* 22n.

Chapter 8

Cicero must have **assessed the fine at** much more than **750,000 denarii** (= 3 million HS) – he estimated the losses to the Sicilians at 100 million or 40 million HS (*Div. in Caec.* 19, *Verr.* 1.56). His gifts from **the Sicilians** reflect the regular practice of Roman advocates (ch. 7n.), but Plutarch stresses Cicero's rectitude by saying that he himself made **no profit**.

Cicero gave the usual games as **aedile**, though these were not spectacular, and pursued his career as a defence lawyer. When Hortensius retired, Cicero became the supreme pleader.

On Cicero's estates and wealth see ch. 7n. The Greek says Arpi in Apulia not **Arpinum** in Latium; the **farm** put vaguely **near Naples** is probably Cicero's villa at Cumae but possibly that at Puteoli; for that at **Pompeii** cf. *Att*. 1.20.1. Note also Cicero's villas at Tusculum (ch. 40) and Formiae. **Terentia** had a half-sister or cousin who was a Vestal Virgin (ch. 10n.), was probably herself of patrician* birth and certainly was very wealthy (hence the size of her **dowry**, 400,000 HS; Moles' text has 120,000 denarii, = 480,000 HS). Cicero as a 'new man'* needed such a connection, and the marriage was successful despite his wife's formidable nature (chs 20, 29, *Cato* 19.3). The **legacy** of **90,000** denarii (= 360,000 HS) may be that of *Att*. 14.10.3, 11.2. His **Greek** associates included Diodotus and Archias, the **Roman** ones Atticus and Varro. On Cicero's **health** see ch. 3n.

The house of Cicero's **father** was in the fashionable *Carinae* quarter on the Esquiline Hill. Cicero did not buy his house on **the Palatine** overlooking the forum until 62 BC (ch. 24n.), and the motive for this move is also attributed to Marius (*Marius* 32.1). Nor will Cicero's **visitors** have been as numerous as those of **Crassus** or **Pompey** (see Moles), and Pompey did not court Cicero until 66 BC (*Pompey* 30n.).

Chapter 9

Cicero **stood for the praetorship** of 66 BC, and after two interruptions to the voting he **came out at the top of the poll** for the third time (Cic. *Leg. Man.* 2). In 67 BC Cicero was amongst the opposition to the tribune Cornelius (*Pompey* 23n.), but he was in favour of Gabinius' bill giving Pompey the command against the pirates (id. 25-6nn.). This might win Pompey's support for Cicero's eventual candidature for the consulship, and Cicero went further in this direction by speaking for the Manilian law (id. 30n.).

In 66 BC Cicero delivered one of his most admired speeches, the *Pro Cluentio*, in which for the first time he promulgates his programme of the 'concord of the orders' (*concordia ordinum; Cluent*. 152-4). As praetor he was also president of the **extortion** court and **handled the legal cases** of some popular politicians; and his reputation with the people remained intact when the historian C. **Licinius Macer**, who was **supported by Crassus**, was **convicted** (Cic. *Att*. 1.4.2). Macer, who wore mourning clothes and his hair long during the trial, presumably **died** of a heart attack, though Valerius Maximus (9.12.7) says he choked himself with his handkerchief. Cicero's treatment of **Manilius** on the other hand aroused **great popular indignation** (**ten days** was in fact the normal period), and he was forced to promise that he would **take on personally the defence of Manilius**. Further on this trial, for extortion not **peculation**, see Seager 57-8. In 66 BC Cicero also took under his wing the young M. Caelius Rufus.

Manilius was eventually condemned in 65 BC for treason, despite being defended by Cicero, who then successfully defended Cornelius against a charge of treason. This increased Cicero's popularity as well as his favour with **Pompey (who was** in the East), but it displeased the Optimates*. In the same year Cicero opposed Crassus' attempt to annex Egypt in the *De Rege Alexandrino* (*Pompey* 42n.), but he was now concerned chiefly with his candidature for the consulship. The **speech in front of the people** (*contio*) was part of his attempt to win popular support, and **the oligarchical party** (i.e. the Optimates*) were in the event forced to back his candidacy (ch. 10).

On P. **Vatinius** and his **neck** cf. ch. 26. Cicero, who attacked Vatinius at the trial of Sestius in 56 BC (*In Vatinium*), was forced by Caesar and Pompey to defend him in 54 BC (ch. 26; Cic. *Fam.* 1.9.19). Vatinius was genuinely grateful.

Chapter 10

In his candidature for **the consulship** Cicero had Atticus to exert his influence on leading members of **the nobility*** such as Hortensius, Lucullus and the Metelli; and he could hope for the support of the absent Pompey and hence many **of the people** (on Pompey's **war with the kings in Pontus and Armenia** see *Pompey* 31-42nn.). Cicero also had influence with the equites*, young nobles* (through his patronage of men like Caelius) and the country towns. Nevertheless, **the nobility*** would nearly always oppose anyone with the status of a 'new man'*, and it was Cicero's good fortune that his candidacy coincided with that of L. Sergius Catilina (**Catiline**), whose election the nobility* was determined to prevent.

Catiline was notorious as a result of his actions under Sulla and as governor of Africa in 67-6 BC. His subsequent trial for extortion precluded his candidacy for the consulship of 65 BC, but he was acquitted. He was probably not involved in the 'First Catilinarian Conspiracy' and late in 64 BC was to be acquitted of murders committed during the Sullan proscriptions (*Caesar* 5, 7nn.). These allegedly included that of **his own brother** (cf. *Sulla* 32.2), or rather his brother-in-law Q. Caecilius, and of his stepson (Sall. *BC* 15.2). Also, he supposedly committed incest with **his own daughter** Orestilla, and was acquitted in 73 BC of seducing the Vestal Virgin Fabia, half-sister of Cicero's wife Terentia. The blackening of his character was largely due to Cicero (*Cat.* 1.26, *Cael.* 12-14) and Sallust (id. 5.1-8, 15-16), and their influence on Plutarch's account is evident. Plutarch's own conservative bias, however, is especially evident in this chapter.

The reasons for discontent at Rome in 63 BC stemmed from the war in the East, which led to a shortage of money in the city. Further, many of Sulla's veterans, who had settled in **Etruria** and other parts of Italy, had financial problems, and those who had been dispossessed had grievances, so too the sons of the proscribed; and many nobles* were in debt through extravagance.

Another factor which should be borne in mind was the imminent return of Pompey (*Pompey* 43n.). There were fears that he might make an attempt at dictatorship, and this would be facilitated if Catiline were consul (giving him an excuse for armed intervention). Equally, Pompey's absence might be exploited by the **revolutionaries** (Sall. *BC* 16.5).

On the Sullan **constitution** see Keaveney ch. 9; it had been modified more than once already (*Pompey* 22n.). The conspirators' **pledges of faith** also allegedly included the drinking of human blood (Sall. *BC* 22.1; for the sacrifice cf. Dio 37.30.3). The corruption **of the young men** derives from Cic. *Cat.* 2.7-8, *Cael.* 12; Sall. id. 14.5-7. N.B. **rotten** is better translated as 'sick' to preserve the metaphor in the Greek (sim. chs 18, 36, 37; *Pompey* 55n.).

Chapter 11

Faced with the candidacies of Catiline and **Gaius Antonius** Hibrida, the Optimates* had little choice but to **put Cicero forward for the consulship**, despite his origins in the equestrian* class (sim. Sall. *BC* 23.5-6). Antonius had been expelled from the senate by the censors of 70 BC (*Pompey* 22n.) but had been re-elected praetor for 66 BC with Cicero's help. For his alliance with Catiline cf. ch. 12; Sall. id. 21.3. The supporters of Pompey helped ensure that Cicero came top of the poll, and he was justifiably proud of his achievement, accomplished in the earliest permitted year (*suo anno*).

That Catiline planned a revolution before 63 BC and that his candidacy was therefore designed **to obtain first a position of strength** is most unlikely. Note that Plutarch repeatedly employs a simple senate/people antithesis (sim. *Pompey* 21.4, 22.3, *Caesar* 14.3), and their acting in concert here is exceptional (see Pelling [3] 166-75).

Chapter 12

Cicero's **considerable preliminary difficulties** began with an agrarian bill of **the tribunes**, led by P. Servilius Rullus. Rullus proposed setting up **a commission of ten** for five years with praetorian (not **unlimited**)

123

power (*imperium**) throughout the empire. Only 17 of the 35 tribes chosen by lot were to be involved in the election of the commissioners, who were to raise money by the sale of **public land** both **in Italy** and abroad in order to buy land for distribution to the poor; they were also to **found new cities** (i.e. colonies; the other activities are not mentioned by Cicero). The beneficiaries would include Pompey's veterans, as well as the urban poor. Cicero in his speeches *De Lege Agraria* argued before **the senate** on 1 January and then **the people** that neither Pompey nor the people would benefit from the law: it interfered with Pompey's command in the East, and the commissioners were mere profiteers – Cicero himself was the true *popularis**. The people were swayed by Cicero's oratory, and the bill probably was never even put to the vote (*Pompey* 42n.).

Cicero implies that among the **eminent people** who supported Rullus' bill were Crassus and Caesar (*Leg. Agr.* 2.44), though Rullus was probably acting initially on Pompey's behalf. Antonius is connected with the tribunes by Dio (37.25.3) and suspected of involvement with Catiline by Cicero (*Sest.* 8). He was allotted Cisalpine **Gaul** as his province but received **Macedonia** from Cicero, a deal perhaps arranged in January (Sall. *BC* 26.4 with McGushin). Cicero also renounced his claim to Cisalpine Gaul, and remained in Rome to take **the chief rôle in the defence of their country** (similar imagery of first and second actors occurs in Cic. *Att.* 1.16.12, which Plutarch used as a source; see Moles). It was then Antonius who in November was given the command against Catiline in Etruria.

Plutarch's reference to Cicero's speech **before the people** may refer to a lost fourth speech, since at *Leg. Agr.* 3.1.1 **the tribunes** are absent. **The rest of the measures** included one to restore rights to the sons of the proscribed and cancel debts, which Cicero blocked (*Caesar* 7n.). For other acts of Cicero in this year see *Pompey* 42n.

Chapter 13

On the power of oratory, of which Cicero's speeches provide the ideal Roman example, cf. ch. 39, *Demosthenes* 5.4, *Comp. Dem. Cic.* 2; Wardman 224; and further on this passage see Moles. While Cicero's oratory had **charm**, Demosthenes' was 'harsh and bitter' (*Demosthenes* 11.5, cf. *Comp. Dem. Cic.* 1.4).

L. (not **Marcus**) Roscius **Otho** as tribune (not **praetor**) in 67 BC passed his law in fact restoring the reservation of fourteen rows of **seats...in the theatre** for the equites*. Otho had vetoed the Gabinian law (*Pompey* 25n.) and was probably praetor in 63 BC when Cicero spoke to **the people** on his behalf and **reprimanded them** (only fragments of his speech survive).

Chapter 14

The consular elections for 62 BC brought Catiline back into the limelight. He proposed the cancellation of debts and had strong backing in **Etruria** among the Sullan veterans, who were led by the ex-centurion L. **Manlius**. He was also thought to be supported by Crassus and Caesar, whom Cicero accused of complicity in Catiline's plot in his lost work *On His Policies* (*De Consiliis Suis*; cf. *Crassus* 13.2-4). Cicero may have wanted to provoke and crush a rising before **Pompey** had the chance to use his army in Italy. He also wanted to ensure that the consuls of 62 BC were reliable and claimed to have arranged for Lucullus' delayed Eastern triumph to be celebrated just before the elections in July, so that Lucullus' veterans could vote for his legate L. Licinius **Murena** (*Mur*. 37-8). In addition, Cicero at first backed Ser. Sulpicius Rufus, who persuaded him to pass a severe law against bribery. This was, however, aimed against Murena, whom Cicero was to defend in November (ch. 17n.). Cato, who joined in the prosecution, also with Sulpicius threatened to indict Catiline, and he in turn made threats against the state which were reported to Cicero by Fulvia (ch. 16n.). Cicero therefore had the senate decree a postponement **of the elections** and question Catiline **on the subject**. Cicero later declared that he also had **information** about a plot **to kill** him during the elections (*Cat*. 1.11), but Plutarch's version that Cicero did not have enough proof **to convict a man like Catiline** is not fully convincing. The senate, in any case, was not impressed by Cicero's arguments, and Catiline left triumphant. To make his point Cicero then arrived at the elections **wearing a breastplate** and with a bodyguard, but the elections were held without trouble (for the indignation of **the people** cf. Dio 37.29.5). At the last moment opinion swung away from Sulpicius to Murena, who despite his later acquittal had indeed indulged in lavish bribery. He was elected with D. Iunius **Silanus** (married to Servilia, Cato's half-sister; *Pompey* 42, *Caesar* 8nn.). It may be that only now did Catiline seriously begin preparations for a revolution, and if so Crassus and Caesar would have ended any support for him.

Further on the *De Consiliis* see Rawson, E., 'History, Historiography and Cicero's *Expositio consiliorum suorum*' *LCM* 7 (1982) pp. 121-4; Moles, J.L., 'Plutarch *Crassus* 13.4-5 and Cicero's *De consiliis suis*' *LCM* 7 (1982) pp. 136-7; ch. 30n. This chapter sees the first of several escort scenes in the *Life*, which indicate the moments when Cicero's public support was at its greatest (cf. chs 16, 19, 22, 33, 43; contrast 31; see further *Pompey* 13n.).

Chapter 15

Catiline's army now **began to gather together**, especially at Faesulae **in Etruria** under Manlius. Catiline himself remained in Rome to allay suspicion, but Cicero may have been kept informed by Fulvia. It was on 20 October that Cicero received the visit from **Crassus** (on his suspected involvement with Catiline see ch. 14n.), M. Claudius **Marcellus** (cos. 51 BC) and Q. Caecilius **Metellus** Pius **Scipio** (cos. 52 BC). Cicero promptly **convened the senate** on 21 October, and **Quintus Arrius** (? pr. 64 BC) reported on events **in Etruria**. Cicero delivered a speech predicting that **the day fixed for going into action** would be 27 October, and that a massacre would take place at Rome on the 28th; and the senate passed its ultimate **decree*** (*Crassus* 13.2-3; Cic. *Cat.* 1.7).

The precise details and dating of these events remain unclear. Plutarch's **soon afterwards** has been taken to imply that the elections were postponed until September, and Suetonius records that 'the debate on Catiline's conspiracy' took place on the same day as the birth of Octavian (*Augustus* 94.5; i.e. 23 September). This cannot mean the debate at which the *s.c.u.* was passed and might refer to the meeting of ch. 14, but neither Suetonius' story nor Plutarch's vague chronology can be pressed (see Stockton App. A). Dio's account suggests (37.31) that there may have been two meetings of the senate on 20/21 October. Note also that the reports were coming from Etruria long before the debate in October, and Plutarch conflates these (see Pelling [2] 127).

Chapter 16

Cicero was now confident that he was **armed with** the power to put down the conspiracy. He **entrusted the conduct of affairs** in Picenum and Gaul to the praetor Q. Caecilius **Metellus** Celer, while **he himself** raised a force and for Rome's safety sent the companies of gladiators to Capua and elsewhere (N.B. a second escort scene; see ch. 14n.). October passed without incident in Rome, then at the beginning of November an unsuccessful attempt was made on Praeneste, and L. Saenius read a letter in the senate confirming that Manlius had risen on 27 October. As alarm in Rome increased, L. Aemilius Paullus initiated a prosecution against Catiline for violence, and Catiline offered to place himself in voluntary custody. Catiline remained free, however, and on 6 November held a conference of the leading conspirators at the house of M. Porcius Laeca. **He decided** to leave Rome and **join Manlius and his army**, while the others were to **make an end** of Cicero and seize the city. The equestrians* C. Cornelius and L.Vargunteius volunteered to kill Cicero when they went as clients* **to pay him their respects** (*salutatio*), but Cicero had been warned by **Fulvia** and set guards round his house (Plutarch and App. *BC* 2.3 confuse Cornelius with one of the leading conspirators, C. Cornelius **Cethegus**; **Marcius** is an error). He then **convened a meeting of the senate**, probably in fact on 8 November, in the **temple of Jupiter Stesius** (**or Stator**, i.e. 'who makes stand firm', symbolic but also more secure than the senate house). **Catiline also attended...intending to defend himself**, and Cicero is the source for the unlikely report that **no senator** would greet or **sit near him** (*Cat.* 1.16, 2.12). Cicero now delivered his famous *First Catilinarian*, in which he attempted to drive Catiline from Rome (**told him to leave** is an exaggeration; for the **city wall** quote cf. id. 1.10). He subsequently **left the city** for Etruria via Arretium, raising the Eagle standard of Marius and assuming **the rods and axes of a magistrate in office** (Sall. *BC* 36.1, 59.3; on the fasces see *Pompey* 19n.). To begin with Catiline only had a few **armed men** with him, but he eventually raised **a force of some 20,000** (App. *BC* 2.7). By mid-November it was a situation of **open war and Antonius was sent** to oppose Catiline.

Fulvia, who is called 'a worthless prostitute' by Florus (2.12.6), was the mistress of Q. Curius, a notorious gambler and one of those expelled from the senate in 70 BC (*Pompey* 22n.). Curius himself eventually became an informer.

Chapter 17

The day after Catiline's departure Cicero delivered his *Second Catilinarian* before the people. **The remains of Catiline's corrupt crew** were led by P. **Cornelius Lentulus** Sura (cos. 71 BC), who had been expelled from the senate in 70 BC and was now praetor (the Cornelii were a patrician* **family**). For Lentulus' oracle cf. Cic. *Cat.* 3.9; Sall. *BC* 47.2; he was **quaestor** in 81 BC, but his **trial** is otherwise unattested. It was **Cornelius** Cethegus who complained about the inaction of his associates (Sall. id. 43.3).

November also saw the prosecution of Murena for electoral bribery (*ambitus*; cf. ch. 35, *Comp. Dem. Cic.* 1.5; Cic. *Pro Murena*; ch. 14n.). Cicero's witty defence included little that was relevant to the charge, but it ensured Murena's acquittal. On **the Sibylline books** see *Caesar* 58n.; and on **Cinna** see *Pompey* 3n.

Chapter 18

The conspirators' plans included a concerted **attack** on Rome from inside and outside during **the Saturnalia** (on which see *Pompey* 34n.). On 16 December the new tribune L. Calpurnius Bestia was to stir up the people against Cicero for provoking a war without just cause, and the next night the city was to be set alight in twelve (not 100) places. Cicero and other leading senators were to be assassinated, and Catiline would seize Rome. For the conspirators' fear of **Pompey** see ch. 10n. Cicero finally made the breakthrough against them when they contacted the **ambassadors of the Allobroges** in Rome to complain about Roman oppression (Plutarch alone says there were **two**). They were not ready for **a revolt,** however, and informed their patron* Q. Fabius Sanga, who in turn told Cicero. The **evidence** Cicero required was provided by the **letters** carried by **Titus** Volturcius, which **urged Catiline to set free the slaves.** On 2 December Cicero sent two praetors (L. Valerius Flaccus and C. Pomptinus) to lay **an ambush by night** at the Milvian Bridge, and Volturcius and others were arrested and handed over to Cicero early on 3 December (Cic. *Cat.* 3.4-6; Sall. *BC* 40-1, 44-46.1).

N.B. the translation **on a small scale or trivial** does not indicate the sickness metaphor in the Greek ('remediable'; see further ch. 10n.).

Chapter 19

Cicero immediately summoned the unsuspecting leaders of the conspiracy to his house and arrested them. Some leading senators advised him to open the letters, but Cicero did not wish to arouse suspicion by breaking the seals. He therefore **assembled the senate in the temple of Concord** and, tipped off by the Allobroges, ordered another praetor **(Gaius Sulpicius)** to search **the house of Cethegus,** where **an enormous quantity** of arms was found (Cic. *Cat.* 3.6-8; Sall. *BC* 46.2-6).

In the temple Cicero **examined the informers** (Cic. *Cat.* 3.8-15; Sall. *BC* 47). Plutarch's account is careless: Volturcius was **voted immunity,** and he reported Lentulus' plans; then the Gauls told of their meetings with the conspirators; finally the letters were read out, and the authors confessed. Although there remains room for doubt over the Allobroges' precise role, any idea of a plant by Cicero should be dismissed. Note that there is no mention in Cicero and Sallust of the consul-designate D. **Iunius Silanus** or C. Calpurnius **Piso** (cos. 67 BC; for their role in the later events see ch. 20n.). The **three consuls** are Cicero and the consuls-elect, Silanus and Murena; the **praetors** would presumably include Sulpicius, Flaccus and Pomptinus.

The senate now passed a vote of thanks to Cicero, Antonius and the praetors who laid the ambush, and an unprecedented thanksgiving to the gods in honour of a magistrate not exercising a military command. It also ordered the conspirators **to be kept under arrest** in private custody, Rome's prison being inadequate. Lentulus was persuaded to resign **his office,** since a magistrate could not normally be deposed or punished. He **laid aside the purple-bordered** toga worn by higher magistrates and free-born sons (ch. 44), and was delivered to the aedile P. Lentulus Spinther. **His associates were then handed over** in fact to other senators, including Crassus, and of these Caesar and Cn. Terentius were praetors-elect. Catulus may now have called Cicero 'Father of his Country', and another consular, L. Gellius Publicola, asserted that he deserved the civic crown (ch. 23n.).

Cicero promptly reported these events to **the people** in his *Third Catilinarian*. Only Plutarch says that Cicero then spent the night at **the house of a neighbouring friend** due to the celebration in his own of the Bona Dea **rites** (on which see *Caesar* 9n.; N.B. the escort scene: see ch. 14n.). Cicero may well have been anxious as to how he should proceed, despite the passing of the senate's ultimate decree*. He discussed the matter with a **very few** friends, including his brother (ch. 20). Plutarch takes the opportunity to include a big moral choice scene (cf. chs 29, 31, 32, 37, 38, 41; see Moles).

Chapter 20

The story of the divine **sign** derives from Cicero's lost poem on his consulship (Servius on Verg. *Ecl.* 8.105, placed before his election; Dio 37.35.4, placed at dawn on 5 December). The Vestals' interpretation of the sign may have been influenced by Fabia, Terentia's half-sister, whom Catiline had been charged with seducing (ch. 10n.). On **Terentia** see ch. 8n. Cicero's remark may have been made in his prose work on his consulship (as Moles). For **advice** given to Cicero by his **friends** and relations see ch. 1n. The former included the learned **Publius Nigidius Figulus** (pr. 58 BC), a Pythagorean, magician and expert on Etruscan religion whose influence is certainly historical (Cic. *Fam.* 4.13.2) but perhaps exaggerated by Plutarch.

Next day (4 December) the senate in fact received the testimony of L. Tarquinius that Crassus was involved in the conspiracy. This is highly unlikely, as Crassus had previously given Cicero information about the plot (ch. 15); and Cicero would not allow Caesar to be implicated by his enemy Catulus and C. Piso. On 5 December the senate was surrounded with guards as it met in the temple of Concord to debate the pressing problem of **the punishment of the conspirators**. Despite Cicero's *Fourth Catilinarian* and the account of Sallust (*BC* 50.4-53.1) not all the details of the meeting are clear. Moles, indeed, argues that there may have been two debates, in which case Plutarch's **next day** is not so much an error as a conflation. Cicero called on D. **Silanus** as the senior consul-designate to **give his opinion first**. His proposal of **the supreme penalty** was taken to mean 'death', and Murena (the other consul-designate) and the fourteen consulars present **supported this motion**; Caesar, now praetor-designate, did not (ch. 21; *Caesar* 7.7-8).

Against Plutarch's view that Caesar was **already** on **the path** to **monarchy** see Caesar 28n. **The information laid against** Caesar came from Catulus and Piso (above); later Cicero himself implausibly implicated Caesar in his *De Consiliis Suis* (ch. 14n.). If Cicero did not fear Caesar himself, he may have been wary of his powerful **friends**, especially Crassus.

Chapter 21

Caesar's **proposal** was in fact life imprisonment (an unusual punishment in the ancient world), not a delay **until final victory over Catiline had been secured** (*Caesar* 7n.; on Caesar's ability as a speaker see id. 3n.). It was probably now that Ti. Claudius Nero moved a postponement of the decision, and Cicero was forced to intervene with his *Fourth Catilinarian* to demand a vote on the proposals of Silanus and Caesar (Cicero does not explicitly support **the first proposal** of Silanus in the published version of the speech; see Moles). Silanus then **took up a different position,** and the senators now supported Caesar's proposal, among them Cicero's **friends** and brother (it would be **to the advantage of Cicero,** but this will not have been a major consideration at this stage). At length, however, **Catulus** opposed it; then M. Porcius **Cato** attacked Caesar and swung the debate, a remarkable achievement for a tribune-designate. On Cicero's motion the senate voted for **the death sentence.** According to Plutarch alone Caesar then caused uproar by opposing **the confiscation of** the conspirators' property, **appealed to the tribunes in vain** and was escorted out of the meeting by Curio (*Caesar* 8n.).

Chapter 22

Again, many of the details of this chapter are only recorded by Plutarch and are elaborated. Note that the conspirators had not **been distributed...among the praetors** (ch. 19n.) but were led to the prison by them (Sall. *BC* 55.2); nor were they handed over **to the public executioner,** rather to the three magistrates concerned (*tresviri capitales*). Cicero, who **shouted out** '*vixere*', was now seen as **the saviour** of Rome (for **founder,** deriving from the Greek appellation of a city's benefactor, see Moles). The theme of Rome's **safety** being ensured by Cicero as a statesman rather than a general recalls his own proud proclamations on these lines (e.g. *Cat.* 3.15, 4.20-1), and similarly Cicero himself boasts how he put down the conspiracy without **civil strife** (id. 3.23-5). His public support is indicated by the escort scene (ch. 14n.). The effect of the news on **those who had flocked to join Catiline** is reported in Sall. id. 57.1. The remainder **joined battle with** Antonius' legate M. Petreius at Pistoria in January 62 BC, where Catiline was defeated and killed.

Chapter 23

The new **tribunes** for 62 BC, including Cato, **Metellus** Nepos and Calpurnius **Bestia, came into office** on 10 December (**Caesar** did not become **praetor** until 1 January – Plutarch has conflated events). On the last day of his consulship Cicero attempted to make his farewell address to **the people** from the speakers' platform in the forum (**rostra**), but Nepos through his veto only allowed him to take the traditional **oath** that he had obeyed the laws (Bestia's involvement is not mentioned in the other sources – this seems to be more conflation). The people's confirmation of Cicero's alternative **oath of his own** then naturally made Nepos and his colleagues **all the more angry** (Cicero in fact swore that the state had been saved by him *alone*, *Pis.* 6-7, *Fam.* 5.2.7). Nepos and **Caesar** were attacking Cicero on the ground that he had put Roman citizens to death without trial. Further on this knotty problem see Stockton 136-8.

Nepos and Caesar kept up the pressure on Cicero in 62 BC, Nepos proposing the **law...for the recall of Pompey** and **Cato** forming the opposition (*Cato* 26-29.2; Dio 37.43). Plutarch says their professed motive was **to put an end to the tyranny of Cicero**, which may well reflect the opinions being expressed by popular politicians at this time, but the official reason for Pompey's recall was to defeat Catiline.

Cicero's title of **father of the fatherland** (*Pater Patriae*) may have first been voted by the senate after the questioning of Lentulus and the other conspirators (ch. 19n.). Cicero (*Pis.* 6) says Catulus proposed this in the senate (cf. Pliny, *NH* 7.117 on **the first**).

Chapter 24

Cicero was now one of his country's leading statesmen (*principes civitatis*) and was probably asked for his opinion first by the consul during senatorial debates. The trials of the minor conspirators began in 62 BC, with guilty verdicts being passed on all but P. Sulla, whom Cicero defended (cf. *Sulla* 5-7). Cicero's position, however, was threatened by the rise of Cato and the attacks of men like Nepos and L. Manlius Torquatus, who accused him of tyranny. Cicero certainly alienated many leading Romans by his boasting over his suppression of the conspiracy (below), though **his books and writings**, including his Greek monograph and epic poem on his consulship and the secret *De Consiliis Suis* (chs 2, 14, 30, *Caesar* 8nn.), acted as a preliminary defence against possible charges over his execution of the conspirators (see Rawson 90-1). Occasionally Cicero tried to adopt a conciliatory position, but his long letter to Pompey was not well received (*Pompey* 42n.). Cicero's other extant speech from 62 BC is the *Pro Archia*, in which he defended the citizenship status of his old teacher (ch. 2n.). Cicero had hopes that Archias too would compose a poem on his consulship. Near the end of the year Cicero bought his house on the Palatine Hill from Crassus (Cic. *Fam.* 5.6.2). He had to borrow heavily, and one of his creditors was P. Sulla, which caused him some embarrassment. Cicero was also involved financially with Antonius, whose exactions in Macedonia were becoming notorious. Further on his debts see ch.7n.; and on his houses ch. 8n.

On Cicero's **obnoxious** self-glorification cf. ch. 36; Dio 38.12.7 (with **boring and tedious**). Many speeches refer to his actions, and others **grew tired of hearing** about them. For Cicero's **sayings,** concerning Greek philosophers and orators of the past, cf. Cic. *Acad.* 2.119 (**Aristotle**), *Brut.* 121 (**Plato** and presumably **Theophrastus** – Cicero simply writes 'who sweeter than Theophrastus?'), *Orat.* 26 (**Demosthenes,** whose **longest** speech was the *On the Crown* – with Moles, Plutarch means one can never have too much of him). **Those who try to copy Demosthenes** are the Roman 'Atticists' like Asinius Pollio, Brutus and Calvus. The **letter** in question is not extant but is also referred to by Quintilian (10.1.24, 12.1.22). Cicero frequently **praises Demosthenes,** but does so especially by imitating his **speeches** against Philip of Macedon (ch. 45n.). As for **scholars of his own time, Cratippus** was the leading member of the school founded by Aristotle (Peripatos or Lyceum; **the Areopagus** was Athens' oldest council, made up of ex-archons). Cicero entrusted **his son** Marcus to the care of **Herodes,** and he did study **with Cratippus** in Athens (45/4 BC, cf. ch. 49). Unfortunately he also gained a reputation for indulging in **heavy drinking** (Pliny, *NH* 14.147), and he was forced by his father to dismiss the distinguished rhetorician **Gorgias** (Cic. *Fam.* 16.21.6; on Gorgias see *OCD* s.v. Gorgias [2]). The **Greek letters** do not survive, but this reference indicates one of Plutarch's sources (Intro. 4). For Plutarch's readiness to condemn Greeks see Jones 107. **Pelops** will have been an influential citizen of **Byzantium,** from where Cicero expected **honorary decrees** for his attack on L. Piso in 55 BC over his misgovernment of his province (cf. *Pis.* 86; ch. 35n.).

Chapter 25

Another criticism of Cicero is that he could not control his tongue, and although witty he tended to go too far (ch. 27).Yet he of all people was aware of the accepted limits of **good manners** (or 'propriety', *to prepon*) in oratorical theory (see Moles). The record of Cicero's remarks here will derive from the collection of Tiro (ch. 1n.).

Cicero's defence of T. **Munatius** Plancus Byrsa took place before the latter's tribunate in 52 BC, after which he was prosecuted by Cicero and exiled (*Pompey* 55n.). **Sabinus** could be T. Vettius Sabinus (pr. 59 BC; Cicero also used the **darkness** imagery at the trial of Cluentius, Quint. 2.17.21). Cicero's speeches for and against **Crassus** reflect the regular training of an orator. Crassus, who was a Peripatetic, makes a joke out of **the Stoic doctrine**, which refers to moral virtue, and Cicero cleverly responds by alluding to Crassus' **reputation of being...fond of money**. Crassus had two sons, Publius and Marcus, and the story here refers to the latter. **Axius** was probably Q. Axius, a member of a banking family from Reate (see Ward 292 n. 11). The point of the pun is that in Greek *axios Krassou* could mean either 'worthy...of Crassus' or 'Axius, son of Crassus'.

Chapter 26

Crassus **set out for Syria** in November 55 BC. He and Cicero had fallen out over Gabinius, and their reconciliation, in fact instigated by Caesar and Pompey, took place shortly before Crassus' departure at a dinner in the villa of Cicero's son-in-law Furius Crassipes. Cicero then defended Crassus' command against the attack of the new consuls of 54 BC (*Fam.* 1.9.20). On **Vatinius** see ch. 9n. Cicero's cursing of **'the man...who told the lie'** may refer to both the messenger and Vatinius (as Moles). The **decree** of Caesar is his second agrarian bill (*Caesar* 14n.). This in fact favoured the urban poor rather than Pompey's (not **his**) **soldiers**, who benefited from the first agrarian bill. **Lucius Gellius** is presumably Publicola (cos. 72 BC). For the story of Octavius (**Ocatvius** is a misprint) and his pierced ear, which implied both Libyan and servile origins, cf. Macrob. 7.3.7. The remark of **Metellus Nepos** may have been made during his tribunate in 62 BC, when Cicero gave evidence against the minor Catilinarian conspirators. Cicero's questioning of Nepos' birth was a standard device, also used against Cicero himself (ch. 1n.). The identity of Nepos' **mother** is unclear (see Wiseman, T.P., 'Celer and Nepos' *CQ* 21 [1971] pp. 180-2). Nepos was in fact suspended from **his office as tribune** before fleeing **to Pompey** (*Pompey* 42n.); **Cicero's comment** refers to Nepos' elevated (i.e. high-flown) style of speaking. **Sextius** should read 'Sestius', whom Cicero defended in 56 BC.

Chapter 27

'**Adrastus**' was a legendary king of Argos, whose daughters Argeia and Deipyle married Polynices (in exile from Thebes) and Tydeus (in exile from Calydon). **Lucius** Aurelius **Cotta** was consul in 65 BC and **censor** in 64 BC. **The verse** is perhaps from Euripides' lost *Oedipus* (frg. 378N) and refers to Laius, father of Oedipus who was warned by the oracle of **Apollo** that if he had a son, the son would kill him. Cicero's remark to **Gellius** is a play on the phrase used by slaves to claim their freedom (*in libertatem reclamare*). On **Faustus** Sulla see *Pompey* 42n.; Plutarch once more refers to Sulla's proscriptions.

Chapter 28

The two major events of 62 BC were the return of Pompey (*Pompey* 42-4nn.) and the Bona Dea **scandal** (*Caesar* 9-10nn.).

Chapter 29

There seems no reason to doubt that to begin with **Cicero was a friend of Clodius** (N.B. **he had come to his house...matters**). Clodius' trial, however, became a political affair. Cicero had little choice but to side with Pompey against him, and he proceeded at the trial in May 61 BC to demolish Clodius' alibi that he was **staying at** Interamna (*Pompey* 44, *Caesar* 10nn.). See Epstein, D.F., 'Cicero's Testimony at the *Bona Dea* Trial' *CP* 81 (1986) pp. 229-35. Plutarch's alleged motive for Cicero's action, the hostility of **Terentia**, is very doubtful, but is part of another moral choice for Cicero (see Moles; ch. 19n.). However, Terentia may indeed have hated Clodius (cf. ch. 30), because his prosecution of Ca-tiline for seducing the Vestal Virgin Fabia (Terentia's half-sister) hu-miliated Fabia and damaged her own reputation (ch. 10n.). **Clodia**, on the other hand, would not have wished **to marry Cicero**, whatever the rumours (she **lived close by** on the Palatine). She was the notorious **wife of Metellus Celer** and probably the Lesbia of Catullus' poems. Her nickname **Lady Farthing** (*Quadrantaria*), which implied she was a cheap tart, perhaps reflects a joke played on her by **one of her lovers**. M. Caelius called her *quadrantaria Clytaemnestra* since she was sus-pected of murdering her husband, and Cicero makes play with the nickname in *Cael.* 62. **The smallest copper coin** was the *quadrans*, worth one quarter of an *as* (4 *asses* = 1 HS).

This Clodia may have been the middle of the three sisters; it was probably the **youngest** who was divorced by L. **Lucullus** on his return to Rome from the East, where Clodius had tampered with his troops (*Pompey* 30n.). She then married Q. **Marcius Rex** (cos. 68 BC).

At the trial **many** of the Optimates* were ranged against Clodius, but Crassus bribed the jury to acquit him (see *Caesar* 10n., also on the **undecipherable** ballots and Caesar's remark). For Cicero's reaction and his reply to Clodius concerning **his evidence** cf. *Att.* 1.16.6-10 (Catulus' remark is at id. 1.16.5). Cicero says that thirty-one voted for the acquit-tal. **Tullus** may be Thyillus, a Greek poet (see Wiseman, T.P., *Cinna the Poet* [Leicester, 1974] pp. 145-6).

Chapter 30

Plutarch now jumps to Clodius' actions in 59 BC; on events in Rome

134

during 61/59 BC see *Pompey* 44-8, *Caesar* 13-14nn. In 60 BC Cicero was much concerned with the break between the senate and equites* over the Asian taxes, and he continued his attempt to win over Pompey. He also began publishing the material on his consulship, the speeches of 63 BC, a history in Greek and perhaps Latin, and his epic poem. His thoughts then turned to Caesar's approaching consulship, declining an invitation to join the 'First Triumvirate'. In 59 BC Cicero refused to serve on the land commissions set up by the first agrarian bill, and he probably attacked Caesar during his unsuccessful defence of Antonius – in the afternoon of the same day Clodius was transferred to plebeian status (*Pompey* 48n.). By April Cicero was at Antium, fed up with the ingratitude of the Optimates* and composing the secret work *On His Policies* (ch. 14n.). He was, however, becoming increasingly anxious about the violent methods of Caesar, the intentions of Pompey and his own expected prosecution by Clodius. From *Att.* 2.18 (June 59 BC) Cicero is back in Rome. He was assured by Pompey of his support against Clodius, but Pompey's feelings towards him changed after the attempted assassination in which Cicero was implicated.

Clodius entered his tribunate on 10 December 59 BC and **won over the people by** his popular legislation, which included free corn distributions and the revival of the **political clubs** (*collegia*; see *Pompey* 52n.). He then began organising gangs of armed slaves and freedmen in the guise of these clubs. L. Calpurnius Piso, the senior consul of 58 BC, at first treated Cicero respectfully, but in late January or early February Clodius bought his support, and that of the other consul Gabinius, by a special bill giving them five-year commands in **Macedonia** and Cilicia (which was later changed to **Syria**). On the same day a second bill was passed interdicting from fire and water anyone who had put Roman citizens **to death without a trial** (Cic. *Sest.* 25, 53, 55). This was clearly aimed at Cicero, who **put on mourning** and begged for support but was met **with mud and stones** (cf. App. *BC* 2.15; Dio 38.14.7).

Crassus had been **an open enemy** of Cicero since the trial of Macer (ch. 9). On Caesar's departure for **Gaul** see *Caesar* 14n. Caesar in fact offered Cicero **an appointment on his staff** (ibid.), and offended by his refusal was ready to encourage Clodius' actions against Cicero (*Pompey* 46n.). The story of **a reconciliation** presumably refers to Clodius' deception of Cicero at the start of the year (Dio 38.14.1-3). Caesar's **speech** was made **to a meeting of the people** (*contio*) in the Circus Flaminius perhaps early in March. In it he refused to condemn Cicero outright (Dio 38.17.1-2).

Chapter 31

The demonstration on the Capitol by **gentlemen outside the senate** (i.e.

equites*) from all over Italy was followed by a delegation to **the senate**, which **met** in the Temple of Concord and voted also to put on **mourning**. **The consuls** Piso and Gabinius issued a joint edict forbidding this, and Gabinius then barred one of the leading equestrians, Cicero's friend L. Aelius Lamia, from coming within 200 miles of Rome (Cic. *Red. Quir.* 8 – 20,000 people, *Sest.* 26-9). Cicero was now faced with the moral choice of **exile** or **armed force** (see Moles; ch. 19n.). First he visited **Piso** with his **son-in-law** C. Calpurnius **Piso** Frugi (on whom see further ch. 41n.) and was justifiably angered by the consul's attitude (Plutarch conflates two meetings, one of Cicero and Piso and a second of Piso and the senators; see below and Moles). This was followed by the public meeting held in the Circus Flaminius by Clodius, at which the consuls expressed their disapproval of the execution of the Catilinarian conspirators, but Caesar would not support retroactive legislation (ch. 30n.). **Pompey**, meanwhile, had retired to **his country house in the Alban hills**. His attitude towards Cicero had now changed (*Pompey* 48, *Caesar* 14nn.), and he may have decided to allow Clodius his head to prevent trouble from him (as Seager 104). Pompey was therefore cynical rather than **ashamed**, and he refused to see Cicero (the embarrassment that led him to slip **out of the house by another door** then seems unlikely; cf. *Pompey* 46.5; Dio 38.17.3; for his marriage to Caesar's daughter see *Pompey* 47n.). He also referred a deputation of senators to the consuls; they were in turn dismissed by Piso, and at a meeting in Cicero's house advised him to leave the city (further on advice given to Cicero by his friends see ch. 1n.). Cicero now felt doubly **betrayed** (*Att.* 3.7.2, 15.2) but accepted the advice **to go into exile** (**Lucullus** is probably M. Lucullus, cf. *Pis.* 77). The **argument** that **the people...would soon feel the need of Cicero again** was at once undermined by Clodius' second bill (ch. 32).

Cicero **dedicated** his **statue of Minerva** in the temple of Jupiter on **the capitol** both to preserve it and put it (and Rome) under Jupiter's protection (Cic. *De Leg.* 2.42). Then he left Rome **secretly in the middle of the night** (c. 20 March), his prestige (*auctoritas*) in ruins; and the pathetic escort scene stands in stark contrast to the escorts Cicero had received when popular (ch. 14n.). He was making for **Sicily** because he had been quaestor there, had secured clients by his prosecution of Verres and was friendly with Vergilius (ch. 32). N.B. **because of Clodius** is probably a mistranslation of the Greek *di'ekeinon*, which should refer to Cicero (as Moles).

Chapter 32

Clodius now **carried through a vote** exiling Cicero by name, confiscating his property and forbidding further discussion of the matter. Cicero states that the distance of exclusion was **400 miles** from Italy (*Att.* 3.4). Therefore his friend C. **Vergilius** Balbus (pr. 62 BC, propraetorian governor **of Sicily** 61-58 BC) told **him not to land in Sicily** (Cic. *Planc.* 95-6). Cicero was staying at the **estate** of Sicca at **Vibo** (not of **Vibius**), whence he now made for **Brundisium** (Sicca could not have heard of the second bill before Cicero's arrival). On the way he was **escorted** by the people of the towns, which were loyal to him. Sicca was Cicero's **prefect of engineers** (*praefectus fabrum*), in this context a civil post dealing with public works; Vibo, already called such in Cicero's time, was actually in Bruttium, south of **Lucania**.

Cicero's crossing to **Dyrrhachium** was delayed by bad weather according only to Plutarch (sim. with the **earthquake** and **soothsayers**). His **miserable** state of mind is reflected in a farewell letter to Terentia (*Fam.* 14.4). Cicero was met on landing by Cn. Plancius, the quaestor of Macedonia, who escorted him to his official residence at Thessalonica (technically within the 400 miles) arriving on 23 May. During his exile Cicero was **disconsolate**, even threatening suicide. He faced the choice between devoting himself to Greek culture and clinging to his hopes of a return to politics (see Moles; ch. 19n.). He chose the latter, and it is clear that he almost suffered a nervous breakdown. Plutarch's account is very similar to his version of the exile of Cicero's Athenian parallel (*Demosthenes* 26.5-7), while Cicero's obsession with Rome is as damaging as that of the Athenians with Sicily (*Pericles* 20.3).

Plutarch's statement that Cicero preferred to be called **a philosopher** to **an orator** is his invention and leads to a discussion of **public opinion**. A philosopher **in politics** has to be on his **guard** not to be swayed by the false opinions and passions of the general public, but Cicero has abandoned his philosophical reason and adopted the public opinion of the dreadfulness of exile. He has additionally, he feels, lost his public reputation, hence he is inconsolable. For a full analysis of this passage see Moles (who translates *tois ektos* as 'those outside', i.e. the many, rather than **what is outside oneself**).

Chapter 33

Clodius immediately destroyed Cicero's **villas** at Tusculum and Formiae and **burned down his house** on the Palatine, replacing it with a shrine with a statue of **Liberty** (**no one would buy anything** is an exaggeration; cf. Cic. *Dom.* 108, 116). His uneasy relationship with Pompey also began to fall apart almost at once, as he interfered with Pompey's Eastern **arrangements** (*Pompey* 48-9nn.). This determined Pompey to work **to have Cicero recalled**, as did an alleged assassination attempt (*Pompey* 49n.). Caesar reluctantly consented to the recall in November, and the movement to secure this gained momentum after Clodius' tribunate ended (**the senate decided** to concentrate on it, *Att*. 3.24.2). The tribune Q. Fabricius proposed a recall bill, but on the day of the voting (25 January 57 BC) Clodius instigated a riot in which Sestius and other tribunes **were wounded in the forum** (according to Cicero Sestius **was left** for **dead, Quintus** simply hid behind the bodies, *Sest*. 75-9). This prompted Pompey finally to mobilise his clients* and add them to the gangs of Sestius and Milo. The senate passed the consuls' motion recalling Cicero by 416 votes to 1, and **the people** ratified the decree in the Centuriate Assembly on 4 August (*Pompey* 49.3; Cic. *Red. Sen.*, *Red. Quir.*).

Milo first tried to **prosecute Clodius** in February, but was stopped by Metellus Nepos and so turned to the use of violence.The senate commended **the cities which had afforded hospitality to Cicero** in May and those who had come to Rome to vote in July. The decree concerning Cicero's **houses** was not finally passed until 2 October: the consuls assessed his compensation at less than he had hoped, and Cicero was short of money. He reached Brundisium on 5 August and **came home to** Rome on 4 September (Cic. *Att*. 4.1.4-5; he left in March 58 BC, over **sixteen months** previously). His **later** remark is in *Red. Sen*. 39. For his reconciliation with **Crassus** and the admiration of **Publius** cf. *Crassus* 13.4; Epstein 10-11. Note again the escort scene (ch. 14n.) and the extraordinary reception on Cicero's arrival at Rome, as he regains his former public support.

Chapter 34

Plutarch now jumps to the second half of 56 BC (see *Pompey* 49-51nn. for Cicero's activities in the meantime). After Luca, Cicero was forced to support the triumvirs and he delivered his *On the Consular Provinces*. Clodius, who had attacked Cicero's house and attempted to assault Cicero himself in November 57 BC, now once again tried to pull down Cicero's house but was stopped by Milo. He was then condemned by the senate. Cicero perhaps at this point delivered before the senate his speech *Concerning the Response of the Soothsayers*, in which he argued the need for unity between the Optimates* and triumvirs. It was after this that Cicero indeed clashed with Cato over **the tablets**, in fact only the one on which Clodius' second law against him was inscribed. Cicero removed it, Clodius restored it, and Cicero took it to his house while Clodius was **out of Rome.** He argued in the senate that **none of** Clodius' laws was **valid**, due to the fact that his adoption into a plebeian* family had been irregular. Cato was forced to speak **against Cicero** because of his mission to Cyprus, which Clodius had devised for just such an occasion (*Cato* 40; Cic. *Sest*. 60). Hence **a certain amount of ill-feeling** arose between the two (see Epstein 39).

138

Chapter 35

Cicero's mood hardly improved in 55 BC, during the second joint-consulship of Pompey and Crassus. He remained on good terms with Pompey, but was at odds once again with Crassus over Gabinius, until Pompey forced their reconciliation (ch. 26n.). Cicero's relationship with Caesar improved during 54 BC, when his brother transferred to Gaul from Pompey's staff and Caesar made Cicero a substantial loan (*Caesar* 23n.). In addition, Cicero was forced to speak for Vatinius (ch. 9n.), and then came the ultimate indignity – after giving evidence against Gabinius at his treason trial, he was made to defend him at his trial for extortion. Finally, he represented Caesar's friend Rabirius Postumus.

In this chapter Plutarch jumps $3^1/2$ years to 52 BC; for events in 54/2 BC see *Pompey* 54-5nn. Cicero lost his nerve on the last day of Milo's **trial** in the face of Pompey's **soldiers** and the threats of Clodius' supporters, and Milo went into exile at Massilia (cf. Ascon. 30-42C). Cicero's arrival in the forum **in a litter** is only related by Plutarch. Cicero several times admits to a lack of confidence when speaking (e.g. *De Orat.* 1.121, *Acad.* 2.64). For the trial of **Murena** (he was prosecuted by Ser. Sulpicius and **Cato** and defended by **Hortensius**, Crassus and Cicero) see ch. 17n. Plutarch's report of Cicero's defence hardly fits with *Cato* 21.5 or the *Pro Murena* as published (see Moles). Likewise, Plutarch's account of Cicero's defence of Milo is dramatised.

Chapter 36

Cicero was probably appointed augur on the proposal of Pompey and Hortensius **in the place of the younger Crassus** after the latter's death at Carrhae in 53 BC and six months before Milo's trial (see Moles). Cicero did not believe in the interpretation of omens given (mostly) by birds, but this was an important political position (see Rawson 139-40).

Pompey's law on provincial government (*Pompey* 56n.) led to a shortage of qualified candidates, and those who had refused a province were now utilised. The East was a major area of concern since Crassus' **disaster in Parthia**, hence in spring 51 BC Bibulus was sent to Syria and in June Cicero unwillingly left Brundisium for **Cilicia** to replace Ap. Claudius. Cicero took experienced legates with him to Cilicia, including his brother Quintus and C. Pomptinus, the praetor of 63 BC (ch. 18n.). As secretary he had the highly educated slave Tiro, who was soon to be freed and would eventually be responsible for preserving Cicero's correspondence. Cicero reached Laodicea on 31 July – he reckoned his term of office began on that date and fervently hoped it would not last longer than a year. He then went to join his army of two under-strength and discontented legions (he would not, therefore, have had **12,000**

infantry, a conventional figure for two legions of 6,000 men each). In late August the Parthians under Pacorus, son of Orodes, crossed the Euphrates into **Syria**, and Cicero moved to defend the threatened **Cappadocia**. He met the young **King Ariobarzanes**, whose care had been entrusted to him by the senate, and successfully secured his safety before marching back into Cilicia. He next attacked the tribes of **Mount Amanus** (the boundary between Cilicia and Syria), and after his victory, largely won by Pomptinus, was acclaimed '**Imperator**'* by his men (Cic. *Fam.* 2.10). Cicero maintains that his approach then caused the Parthians to retreat in panic from Antioch before being attacked by Cassius. Bibulus finally arrived in Syria at this point, immediately to lose a cohort, while Cicero besieged and captured Pindenissus. He now desired a vote of thanksgiving and a triumph to help him recover his lost prestige, hence his long letter to Cato (*Fam.* 15.4), and the former was voted despite Cato's opposition. Cicero responded politely to Cato, but was most upset by this and by Cato's proposal of twenty days' thanksgiving to Bibulus, his son-in-law. From Pindenissus Cicero moved to Laodicea, where he carried out judicial business (below), while becoming increasingly anxious both about the Parthians in Syria and about the prospect of being detained in Cilicia. Fortunately the Parthians were recalled by Orodes, and Cicero felt justified early in August in handing his province over to his new quaestor, C. Coelius Caldus. He then headed via **Rhodes** to **Athens**. After an enjoyable stay there with the philosopher Aristus, brother of Antiochus, he returned to Italy on 14 October (for Antiochus and his **past** visit see ch. 4n.).

Cicero was immensely proud of his **considerate** acts **as governor**. These were prompted by Cato's close scrutiny of provincial government and Cicero's own remarks and writings on the subject, as well as by his relationship with the equites*. Cicero claimed **he saw to it that the cities regained their financial stability**, by not requisitioning supplies or requiring **presents** and by persuading ex-magistrates to repay **what they had embezzled** (*Att.* 5.16.2-3, 6.2.4-5). He also kept firm control over his staff and permitted freer access to himself than was normal (for his early rising cf. id. 6.2.5). Nevertheless, his dealings with Brutus, concerning a loan to Ariobarzanes and his creditors from Salamis in Cyprus, did not match his lofty ideals; and Cicero faced further problems connected with the rapacious governorship of his predecessor Ap. Claudius (see Rawson 177-80). Brutus was Cato's nephew and a friend of Atticus, while Appius was a member of one of Rome's leading families and was closely connected with Pompey and Brutus, both by marriage and politically. Cicero's dilemma in dealing with these men is therefore evident and was increased when his daughter Tullia married Dolabella, who was prosecuting Appius for treason.

Another important figure during Cicero's governorship is M. **Caelius** Rufus, his pupil (ch. 9n.) and confidential correspondent. Caelius (aedile 50 BC) determined to emulate Milo in putting on spectacular games, hence his request for **some panthers** (Cic. *Fam.* 8.2.2, 9.3). Cicero grew tired of such requests and tried to make light of the matter (though with a sting and certainly not **in a mood of self-glorification**) with his comment that the panthers **had all run off to Caria in indignation** (id. 2.11.2). Caelius then raised more problems for Cicero by falling out with Appius.

For events in Rome during Cicero's proconsulship see *Pompey* 57-8, *Caesar* 29-30. Note another example of sickness metaphor (**fever**); see ch. 10n.

Chapter 37

Cicero reached Rome on 4 January 49 BC and stayed outside the city, hoping for a **triumph**, but this was ruled out by the civil war. He continued to receive friendly letters from Caesar and his agent Balbus, but his real sympathies lay with Pompey, whom he hoped to persuade to avoid war. Cicero's **interviews...with Pompey** included meetings on the way to Rome, on 10 December 50 BC in Campania (*Att.* 7.4.2) and on 25 December at Formiae (id. 7.8.4), and he made further unsuccessful attempts to reconcile the two men when he reached Rome (*Pompey* 59n.). Pompey **abandoned the city** on 17 January (see id. 61n.), and Cicero made the decision to do likewise on the next day. The 'quote' from Cicero's **letters** is an amalgamation of various passages but especially *Att.* 8.7.2 ('I have someone to flee from but no one to follow'; see Moles). Cicero had recommended the young lawyer C. **Trebatius** Testa to Caesar, and he served in Gaul (*Caesar* 23n.). His letter in late January (*Att.* 7.17.3-4) is reworked here by Plutarch: Caesar asked Cicero to remain near Rome, and a surprised Cicero **replied** (without anger) that this would be a difficult course of action (he told Atticus he would act as became his 'duty and dignity').

At Formiae Cicero began months of agonising over his moral choice (on which see Moles; ch. 19n.). He had been assigned the defence of Capua but gave up this command for one on the Campanian coast. He was still uncommitted, however, and it was with great reluctance that he set out to join Pompey in Luceria. He turned back on learning that Caesar had blocked the route, but his hopes of Pompey saving Italy were finally dashed by Domitius' surrender at Corfinium (*Pompey* 62n.). He then met Caesar at Formiae (*Att.* 9.17-18; *Caesar* 35n.) but refused to return to Rome. Caesar and Antony warned him not to leave the country, but on 7 June Cicero finally left Italy.

Note again the sickness metaphor in this chapter (**things had gone too far for any remedy**).

Caesar set out for Spain early in April (*Caesar* 36n.), and Cicero joined Pompey's camp, where he clearly was distressed (Cic. *Fam.* 7.3.2). Plutarch depicts another big moral choice scene, this time with advice from Cato which stems from the Stoic doctrine of Panaetius (see Moles, also on the parallel with *Demosthenes* 13.2; ch. 19n.).

Cicero's letters dry up after his departure from Italy, and this chapter of Plutarch is our main source for his actions in the camp (further on his jokes see ch. 1n.). **Domitius** is L. Domitius Ahenobarbus (cos. 54 BC) who was killed at Pharsalus; on **Theophanes** see *Pompey* 32n. (**chief of engineers** means adjutant). **The Rhodians** lost **their fleet** on its way to Pompey, whom Caesar was **besieging** in Dyrrhachium (Caes. *BC* 3.26-7). **Lentulus** is L. Cornelius Lentulus Crus (cos. 49 BC) who was killed in Egypt (*Pompey* 80n.). **The defeat** must refer to events at Dyrrhachium not Pharsalus. **Nonnius** may be M. Nonius Sufenas (? pr. 52 BC). Cicero's comment about **Labienus** will have been made at Dyrrhachium after Labienus brought news of Pharsalus (Cic. *Div.* 1.68).

Chapter 39

Cicero will have been at Dyrrhachium with **Cato** during **the battle of Pharsalus**, perhaps using **ill health** as an excuse. Cato had been left there with fifteen cohorts by Pompey. After Pharsalus the Pompeians crossed to their naval base on Corcyra, and Cato offered Cicero, **as an ex-consul, command** of the remaining forces (the scene after his refusal may be exaggerated; cf. *Cato* 55.3; **young Pompey** is Gnaeus). Cicero then went to Patrae in the Peloponnese, and a letter came from Dolabella giving him permission to return to Italy.

Cicero **put in to Brundisium** in mid-October 48 BC. He was still in ill health, but at least the Caesarian commander at Brundisium, Vatinius, was now on good terms with him. Cicero had no desire to join the Pompeians in Africa, and he had family problems: Quintus via his son was slandering him before Caesar; Tullia's husband Dolabella was at odds with Antony (*Caesar* 51n.); and his own marriage may have been in trouble (ch. 41n.). Cicero's major concern, however, was how he would be treated by Caesar, who was long **delayed** in **Egypt** and then **Asia** (*Caesar* 48-50nn.). Caesar calmed his fears in a letter (Cic. *Fam.* 14.23), and Quintus and his son were forgiven; but Cicero remained uneasy until Caesar **landed at Tarentum** in September 47 BC, and he was allowed to return to Rome.

Cicero says that he wrote his **encomium on Cato** on the wishes of Brutus, who also wrote a *Cato* (*Orat.* 35, cf. *Att.* 13.46.2). In it he extolled Cato as the epitome of Roman virtue. Caesar was irritated, not wishing Cato to be set up as a martyr to Republicanism, and after Munda he began his 'Anti-Cato' in two books (Suet. *Caesar* 56.5). Caesar's attack on Cato's private life, however, went too far. His likening of Cicero to the great Athenian statesman and orator **Pericles** is high praise, but **Theramenes** had the reputation of being untrustworthy.

Cicero defended Q. **Ligarius** in October 46 BC, having worked with Ligarius' brothers for his recall from exile (*Fam.* 6.14.2; *Caesar* 55n.). He was prosecuted by Q. Aelius Tubero over his anti-Caesarian actions in Africa. Plutarch's story seems unlikely, since the references to **Pharsalus** in the published speech are not of the kind to arouse such emotions (*Lig.* 9, 28; see Moles); but it may hint at one of Caesar's epileptic fits.

Chapter 40

Cicero's career now seemed over, and he had little choice when he **retired from public life and** devoted himself to study. Still, he was careful to keep on favourable terms with Caesarian supporters such as Hirtius and Dolabella, despite the latter's divorce from Tullia (ch. 41, *Caesar* 55nn.). Cicero first produced his history of Roman oratory, the *Brutus*, which included praise of Caesar's style (251-62). Also addressed to Brutus is the *Stoic Paradoxes*, which may have led Brutus to request the *Cato*. After the *Cato* came another treatise on oratory, the *Orator*, which included an attack on the new 'Attic' style (28-32).

A visit to **Tusculum** in June 46 BC with Varro perhaps prompted Cicero's renewed interest in **philosophy** (*Fam.* 9.6.4-5), as also did Brutus' book *On Virtue* (*Fin.* 1.8). Writing philosophy in Latin immediately raised the problems of vocabulary and syntax, and Cicero coined new **Latin names** for Greek originals:

phantasia	= *visum* (*Acad.* 1.40)	=	image
synkatathesis	= *adsensio, adprobatio* (*Acad.* 2.37)	=	assent
epoche	= *retentio adsensionis* (*Acad.* 2.59)	=	suspension of judgment
katalepsis	= *comprehensio* (*Acad.* 1.41)	=	comprehension
atomon, ameres	= *individuum* (*Fin. 1.17*)	=	atom, indivisible
kenon	= *inane* (*Fat.* 24)	=	void

Almost all of his philosophical works date from the period 46 to 44 BC and are especially concerned with presenting older ideas, chiefly those of the New Academy (ch. 4n.). These include *Academica* and *De Finibus* (45 BC); *Tusculan Disputations*, *Protagoras* and *Timaeus* (translations of Plato, both lost), *On the Nature of the Gods, On Divination* and *On Duties* (not one of the **dialogues,** sim. the *Stoic Paradoxes*; all 44 BC).

For Cicero's poetry see ch. 2n.; and on his estates see ch. 8n. The letter with the **life of a Laertes** quote is not extant (Odysseus' father Laertes lived in the country). Cicero defends his rare visits **to Rome** at *Fam.* 9.15.3 (for his role in proposing **honours for** Caesar cf. *Caesar* 57.2, 57n. on **Pompey's statues**).

Chapter 41

This chapter brings together several themes which are prominent in the *Life*. These include: Cicero cannot now write his **history** or retire into intellectual life (cf. ch. 43, **he agreed..to Rome**); the problems of his private life ruin his judgment in both private (his **marriage** to Publilia) and public affairs (cf. chs 44-5 re. Octavian); he has key choices to make which will bring success or failure (*authaireta*, **brought upon himself**, is better translated as 'through his own choice'; cf. chs 43 **he agreed**, 45 **he imagined that...influence**, 46 **he too realised...himself**; see further ch. 19n.); the struggle between his passion and reason, reflected in his marriage, will have serious consequences (cf. ch. 45 **hatred...passion for distinction**, 46 tragic infatuation leads him to support Octavian, but **soon afterwards he too realized...country**, 47 **terrible thoughts and desperate plans**). See in greater detail Moles' analysis of 41.1.

Cicero **divorced his wife Terentia** in 46 BC. Trouble may have been brewing since his return to Italy at the end of 48 BC, but she had hardly **allowed him to set out** for Greece **without sufficient means** (*Fam.* 14.7). Cicero in fact wrote to Terentia on his return telling her not to come to Brundisium, and the problem came to a head in the summer of 47 BC. It was financial, and there was also the episode of Tullia's **long journey** in 47 BC (*Att.* 11.17, 17a.1; she was no longer **a young girl** but was over thirty). There is no other evidence that Terentia **stripped Cicero's house**.

After Cicero's return to Rome his pregnant daughter Tullia was divorced from Dolabella in c. November 46 BC, and Cicero also had the worry of his son Marcus, who wanted to join Caesar in Spain. He was himself planning to remarry, finally choosing his **extremely rich** ward Publilia, perhaps in December 46 BC (*Fam.* 4.14.3). With the marriage control of Publilia's estate passed to Cicero, hence the allegations that he married her in order **to use her money for satisfying his creditors**. For the version of Tiro cf. Dio 46.18.3 (on Tiro see chs 36, 49nn.); the reference to Antony's reply to the **Philippics** indicates one of Plutarch's sources (Intro. 4). Cicero's life was dramatically changed, however, when Tullia **died** at Tusculum in February 45 BC, soon after giving birth to a son at Cicero's house in Rome – and Cicero divorced Publilia (**the house of Lentulus** is also wrongly mentioned by Ascon. 5C). Tullia's first **husband**, C. Calpurnius **Piso** Frugi (ch. 31), had died before Cicero returned from exile in 57 BC. Tullia had then married Furius Crassipes, then P. Dolabella in 50 BC (a patrician*, he was adopted in 48 BC by a plebeian* named **Lentulus** so that he could stand for the tribunate). Tullia's death affected Cicero deeply, and he withdrew to his new secluded house at Astura. Here he wrote a *Self-Consolation* and received letters of consolation from among others Brutus, Caesar and Ser. Sulpicius. Note that the text of Plutarch says Cicero was visited by 'philosophers', which is usually emended to **friends** (but see Moles).

Cicero **had planned** his Roman **history** in the late 50s BC and resumed the idea in November 44 BC (*Att.* 16.13c.2).

Chapter 42

Cicero finally returned to Tusculum in the summer of 45 BC, greatly concerned with personal and business matters (see Rawson 250-3). He was now on good terms with **Brutus**, but he left Tusculum for Arpinum near the end of June partly to escape Brutus' visits. Cicero then returned to Rome to defend King Deiotarus in Caesar's house: clearly he was at least formally on good terms with Caesar, and in December invited him to dinner near Puteoli (*Att.* 13.52). It is hardly surprising, then, that Cicero was not informed of **the plot** to assassinate Caesar, despite his friendship with Brutus. He allegedly called out Cicero's name after the deed had been done (Cic. *Phil.* 2.28, 30), but Cicero did not remain in the senate to give his endorsement. He did, however, go up to the Capitol and advise the assassins to summon the senate (*Att.* 14.10.1), but they began negotiations with Antony (*Caesar* 67n.). **Antony, as consul, called a meeting of the senate and said a few words on** compromise, which Cicero supported, and an **amnesty** for the assassins was voted (*Caesar* ibid.; the **proposals** over assigning **provinces** were the ones which **came to nothing**). For subsequent events in Rome see *Caesar* 68n.

Chapter 43

After Brutus and Cassius fled, Antony was left in control of Rome. Cicero, who was not as yet **again becoming a power in the state**, also left and was soon unhappy with Antony's behaviour. Antony was courteous towards him, however, as was Octavian, whom Cicero met in April. Cicero planned to return to Rome for a meeting of the senate on 1 June and then travel to Athens to visit his son, who was studying there (ch. 45); but A. **Hirtius**, one of the consuls-designate (with C. Vibius Pansa), advised him not to go to the city. Cicero therefore asked the consuls for a legateship and accepted a nominal **appointment on Dolabella's staff** (*Att.* 15.8.1, 11.4). He could see another civil war looming and decided to go to Greece, finally leaving Italy in July (there is no other evidence that he made an agreement **with Hirtius and Pansa**). He reached Syracuse in Sicily on 1 August but was driven back to Italy by adverse winds. He then heard of the meeting of the senate on 1 August, of the hope that Brutus and Cassius might reach agreement with Antony, and of the criticisms of his own absence (**Antony's behaviour** was in fact a response to the growing popularity of Octavian). L. Piso had attacked Antony, and was praised for this by Brutus when he met Cicero on 17 August.

There were, then, various groups in the senate with whom Cicero might work to dispose of Antony. Further, there was Octavian, who had been studying at **Apollonia** in Illyricum and had returned to Italy in April on hearing of Caesar's death (Cic. *Att.* 14.10.3; on Plutarch's chronology here see Moles). Cicero returned to a great **welcome** (at least according to Plutarch's escort scene) but refused to attend the senate on 1 September, when Antony would propose honours to Caesar (for his excuse cf. *Phil.* 1.12, 28). **Antony was extremely angry** at Cicero's absence, though *Phil.* 1.12-13 shows that Plutarch exaggerates (and he invents the protest of **many people**; on this and the **sureties** see Moles); but Cicero thereby avoided offending Antony even more by attacking him. Next day Antony himself was absent when Cicero delivered his mild *First Philippic*, to which Antony replied violently on 19 September, again in Cicero's absence (hence their formal enmity, on which see Epstein 23, 43). Cicero now pinned his hopes on Brutus and Cassius, while preparing his *Second Philippic*, and left Rome for Puteoli.

According to *Antony* 15.1 Caesar's **estate** amounted to 24 million **drachmas** (= 96 million HS); for his legacy see *Caesar* 68n.

Chapter 44

On 1 November 44 BC Cicero received a letter from Octavian (*Att.* 16.8) – he had bribed the veterans settled in Campania and wanted Cicero's backing against Antony. Cicero, who was worried about Octavian's youth, advised him to go to Rome but would not do so himself, despite Octavian's repeated entreaties. He was waiting for the expiry of Antony's consulship and was contemplating his proposed history (ch. 41n.). He finally returned on 9 December to deal with financial problems and attended the senate on 20 December to discuss D. Brutus' edict of allegiance to the senate and people: his *Third Philippic* induced the senate to recognise Octavian and order the governors to stay in their provinces. Cicero then claimed in the *Fourth Philippic* that Antony had effectively been declared a public enemy, and he believed this was the day on which he began to rebuild the Republic (*Phil.* 5.30, *Fam.* 12.25.2).

Cicero's meeting with L. Marcius **Philippus** (cos. 56 BC, second husband of Atia) and C. Claudius Marcellus (cos. 50 BC, husband of Octavia) is unattested elsewhere but accepted by Moles. In the tradition the **dream** here attributed to Cicero was in fact that of Catulus (Suet. *Augustus* 94.8; Dio 45.2.3-4), but note that at the time of Catulus' death (before May 60 BC) Octavian was only about two and a half years old. Cicero's dream was that Octavian was let down from heaven by golden chains and handed a whip by Jupiter (Suet. id. 94.9), while the dream that Octavian was destined to make **an end of civil wars** (perhaps part of the previous dream) comes from Augustus' *Autobiography*. For Plutarch's view that only a monarch sent by the gods could save Rome see *Pompey* 70n.; further on dreams see id. 32n.; and on the boys' **purple-bordered togas** see ch. 19n.

Octavian's **father was** the wealthy equestrian* C. **Octavius**, who in fact became praetor (61 BC), governed Macedonia and was proclaimed 'Imperator'*. His **mother was** Atia (not **Attia**), daughter of M. Atius Balbus and Julia. For Caesar's **will** see *Caesar* 56, 68nn. Octavian **was born** on 23 September 63 BC.

Chapter 45

This chapter has traditionally been one of those cited to show Plutarch's lack of political insight, here a failure to understand Cicero's attempt to play Octavian off against Antony before discarding him (see Intro. 3). Moles defends Plutarch, emphasising the historicity of the lure of a second **consulship** with Octavian which proved too great for Cicero. Plutarch's division of **spoken** and real **reasons** recalls Thuc. 1.23.5-6, and Cicero's **hatred of Antony** is also noted in *Brutus* 22.3; Dio 45.15.4. Note also the tragic and ironic reversal of roles: Cicero thinks he is using Octavian, but in truth it is he who is making use of Cicero's passion for power.

For Octavian calling Cicero **'father'** cf. Brutus in Cic. *Ad Brut.* 17.5. Plutarch then exaggerates Brutus' reaction, reflected in *Ad Brut.* 25.7 (which is Brutus to Cicero; see further Moles; Intro. 4, also on **Caesar himself admitted**). On the **command** given to **Cicero's son** Marcus cf. *Brutus* 24.2, 26.2 (his **successful undertakings** early in 43 BC); Cic. *Ad Brut.* 2.6, 5.2, 12.1. Brutus left for **Athens** in August 44 BC.

The first half of 43 BC saw Cicero's **power in Rome** reach **its greatest height**. By now Antony was besieging D. Brutus in Mutina, but Cicero delivered an attack on him which became the *Fifth Philippic*. He thereby secured a command for Octavian, with dispensation to stand for office early (on **the lictors** see *Pompey* 19n.). In April Hirtius twice defeated Antony, at Forum Gallorum and a week later at Mutina, and in his *Fourteenth Philippic* (the last extant speech) Cicero proposes the title 'Imperator'* for Hirtius, Pansa and Octavian: he had not yet heard the news of Pansa's mortal wound in the first battle and Hirtius' death in the second.

Antony was now declared an enemy of Rome, but while D. Brutus received a triumph, Octavian was ignored by the senate. It did not help matters when he was informed of Cicero's infamous remark that 'the young man was to be lauded, applauded and then discarded' (*laudandum adulescentem, ornandum, tollendum, Fam.* 11.20.1, 21.1). It is clear that Cicero underestimated both Octavian and the power of Caesar's name, and by the end of July he was worried about how to control the young man (Cic. *Ad Brut.* 26.3-4). He was then compromised by Octavian's proposal of a joint **consulship** (see Moles; Octavian cannot have desired **a good name**, since he was already 'Caesar'). The senate delayed the elections, perhaps promising Octavian a praetorship, but he sent 400 soldiers to Rome to demand a consulship, payment of his troops and also the cancellation of Antony's outlawry. The senate refused, and in August Octavian crossed the Rubicon with eight legions. Cicero was allegedly not in the senate when it agreed to Octavian's candidature, but as three more legions went over to Octavian Cicero grudgingly went to meet him.

Chapter 46

Octavian and his cousin Q. Pedius became suffect consuls on 19 August 43 BC. Cicero left for **Tusculum** (ch. 47), and in Rome a court was established to punish Caesar's murderers. Then Octavian met **Antony and Lepidus** in **Bononia** (Bologna) at the end of October, and the three formed the 'Second Triumvirate'. It was easy enough to share out the western provinces, but to secure land and money for their men they had to resort to proscriptions. This was also the way of ridding themselves of their enemies – and Antony had all the Cicerones put on the **list**, however much Octavian may or may not have tried to persuade him otherwise.

The **more than 200 men** refers only to senators (c. 2,000 equites* were also proscribed), but figures for the total vary in the sources (200 at *Brutus* 27.5; 300 at *Antony* 20.1; App. *BC* 4.5.) Lepidus' **brother** was L. Aemilius Paullus (cos. 50 BC); the sister of L. **Caesar** (cos. 64 BC) married M. Antonius (pr. 74 BC) – both in fact survived. There is an alternative version in *Antony* 19.2 that it was Lepidus who wanted to kill his brother (cf. App. id. 4.12; Dio 47.6.3). On the role of Cicero's **friends** see ch. 1n.

Chapter 47

Cicero's implausible decision **to go secretly to Caesar's home** gives the narrative a tragic texture, which is heightened by the actions of the crow: Cicero is abandoned by men and only cared for by **wild brute creatures.** Additionally, he is suffering **undeserved ill fortune,** another tragic element. For other accounts of Cicero's death cf. Sen. *Suas.* 6-7; App. *BC* 4.19; Dio 47.8.3-4, 11.1-2 (Demosthenes' end was similarly tragic, *Demosthenes* 28.2-29.7). Plutarch's account will derive from Tiro (Intro. 4). **Astura** was south of Antium, and further south still were **Circaeum** (usually Circei) and **Caieta** (the MSS give the alternative form Caietae). For **Brutus in Macedonia** see ch. 45n.; on the deaths of **Quintus** and **his son** Quintus cf. rather differently App. *BC* 4.20; Dio 47.10.6-7. The summer **Etesian winds** blew from the north-west. **Crows** were the messengers of **Apollo** and harbingers of death: hence the end of the tragedy is nigh.

Chapter 48

Cicero's **murderers...were the centurion Herennius** (see Moles) and C. **Popillius** Laenas. Cicero's supposed defence of the latter is not connected with parricide by Appian or Dio (this charge was invented by rhetoricians; for Plutarch's use of it see Moles).

In Appian Cicero is betrayed by a shoemaker and ex-client* of Clodius; his steadfast end is only disputed by Asinius Pollio (in Sen. *Suas.* 6.24). Cicero died on 7 December, just under one month before his **sixty-fourth** birthday. Both Cicero's **hands** are cut off in Sen. *Suas.* 6.17, but it is only his right hand in *Antony* 20.2 (cf. App. *BC* 4.20; Dio 47.8.3; Sen. id. 6.19). Cicero sent the *Fifth* and *Tenth Philippics* to M. Brutus, who replied that they were deserving of Cicero's jesting title **'the Philippics'** (Cic. *Ad Brut.* 2.4, 4.2).

Chapter 49

Antony had Cicero's **head** and **hands** nailed up over the Rostra, possibly on the orders of Antony's wife Fulvia (Sen. *Suas.* 6.17, cf. 6.19 for Antony's exclamation). Pomponia's revenge on **Philologus** is incredible, as Plutarch himself is aware (see Moles; she was Atticus' sister). On **Tiro** see Intro. 4.

For subsequent events see *Caesar* 69n. A better translation than **the son of one of his daughters** is 'one of his grandsons' (i.e. Gaius, Lucius or Agrippa Postumus, sons of Julia). Augustus here shows the typical magnanimity of a victor after the event (*Caesar* 26n.). Cicero's **son**

Marcus fought at Philippi and under Sex. Pompey, but was pardoned and after **the final defeat of Antony** at Actium became consul as **colleague** to Octavian in 30 BC. **The senate** in fact **took down all the statues of Antony** and abolished his memory (*damnatio memoriae*) several months before this (Dio 51.19.3). For the Plutarchean tragic ending with moral redress see *Pompey* 80n.

Glossary

Amicitia: 'friendship', both personal and political (the opposite is *inimicitia*). Modern scholars have tended to identify *amicitiae* with political alliances, but this is an exaggeration. See Brunt [3] ch. 7.; *factio* (below).

Clientela: 'clientship', the system of mutual obligations between patrons and clients whose importance, especially in the electoral sphere, has probably been overestimated by modern scholars. See Brunt [3] ch. 8.

Equites, equestrian order: this term denotes either strictly those who were enrolled into the eighteen equestrian centuries of the Centuriate Assembly (and who were entitled to a public horse), or more generally those with a property qualification of over 400,000 HS. It is applied to those outside the senate, including sons of senators who had not begun their political careers, businessmen (notably the *publicani*, who carried out state contracts) and the propertied classes of the Italian municipalities (sometimes called *domi nobiles*). See Brunt [3] ch. 3.

Factio: another modern theory which needs great modification is that there existed in Roman politics large coalitions ('factions') of politicians bound by ties of kinship or friendship (above). See Brunt [3] ch. 9.

Imperator: the salutation of a general by his troops after a victory. The increasing influence of the army in our period made this the symbol of the military authority. It was Octavian who began to use the title before rather than after his name as a *praenomen* ('forename'); and from this developed the use of *imperator* to denote the supreme power (i.e. 'emperor').

Imperium: the supreme administrative and executive power through which senior magistrates (i.e. dictators, masters of the horse, censors, consuls, praetors, proconsuls, propraetors and certain commissioners) carried out their duties. There were two kinds, *imperium domi* exercised within the boundary of the city (*pomerium*) and *imperium militiae*, the right to command outside Rome.

Nobiles, nobility: descendants in the male line of a consul, forming the dominant and exclusive group in the Roman oligarchy.

Novus Homo: 'new man', the first member of a family to be elected to curule office, used especially of those who reached the consulship and thereby ennobled their family (see above).

Optimates: 'the best people', a propaganda term used of and by those politicians who attached great importance to the role of the senate, and of the small group of leading men (mostly ex-consuls) within it. The *Populares* chose instead to work through the popular assemblies.

Patricians: the group of aristocrats, privileged by birth, who in the early Republic monopolised political power. Those who were not patricians were *plebeians*. In the first century BC they still had some additional prestige and control of a few religious offices.

Populares: see **Optimates**

Senatus consultum ultimum: the 'ultimate decree of the senate', first passed against C. Gracchus in 121 BC, instructed the consuls and other magistrates to protect the state in times of emergency. Since it was a senatorial decree, the constitutional validity of the *s.c.u.* was disputed. Its supporters argued that those against whom the decree was directed had forfeited their citizen rights and could be executed without trial as public enemies (*hostes*); but this did not save Cicero from exile for his part in crushing the Catilinarian conspiracy.

Bibliography

The *Lives* of Pompey, Caesar and Cicero cover a momentous period of Roman history, when the traditional Republican form of government collapsed, to be replaced by the Principate. The course of these events, up to the beginning of the struggle between Antony and Octavian which was eventually resolved at Actium in 31 BC, is traced in the Commentary, but detailed analysis of the trends and reasons behind the fall, as well as of the workings of the political system, is beyond the scope of this *Companion*. The modern literature is vast, but the best general history of the period is still Scullard. More recent works are those of Beard and Crawford (a very readable introduction to the period) and, for the more advanced reader, the collection of essays in Brunt [3]. Among the biographies Gelzer remains essential, Seager provides a detailed analysis of Pompey's political career and Rawson is an excellent introduction to the many facets of Cicero's life. Finally, Plutarch's biographical methods are best studied now through the works of Pelling and Moles.

SOURCES

The works of the major authors are available in translation in Penguins and Loebs (section references in this book are usually to the text of the latter). Useful collections are Sabben-Clare and *Lactor* 7, and for inscriptions Sherk (see below).

WORKS ON PLUTARCH

Barrow, R.H., *Plutarch and his Times* (London, 1967)
Gomme, A.W., *A Historical Commentary on Thucydides, I* (Oxford, 1959) pp. 54-84
Gossage, A.J., 'Plutarch' in Dorey, T.A. (ed.) *Latin Biography* (London, 1967) pp. 45-77
Jones, C.P., *Plutarch and Rome* (Oxford, 1971)
Moles, J.L., *Plutarch: Life of Cicero* (Warminster, 1988)

Pelling, C.B.R., [1] 'Plutarch's Method of Work in the Roman Lives' *JHS* 99 (1979) pp. 74-96

───── [2] 'Plutarch's Adaptation of his Source-Material' *JHS* 100 (1980) pp. 127-40

───── [3] 'Plutarch and Roman Politics' in Moxon, I.S., Smart J.D., Woodman, A.J. (eds) *Past Perspectives: Studies in Greek and Roman Historical Writing* (Cambridge, 1986) pp. 159-87

───── [4] *Plutarch: Life of Antony* (Cambridge, 1988)

Podlecki, A.J., *Plutarch: Life of Pericles* (Bristol, 1987)

Russell, D.A., *Plutarch* (London, 1973)

Wardman, A.E., *Plutarch's Lives* (London, 1974)

BIOGRAPHIES

Bradford, E., *Julius Caesar: The Pursuit of Power* (London, 1984)

Fuller, J.F.C., *Julius Caesar: Man, Soldier, and Tyrant* (London, 1965)

Gelzer, M., *Caesar: Politician and Statesman* (Oxford, 1968)

Grant, M., *Julius Caesar* (London, 1969)

Greenhalgh, P., [1] *Pompey: The Roman Alexander* (London, 1980)

───── [2] *Pompey: The Republican Prince* (London, 1981)

Keaveney, A., *Sulla: The Last Republican* (London, 1982)

Lacey, W.K., *Cicero* (London, 1978)

Leach, J., *Pompey the Great* (London, 1978)

Mitchell, T.N., *Cicero: The Ascending Years* (New Haven, 1979)

Rawson, E., *Cicero: A Portrait* (London, 1975; repr. Bristol, 1983)

Seager, R., *Pompey: A Political Biography* (Oxford, 1979)

Smith, R.E., *Cicero the Statesman* (Cambridge, 1966)

Spann, P.O., *Quintus Sertorius and the Legacy of Sulla* (Arkansas, 1987)

Stockton, D.L., *Cicero: A Political Biography* (Oxford , 1971)

Weinstock, S., *Divus Julius* (Oxford, 1971)

GENERAL HISTORICAL WORKS

Badian, E., [1] *Foreign Clientelae (264-70 B.C.)* (Oxford, 1958)

───── [2] *Studies in Greek and Roman History* (Oxford, 1964)

Beard, W.M. and Crawford, M.H., *Rome in the Late Republic* (London, 1985)

Broughton, T.R.S., *The Magistrates of the Roman Republic*, 3 vols. (New York, 1951-86)

Brunt, P.A., [1] *Italian Manpower 225 B.C.-A.D. 14* (Oxford, 1971)

───── [2] *Social Conflicts in the Roman Republic* (London, 1971)

154

———— [3] *The Fall of the Roman Republic and Related Essays* (Oxford, 1988)

The Cambridge Ancient History IX (Cambridge, 1932)

Cary, M. and Scullard, H.H., *A History of Rome* (London, 1975)

Cornell, T.J. and Matthews, J., *Atlas of the Roman World* (Oxford, 1982)

Crawford, M.H., *The Roman Republic* (London, 1978)

Epstein, D.F., *Personal Enmity in Roman Politics 218-43 B.C.* (London, 1987)

Gruen, E.S., [1] *Roman Politics and the Criminal Courts, 149-78 B.C.* (Cambridge Mass., 1968)

———— [2] *The Last Generation of the Roman Republic* (Berkeley/Los Angeles, 1974)

Lactor 7, *Roman Politics* (1982)

Lintott, A.W., *Violence in Republican Rome* (Oxford, 1968)

McGing, B.C., *The Foreign Policy of Mithridates VI Eupator, King of Pontus* (Leiden, 1986)

The Oxford Classical Dictionary (2nd. ed, Oxford, 1970)

Sabben-Clare, J., *Caesar and Roman Politics 60-50 B.C.* (Oxford, 1971; repr. Bristol 1981)

Scullard, H.H., *From the Gracchi to Nero* (London, 1963)

Sherk, R.K., *Rome and Greek East to the Death of Augustus*, in *Translated Documents of Greece and Rome IV* (Cambridge, 1984)

Sherwin-White, A.N., *Roman Foreign Policy in the East* (London, 1984)

Syme, R., *The Roman Revolution* (Oxford, 1939)

Taylor, L.R., *Party Politics in the Age of Caesar* (Berkeley/Los Angeles, 1949)

Twyman, B., 'The Metelli, Pompeius and Prosopography' *ANRW* I.1.816-74

Wiseman, T.P., *New Men in the Roman Senate 139 B.C.-A.D. 14* (Oxford, 1971)